# A
# Village at Lord's

# A
# Village at Lord's

David P. Demelvan

THE HISTORY OF
THE FIRST TWENTY-ONE YEARS
OF
THE NATIONAL VILLAGE CRICKET
CHAMPIONSHIPS
1972-1992

PUBLISHED
BY

LIZFRAN PUBLICATIONS

© David P Demelvan 1993
ISBN 1-8983150

British Library Cataloguing-in-Publication Data
A catalogue record for this book is
available from the British Library

All rights reserved. Apart from any fair dealings for the purpose of private study, research, criticism or review as permitted under the Copyrights, Design and Patent Act 1988, no part of this book may be reproduced, stored in a retrieval system, or transmitted in any form or by any means, electronic, electrical, chemical, optical, photocopying, recording or otherwise, without prior written permission from the publisher. All enquiries should be addressed to the publisher.

Book Design by Anndawn
Cartoon Illustrations by Bajjer Arts, Wootton Bassett, Wiltshire

Published by Lizfran Publications, P.O. Box 532, Calne, SN11 8XD
Composed from authors disk by
Action Typesetting Limited, Russell Street, Gloucester
Printed and bound in Great Britain by
The Cromwell Press, Broughton Gifford, Melksham, Wiltshire

# Contents

| | | |
|---|---|---|
| | Introduction | 1 |
| 1. | The Brocklehurst's Dream | 9 |
| 2. | A Tot of Whisky At The Birth | 19 |
| 3. | Cricket Can Be A "Bitter Game" | 39 |
| 4. | Fertilizer As A Growing Agent | 71 |
| 5. | The Lean Years | 95 |
| 6. | A Cavaliers Return | 119 |
| 7. | A Villager On The Boundary | 129 |
| 8. | Tales From The Hedgerows | 163 |
| 9. | A Crystal Ball With No Snowflakes | 183 |
| | Appendices | 195 |

# DEDICATION

To The Memory Of
Michael Henderson and the Hon. Findlay Rea
Who contributed so much to the grass roots of cricket

# Foreword

Whenever I used to listen to John Arlott broadcasting, his grand Hampshire burr would conjure up the smell of bat oil and new mown grass, and a vision of white flannels on a village green with a pub and a church in the background.

Cricket started in the wooded countryside of Kent, Surrey, Hampshire and Sussex. It is still flourishing in the countryside all over Great Britain, thanks to village cricket. As far as I am concerned modern Test Matches and county games take second place to the game as still played by villages. It is the root of cricket and an example of how cricket should be played — in a sporting way with the emphasis on enjoyment and fun.

When motoring round the country I can never resist drawing up to watch a village match. Of course it has changed over the years, since I played my first village match against Upwey in Dorset in 1924. No longer does one see the squire, the vicar and the blacksmith appearing together in the same team. There are no more belts and braces, no cow pats nor long grass. Instead of the

## A Village at Lord's

old tin huts many villages have built themselves modern pavilions, often thatched and moulding into the surroundings.

The style of play has altered too. There are not so many mere sloggers, nor does the wicket keeper have a long stop. Thanks no doubt to television the field placing is more "professional" — not necessarily a good thing if it encourages the use of silly points and short legs for bat and pad catches. In fact I often worry about the danger when I see village fielders crowding the bat as they have seen Test cricketers do on the telly. So far I have not seen any helmets and lets hope there never will be any.

The fielding and throwing have improved beyond belief, partly due to the better outfields on most grounds.

There have always been jokes about cricket umpires but my impression is that the standard over all is pretty high. There are still "ours" and "theirs" umpires but there is less dissent and unsporting appealing than in the first class game.

I love the story of the local umpire who gave the visitors' leading batsman out for a doubtful catch behind the wicket. "I didn't hit it. I wasn't out" said the retiring batsman as he passed the umpire, who replied: "Well look in Thursdays Gazette and you will see that you were out." "You look", said the batsman. "I happen to be the editor."

The church has always played an important part in village cricket. My favourite cleric the late Canon Pickles once got his dates muddled, and forgot he had a christening at 4 p.m. His village batted first and at 3.45 he retired, put a surplice and cassock over his pads, took the christening and was allowed back to continue his innings.

In another match a Bishop opened the innings for his village. A young aspiring curate was the opening bowler and in due deference to the Bishop sent up a slow half volley with his first ball. The Bishop promptly hit it right out of the ground.. "I'm sorry young man," he said, "I'm afraid that I have hit you out of your parish." The curate grinned sheepishly but inwardly felt

## Foreword

peeved as he walked slowly back to his mark. He turned, ran in and sent down a vicious bouncer. It hit the rather portly Bishop in his midriff and he collapsed on the ground in agony. The young curate rushed up and said: "I'm sorry my lord Bishop. I'm afraid that I have hit you in the middle of your diocese!"

Since 1972 there has been a new goal for village cricketers — a sort of Utopian prize beyond their wildest dreams. A chance to play at Lord's, the headquarters of cricket. Thanks to the foresight and driving force of Ben Brocklehurst and The Cricketer — ably assisted by Belinda Brocklehurst — the Final of the National Village Championship has been played at Lord's for the last twenty years.

Each year well over six hundred villages from all over the country enter the competition. Only two of them ever get to Lord's, but thanks to the generous sponsorship of firms like Haig Whisky, Whitbread, Norsk Hydro and Rothmans, they have the day of their life. So do the spectators, of whom I have been lucky to be one for most of the twenty years. It's a joy to see their keenness, skill and immaculate turn out, and the sporting spirit in which the Final is always played.

David Demelvan has done a masterly job in creating for us the history of the National Village Championship, with all the many stories of unusual records and amusing happenings behind the scenes. I wish him every success with this book, which I hope will be read and enjoyed by countless village cricketers, who hold the future of cricket in their hands. So long as they continue to play for fun because they love cricket, and maintain all its sporting traditions, then the old phrase "It's not cricket" may mean something once again.

Brian Johnston,
St. John's Wood,
March 1993.

# LORD'S GROUND

**FREE ADMISSION** — **FREE ADMISSION**

## The National Village Cricket Championship
ORGANISED AND SPONSORED BY THE CRICKETER

### THE FINAL SATURDAY, 25th AUGUST, 1990
### GOATACRE (Wiltshire) v DUNSTALL (Staffordshire)

Umpires: P.S.C. STEVENS & W.A.U. WICKREMASINGHE — Scorers: S.T. PITMAN; T. SHILTON & E. SOLOMON

*Goatacre won the toss and elected to bat*    Weather: Hot and Sunny    Pitch: Good

| GOATACRE | | DUNSTALL | |
|---|---|---|---|
| PETE LEAVEY b Shipton | 0 | GEOFF SHILTON ct Leavey, b Rose | 35 |
| MARK HUNT b Crossland | 39 | *PHIL WALLBANK ct Haines, b Angell | 51 |
| JOHN SPENCER ct Higgott, b Shipton | 12 | ROBERT COOPER b Turner | 1 |
| JOHN TURNER ct Crossland b Scrimshaw | 53 | KEITH SHILTON b Angell | 23 |
| *KEVEN ILES ct Boulton, c Shipton | 123 | COLIN BOULTON run out | 21 |
| ANDY DAWSON not out | 12 | CHARLES CROSSLAND b Angell | 2 |
| †JOHN WILKINS not out | 3 | RICHARD INGLES b Dawson | 24 |
| PAUL ROSE Did not bat | | †TONY HIGGOTT ct Dawson, b Angell | 9 |
| JON ANGELL Did not bat | | ABID ALI not out | 31 |
| JONATHAN HAINES Did not bat | | STUART SCRIMSHAW not out | 7 |
| PETE DOLMAN Did not bat | | DAVE SHIPTON Did not bat | |
| 12th Man A. ILES | | 12th man D. GRANVILLE | |
| Extras lb 12 w 10; nb 3 | 25 | b.1; lb 3; w 6; nb 3 | 13 |
| **TOTAL (40 overs) 5 Wkts.** | **267** | **TOTAL (40 overs) 8 Wckts** | **217** |

FALL OF WICKETS
1-0; 2-23; 3-100; 4-220; 5-260

FALL OF WICKETS
1-67; 2-73; 3-114; 4-125; 5-141; 6-143; 7-163; 8-188

*'LEADING FROM THE FRONT'*
*Goatacre's Captain on his way to the competitions maiden century at Lord's.*

BOWLING ANALYSIS
SHIPTON   9 overs 0 maidens 83 runs 3 wickets
CROSSLAND 9 overs 1 maiden  54 runs 1 wicket
SCRIMSHAW 9 overs 2 maidens 35 runs 1 wicket
BOULTON   6 overs 0 maidens 17 runs 0 wicket
ALI       6 overs 0 maidens 41 runs 0 wicket
WALLBANK  2 overs 0 maidens 25 runs 0 wicket

BOWLING ANALYSIS
DAWSON    6 overs 0 maidens 41 runs 1 wicket
SPENCER   5 overs 0 maidens 16 runs 0 wicket
ROSE      7 overs 0 maidens 37 runs 1 wicket
DOLMAN    6 overs 0 maidens 41 runs 0 wicket
TURNER    4 overs 1 maiden   8 runs 1 wicket
ANGELL    6 overs 0 maidens 18 runs 4 wickets
ILES      2 overs 0 maidens 15 runs 0 wicket
HAINES    3 overs 0 maidens 31 runs 0 wicket
LEAVEY    1 over  0 maidens  6 runs 0 wicket

**MAN OF THE MATCH: K. M. ILES**

* Captain    †Wicket-keeper

### RESULT: GOATACRE WON BY 50 RUNS

### A RECORD BREAKING FINAL

Both teams exceeded the previous highest total in a final set by East Brierley with 216 for 4 (40 overs) in 1979. Iles' 123 beat the previous highest innings of 91 not out which he achieved himself in the 1988 final replay at Beckenham. Jon Angell's 4-18 is the 3rd best bowling analysis in a final.

# Acknowledgements

It seems a long time since I received that rather poignant letter from Ben Brocklehurst, affording me the opportunity to write a book on the history of the championships.

His letter raised no objection — but advised me not to expect too much background support from his people, they were far too busy. "If we gave you all the information you needed we would find we were writing the book ourselves!" he said.

He then promptly began advising me on publication and distribution. He sent me an invitation to the Final, together with all necessary passes. As if that weren't enough , he apologised in advance if he might appear to ignore me on the day, because as host there were many people he had to see to. His letter concluded "There won't be much time to discuss your project in detail. Having met you however, we can correspond."

One person I did meet that day was Brian Johnston, who readily agreed to write the foreword. And what a superb piece of work it is. Thank you, Johnners. I hope by the time the book is published I will have managed to bake that cake I promised you!

So, it was these busy people who provided me with a desk at their offices to embark upon my research. For three fascinating days I was afforded every help and courtesy. Lunch when I arrived there was something very special to me. The enthusiasm for the competition was clearly evident at the lunch table. I never did apologise to Ben for commandeering his summerhouse from 8 am. on Friday, not giving it back 'til long after the staff had gone home. At one point he did rescue me, and we strolled round the garden, as he retold various stories. Suitably refreshed I went back to the summerhouse to complete my work.

I returned to Wiltshire physically and mentally exhausted, but content. Not only had I a structured path to complete my research, I had also sampled the tranquil cottage industry environment of "The grass roots of the competition." To Ben, Belinda, Sue and all at Beechanger a very special thanks — for without your assistance and support this book simply could not have been written.

Thanks must also go to Lt.Col. Stephenson, who gave me free access to the library at Lord's. Curator Stephen Green also made me feel extremely welcome. It was a unique experience, sitting at a desk surrounded by volumes of cricket history. When I left on that dark wet December evening, I could not help having a peek at the hallowed sporting arena, with it's rows of empty seats. The pitch looked immaculate. I remember thinking that should we have an Indian Summer by Christmas, it would take but half a day to prepare for a game on Boxing Day. Thank you to the hosts of Village Cricket.

I recall a conversation with Ben, when he expressed his reservations on my contacting past sponsors, particularly from the early years. Current sponsors Rothmans were relatively easy to contact. Although their involvement is comparatively short, they have been most helpful.

Sam Whitbread invited me to Chiswell Street. He didn't think he had much to contribute — but he did. Unknown to him he helped dot the i's and cross the t's. The opportunity to view the banqueting hall was beneficial in getting a taste of the atmosphere that must have prevailed on the eve of finals.

Malcolm Lukey of Norsk Hydro was infectious, he 'phoned. me and we arranged to have lunch. He recalled many happy days

## Acknowledgements

when his company were involved in the competition. Being the type of chap he is, Malcolm entrusted all his records to me, as well as a plaque for my study (when I eventually have one!). He also put me in touch with Tony Huskinson, who imparted a wealth of notes, and fond memories of his involvement when editor of "The Cricketer" annual.

John Haig was the most difficult to locate. After several months of telephone calls and general enquiries, I eventually tracked down Graeme Forrester of United Distillers. Thanks for your help Graeme, and for pointing me in the right direction to complete the sponsorship corporate chain.

Response from the villages was numerically small. However those who did contact me provided a wealth of information. My thanks to "The Cricketer" and Charlie Chester, host of Radio 2 Sunday Soapbox, for their appeals on my behalf.

In hindsight, I am relieved not everyone did respond. If they had I don't know how I would have coped. My particular thanks to Pat Almond of Forge Valley, John Thirkell of Linton, and their good friends from Troon (courtesy of J.P.Angove). Also Freuchie, the champions of Scotland, I hope to meet you one day, Dave Christie. I did not need to write to Methley of Yorkshire, they gave me all the information I needed when I had the pleasure of joining them at Lord's for the 1992 final. Brian Flintoff of Sessay, York Walker of Tofts, David Wickens of Newick C.C., Chris Despres of St.Fagans, and last but not least, Alan Prior who umpired Rowledge's first match — an inspired reflection. My grateful thanks to you all.

The newspapers and photographers who provided such rich reports and photographs to help me build up a picture of events over the years. The list of those whose help I have called upon appears in the appendendices.

Now closer to home. To all at Goatacre C.C., thanks for your help, advice and encouragement, as well as many memorable hours of enjoyment from the boundary. To my dear friend David

Evans, chairman of Wiltshire Cricket Umpires Association, who read the text with the objective eye of a knowledgeable cricket enthusiast. And last, but by no means least, my wife Pauline, for her patience, understanding and hard work typing the manuscript. Without her help I would probably still be on Chapter Three!

To anyone I may have unintentionally missed, my apologies in advance.

D.P.D. May 1993.

# Introduction

Lord's is the undisputed "Mecca of Cricket" and became the eventual home of the Marylebone Cricket Club, some twenty-seven years after its foundation in 1787. This famous ground has hosted many memorable matches since that first game between MCC and Hertfordshire on June 22nd.1814. Wisden and other cricketing books have admirably chronicled much of the history of the first class game. In so doing, I would suggest more has been written about the activities at Lord's than any other cricket ground in the world. After all it is from within those hallowed walls that the laws are administered.

In 1972 a new tradition was established in the national cricketing calendar. The birth of The National Village Championships. Each year since then (save one), the MCC has played host to two villages and their supporters, in a final to decide who will be crowned as the best village team in the land. This is the culmination of a tournament, which in it's early years saw some 800 villages set out on the road to Lord's early in the season. It was later trimmed to 630 to help encourage true villagers to take part. Twenty years on the competition is still a popular event, and has established a unique chapter of it's own in cricket history. The Hampshire village of Hambledon for example, from whom MCC inherited responsibility for the government of the game in 1787, were finalists in 1989. The highest aggregate score in a final is 484 with both sides batting their allotted forty overs. A significant contribution to this mammoth feat was one batsman scoring a century off just thirty-nine balls in forty five minutes. Some statistical pundits are still stumped, being unable to confirm or deny it as the fastest century ever recorded at Lord's?

It is not my intention for this book to be a statistical chronicle of the competition, with a few memorable match reports thrown in. The main theme is centred around those villages fortunate enough to have experienced playing at Lord's. How they made it, together with some of their stories along the way. A competition of this nature would not have survived or been so successful, without sponsors, organisers and of course the hosts. They too have their story to tell.

Ever since the competition's inception the draw has been designed on a specific geographical basis. The intention being for group finalists to play on a regional basis, culminating in one semi-final between the South West and South East. The other between The North and Midlands. This ensured, as far as practically possible, a final between a village from the North and South of Britain. This has gone a long way to enhance the importance of the competition as a national event. It has helped create a bond between villages from opposite ends of the land, which over the years has resulted in some friendlies becoming an annual event. I suspect part of the reason has been to recall memories of their match at Lords, not just for the teams, but their supporters as well. At such reunions, the stories abound of exploits, both strange and bizarre, some possibly tinged with disbelief! All go to demonstrate the importance of this very special competition to the grass roots of the game — The Villagers!

This is not just a simple knockout competition culminating in a forty overs a side final, with the victors receiving "The Cup" and a quick drink at the bar to celebrate afterwards. It is a well organised affair from the start, played to a strict set of regulations. Qualification for both the villages and their players are clearly defined, resulting in a highly respected and well thought out final each year. The organisers ensure both spectators and players alike

# Introduction

enjoy their day The staffing and ground facilities are equal to any of the first class limited over competitions, which as we know are also played at Lord's. As most teams who have had the good fortune to play in a village final will readily agree, it is the achievement of getting there and the experience that is important. To win the cup is looked upon as *'the icing on the cake.'* This is a view shared by their supporters.

Preparations for the final start on the eve of the match. At some point during the day both teams, together with club officials and wives depart for London. Timing depends very much on how far up country they are. If travelling from Northumberland or Durham it would mean the coach departing before first light. Before that if travelling from Scotland.

Whatever time of day it is, proud stalwart supporters are there to see them off to the eve of match hospitalities. This in eager anticipation of meeting again the following day to enjoy a memorable occasion the like of which the village has probably never experienced before. Despite the fact that a club's history may date back a century or more. A prime example of this is the Hampshire village of Hursley Park, founded in 1785. They were beaten finalists in 1984. A great pity for them, as it would have been a fitting accolade to have celebrated their bi-centenary as National Champions. It was not to be however. they were beaten by Marchwiel (Clwyd), their only consolation was having lost by only eight runs. The closest final on record. Even that was short-lived. The following year both Rowledge (Surrey) and Freuchie (Scotland) finished on the same total of 134. Freuchie won on having lost fewer wickets. Some would say a just reward for the long haul the team and their loyal supporters had travelling from the far North. In addition to their national pipers! They are said to be the only Scottish team to have played at Lord's.

Once the team coaches arrive at St.John's Wood, pre-match hospitalities begin. First there is a champagne reception, followed by the evening celebrations. Here the Lord's Banqueting Suite is the venue for dinner, where several famous cricketing personalities are invited guests. Everything possible is done to ensure the country guests are afforded the opportunity to relax. It also provides the ideal atmosphere for everyone to become well acquainted.

Overnight accommodation is provided at an hotel close to the ground, so all are afforded the chance of a good nights sleep before the big day ahead. Not all take the opportunity however, it is not unusual to see players in the bar until 2 a.m. One group, unable to sleep, played "cricket" with a ping pong ball and a rolled up newspaper. I don't find this surprising, after all it's not every day a village cricketer has his skills tested in front of a crowd at the most famous cricket ground in the world. And each person must handle the waiting in the best way suited to him.

The day of the final dawns. First order of the day is breakfast, but thoughts of what is to come can cause jangled nerves, which may well affect the appetite. Some country farmers however are used to a hearty breakfast and will not be put off by the occasion. This is highlighted by an incident on the morning of one final, which also demonstrates how important the competition is viewed and known to professionals who earn their living from the first class game. It was a Saturday in late August, and the third day of the final test at the Oval between England and India. A player, on entering the dining room was overwhelmed by the buffet selection in front of him. So intent was he on his gastronomic jackpot that he collided with a fellow guest. Turning to apologise for his action, he was seized with a mixture of panic and embarrassment, as he recognised umpire Nigel Plews, who was on test duty. His embarrassment was quickly dispelled by the beaming smile on the umpire's face, who retorted in a friendly manner, "After you old chap, it's you who has an important game today. I shall only be standing around at a match across the river." After a brief pause Nigel continued "By the way,

## Introduction

congratulations on reaching the final. Good Luck. Enjoy the game, and pass on my best wishes to all the other players."

Breakfast over, bags packed and farewells said to fellow guests and hotel staff, it is off on the short journey to Lord's. The teams enter by the Grace Gates. From that moment on, they are not just provided with the services extended to those contesting a first class county game, but are accorded the privileges which MCC normally reserve for test match players. For example, a steward is on duty in each dressing room to attend to the needs of the players. Should anyone require a soft drink, clean towel, or anything at all, they only have to ask and the steward will attend to it.

Once the players have established themselves in their respective dressing rooms, it is time for the official photographs. As is the custom, these are taken in the Lord Harris Memorial Gardens. By this time many supporters have arrived at the ground. Despite the fact the professional photographers hold centre stage, anyone is free to use their own camera, and every courtesy is extended to them whilst they capture the scene for posterity.

By now most supporters are on the ground. Places where they are prevented from going are few. Ground staff are helpful in every way. Club secretaries also issue passes to selected club members, in order that they may view inside the pavilion. Only two females are granted permission to step over the threshold, but more about that later.

The players are warming up in the practice nets at the Nursery End. Time is drawing near for the start of play. Supporters' attentions are turned to the main business of the day, THE MATCH! They eagerly take their seats. It has become a tradition to set up camp either side of the electronic scoreboard, opposite Father Time and the Grandstand. One set of supporters commandeer The Tavern Stand, whilst the other congregate in the New Mound Stand. This is a sensible arrangement as everybody is in close proximity to the Tavern Bar, which is open for the duration of the game, thus providing the opportunity for refreshments during play without missing any action in the field. It also enables rival supporters to meet each other and expound on the cricketing feats of their local heroes out in the middle, as well as some of the excitement they have experienced along the road to Lord's. Of course there have been the tight finishes! These have become meat and drink to the seasoned cricket supporter, since the introduction of the limited over competitions. It is how some of the ties have been decided in this unique competition that is so fascinating. Some I have retold in this book. But I am sure for every one I have discovered, there are dozens still to come to light.

The umpires appear from the pavilion and step onto the hallowed turf, closely followed by the fielding side. Practice balls are in evidence, as bowlers turn their arm. The wicket keeper is tested from all angles. That carnival atmosphere which existed for the past few hours, gives way to tension and excited anticipation, heightened by the dulcet tones of Alan Curtis on the Public Address system. A veteran of test match and one day finals, he readily admits to finding it comforting contemplating the village final at the end of August. In his usual professional style he welcomes the visiting teams and their supporters. His preambles always contain snippets of information about the villages and some of their players. The announcement of the result of the toss is wasted on the seasoned rustic supporter. He has already gleaned this information for himself, and is fully aware why the opposition have been put into bat. In all fairness to Alan, this is an invaluable facility much appreciated Those paying up to £40 a ticket for a first class match expect a professional commentary and get it. But the same standard of service is provided in the village final. He always gets details of players correct. Something I found difficult when commentating on a big village match last year. To the experienced hand a watchful eye on the scoreboard may well help in acknowledging a batsman's half century. But

# Introduction

the announcement of a bowler's final analysis, just as he takes up his position at long on in front of his own supporters - well that is Alan's forte! He knows what the fans want. On the two occasions he was unable to commentate, Frank Partridge filled the breach admirably.

The five minute warning bell is history. Practice balls magically disappear, and the new scene shows the fielding captain in earnest discussion with his opening bowler. Fervent arm waving settles the fielders into position. At the same time, both openers are making their way to the wicket. Opening bat takes his guard, as fine adjustment is made to the field. The bowler is at the start of his run up, loosening up with energetic arm swings. A hush descends upon the tiny crowd tucked into one corner of this cricket amphitheatre. The silence is made all the more uncanny by the vast ocean of empty seats, from the Warner Stand to the Nursery End. The batsman surveys the field. Who knows what is going on in the minds of players and spectators alike? Some probably have recollections of an earlier game when the odds seemed stacked against victory. But a flurry of hard hitting, or two quick wickets turned almost certain defeat into victory. Everyone is holding their breath. The proverbial pin can be heard if it drops. After what seems like an age, the umpire lowers his outstretched arm, as the familiar sound of "PLAY" breaks the silence. The Game is On.

In a few short hours one team will be crowned National Village Champions. For a brief period they will receive recognition on national television and radio sports headlines. Local media often give it star billing ahead of first class county reports. Some local stations have taken to giving ball by ball commentary of the match, and some have even done this for the semi-finals.

The following morning, those national newspapers which take the trouble to give a creditable coverage to cricket, will carry a comprehensive report of the match. Proud villagers will empty the shelves in their local newsagents. Press reports and photographs take pride of place in scrapbooks, recording "The Day Our Village Went to Lord's."

I was discussing the merits of the competition with a seasoned supporter who has attended two finals, as official scorer, and summed it up admirably. "The spirit, enthusiasm and camaraderie created as a village progresses through the competition is very special. If someone could find a way to bottle it, they would make a fortune." I certainly agree. The competition has come of age! It has achieved the first milestone by celebrating it's twenty-first birthday in 1992. Hursley Park lifted the cup, at it's second attempt, aged 207. We now look forward to the next milestone, the silver jubilee in 1997.

Should your village be taking part, give them your support to the hilt. Not just in this competition, but in their league and cup matches. It will help them enjoy their game out in the middle, and raise morale. It will also ensure that cricket makes a purposeful contribution to the social side of village life. If you are an avid supporter of the game, with no particular team to support, look out for the village final at Lords towards the end of August. Book yourself a place simply by being there. You don't need a ticket, admission is free and you will not be locked out. You can rest assured it will be an experience to savour. Like a good home-made wine, this competition improves with age.

David P Demelvan,<br>
Goatacre,<br>
September 1992.

# CHAPTER ONE

# The Brocklehurst's Dream

I wonder how many village cricketers are aware of the existence of the National Cricket Association? How ever many there are today, I am confident the number far exceeds those who knew of it in 1970. It was at that time Aiden Crawley was not satisfied enough was being done to raise the association's profile. After the season had finished, he invited Ben Brocklehurst and Jim Swanton (two board members of The Cricketer magazine) to lunch in the committee room at Lord's. The purpose of the exercise was to discuss how best their magazine could help promote the NCA.

I never did find out exactly what was discussed. When lunch was over, Aiden was standing by a window gazing out over a deserted Lord's. After a while he murmured that he had often thought of two village clubs playing on the hallowed turf. Everyone chuckled and went their separate ways, but the seed of an idea had been sown in the mind of Ben Brocklehurst.

Back at his office, Ben sat down with his general manager, Harry Constantine to discuss how to go about breathing life into the idea.

The first thing was to establish what constituted a village. They decided to go through the AA handbook and extract place names with a maximum population of 2500 inhabitants. All right so far! But how were they to make contact? It was considered most effective to address a standard letter to the village pub. Where none existed, it was sent to the local garage, asking for it to be forwarded to the local club secretary.

## A Village at Lord's

These initial steps proved to be a substantial administrative task, it was clear computerisation was called for. In the early seventies computer technology was not what it is today. It was not possible to pick up a 40 megabyte personal computer off the shelf in the local electronic superstore. But Ben knew a neighbour who had access to such facilities. So off went Harry, armed with the essential information to put on disk, before approaching the villages. This would make the next stage easier, if there was to be a next stage.

As I said computers today are not what they were twenty years ago. This monster had been housed in a special room. It was air conditioned and had a time lock. Well Harry was so engrossed in his task, that he failed to notice the warning before the time lock came into operation. The next morning a dishevelled general manager staggered out of the locked room and made his way to a much smaller one! But he had not wasted the night, his task had been achieved.

The next stage was to agree some draft rules. Once this was completed a standard letter was sent out to all villages on computer. The local post office in that particular part of Kent must have had quite a shock, in having to contend with such a large volume of mail. All that was left to do was sit back and wait. It was like concocting your very own home made firework, the outer covering comprising brown or manilla envelopes; light the blue touch paper and stand back. The result could be a glittering cascade, a splutter, or a dull damp squib. Ben and his merry band were not to be disappointed. An almost instant and overwhelming response resulted.

More than a thousand villages had responded. They came from the Highlands of Scotland to the southern tip of Cornwall. From the west coast of Wales to The Wash. Next year was to see an armada of clubs sail on village greens. Little did they know then, on what a hallowed green sea the final battle would be contested. The response may have been overwhelming, but the task of organisation was uncharted waters. Jim Dunbar, secretary of the NCA was approached. He felt the association was not in a position to organise a competition of such magnitude. Ben Brocklehurst was clearly not a man frightened to take up a challenge. The Cricketer had thrown down the gauntlet. Villages all over the country had picked it up. Someone had to see it through. So Ben and his staff soldiered on.

First priority was to analyse those villages that had responded. Almost eight hundred clubs were included in the draw. At first glance round one seemed to be a puzzling hotchpotch of numerical inconsistency. Why not just put all the teams into a hat and draw them out on the same basis as the FA Cup had been done over the years? Yes an administratively simple exercise. The organisers of this competition were not going to be hoodwinked into taking such a simple path. It would have been so easy to do. Our other national sport is blessed, or cursed (whichever way you view it) with a more sound financial and media base. But these people knew the cricket scene. Therefore they opted for a geographical group system. Travelling long distances in preliminary rounds would have been just too prohibitively expensive for players and supporters alike. In later rounds, beyond the group final, it was a different kettle of fish. The Cricketer had engineered the whole draw to ensure travelling was kept to the absolute minimum, right up to the final.

Another administrative aid had also been included. This was the match result card. It had been designed in such a way as to afford club secretaries the opportunity to give an account of the game, together with any unusual incidents. This has proved to be invaluable in the preparation of the annual (published by The Cricketer) each year. The late Findlay Rea, obviously made good use of them in his inspired contributions. A writer rich in talent and an avid supporter of the competition, so sadly missed. The original rules have changed little over the years. When change has been necessary, it has only been with good reason. And then only to improve the competition. Rules of play have always remained the same. When weather vagaries intervene there is feverish reference to the "rule book." In defence of the poor downtrodden match secretaries and umpires, I take this opportunity to include Rule 8 in order to clear up any misunderstanding. While at the same time giving any reader not familiar with the competition an insight into how a match is decided. Rule 8. The laws of cricket as laid down by the NCA for the current year shall apply, together with the following special conditions:

(a) Each side shall bat for 40 overs unless their innings is completed earlier, or unless the captains agree to a lesser number of overs before the match.

(b) No bowler may bowl more than 9 overs. Part of an over will count as a full over only in so far as each bowler's limit is concerned. When it is agreed that a match shall consist of fewer than 40 overs, no bowler may bowl more than one-quarter of the total number of overs to be bowled by his side.

(c) The side which scores the most runs shall be the winner

(d) If the scores are level, the side which has lost fewer wickets shall be the winner,

(e) If still equal, the side which has received fewer balls at the end of the match shall be the winner.

(f) If still equal, the side which has scored more runs at the end of twenty overs shall be the winner.

(g) If still equal, the side which has lost fewer wickets at the end of twenty overs shall be the winner. If still level that is to say, both sides having scored the same number of runs and having lost the same wickets at the end of twenty overs, the result will be decided by a bowling competition. See rule nine

(h) If the side batting second equal it's opponent's score off the last ball of the match, providing that they have lost fewer wickets, then they have won the match and the ball is dead.

(i) If rain or bad light curtails play before the completion of a match, the result shall be in favour of the side which has scored the fastest runs per over THROUGHOUT THE INNINGS, providing that at least twenty have been bowled to the side batting second. If the scoring rates are identical, then the side with the higher score after twenty overs shall be the winners, if still equal, the side which has lost fewer wickets in the first twenty overs shall be the winners. If still equal the result will be decided by a bowling competition. See rule nine.

(j) If the start of a match is delayed by weather or if there is a subsequent interruption, the captains may agree to a lesser

number of overs, the minimum being fifteen.
(k) If the match is abandoned after each side has batted for twenty overs, then Rule 8 (i) applies.

In the event a match fails to produce a result on the scheduled date, Rule 9 comes into force. The re-scheduled match is switched to the visiting team's ground the following week, or an agreed earlier date. If the re-arranged match still failed to produce a result, an alternative way of deciding the outcome was the nerve jangling spectacle of "bowling at the stumps!" Cricket's equivalent of a penalty shoot-out in football. With the ground including car park under water, this proves to be an impossible task. There is of course one last resort. I refer of course to the toss of a coin. On the occasions this scenario has been faced, it has produced some ingenious ways of deciding the outcome of which team would progress to the next round. The methods chosen have been accepted as a valid result by the organisers.

I am sure many captains, on whose shoulders the decision rests, not the umpires, are aware of their loyal supporters. They are left having to rely on their picnic hampers, cricket conversation and a jar of ale, should the bar be open; while the rain continues to tumble down. It would be unfair on them to see their team's fate decided by the toss of a coin. This is where their rustic ingenuity comes to the fore, in providing some form of skilful competition to entertain and produce an honourable result.

On such occasions when the weather is unpleasant, it is of course a favourite topic of conversation. The British are renowned the world over for using it to start polite conversation. In this case it has more profound meaning. Gathering in the harvest could be seriously effected.

Many a farmer in the latter stages of the competition has the task of harvesting his precious crops. At that time he may appear to have an agonising decision to make, the village has reached the quarter-finals of the competition. He may be a sound opening bat, astute leg break bowler, or reliable wicket-keeper. He is bound to play, so who will gather in the harvest? No such delusions of grandeur for such a down to earth man of the soil. It is simply a matter of waiting to see if the skipper has him on the team sheet. Should this be the case, he will oil his bat and tidy up his pads; they may even get a fresh whitening for the occasion. In celebration of his inclusion in the side, for such an important game he may celebrate by buying a new box. The old one after all has seen better days, and besides it may be an astute move under the circumstances. The opposition are obviously not going to be a pushover.

On arrival at the away ground Mother Nature may have provided a scene of blustery black clouds, so be it! At home maybe a hundred miles or more away the sun could be shining. If that be the case, harvesting will go on without the intrepid farmer. He has his new box, fresh white pads, well oiled bat-and a game of cricket to enjoy. Hopefully to win, if not he will make new friends that but for this competition he may well not meet.

I have digressed, in hindsight more than twenty years on the rules have stood the test of time, with very little variation. As I said earlier changes have only been introduced for good reason. Sometimes it is to make life easier for the village clubs competing, or to try and protect true villagers being edged out by superior skill being introduced by some sides. Thankfully few have been brought before the stewards.

In the event a new civic or public utility building is to be constructed, it is not unusual for construction work to be preceded by a ceremonial "laying of the foundation stone", or some other memorial. In attendance are such dignitaries as befits the architectural edifice to be created. In the case of a local town library, the mayor dons the chain of office and obligatory hard hat! Armed with either the silver trowel or spade, depending on the memorial, he or she performs their civic duty in front of invited guests. These are usually local councillors, including the

## The Brocklehurst's Dream

leader of the council, providing he can set aside his butcher's apron for the morning. A member of the local press is also in attendance with trusty photographer. Together they prepare a suitable words and picture story for Friday's edition of the local chronicle. A building of national importance demands a person of higher profile to perform the ceremony. Still in hard hat the ceremony is virtually identical. The only difference being it attracts the national media and most of the invited guests can be found listed in Debrett's Peerage. This ceremony has long been considered essential groundwork before the project can commence in earnest.

The Cricketer were satisfied their groundwork was almost completed and they could soon start the project in earnest. It was now opportune for them to lay the foundation stone. This was done in the form of a press conference, although the participants were members of truly local communities, Ben obviously considered the project deserved more than local recognition. He held the conference in the Long Room at Lord's. Of course the national press were in attendance. The media may have seen this as just a novel village cricket experiment (dictionary definition of experiment "It's a test or trial procedure adopted on chance of it's succeeding").

Ben was determined this particular experiment was afforded every possible opportunity to succeed. At the end of the press conference he was interviewed for the BBC by Christopher Martin-Jenkins. He seized on the opportunity for a sponsor to come forward. Little did he know then how soon that would happen. More good fortune was to follow, it later transpired MCC and Lord's ground staff offered to host the 1972 final at lord's. This was the ultimate ingredient to fire the villagers on. Not only were they to compete for the title of national champions, the two finalists would be contesting a battle of cricketing skill and nerve on the most famous cricket ground in the world.

It would not be proper for me to finish this chapter without giving a special mention to Ben Brocklehurst's wife Belinda. She has put so much into the competition, particularly behind the scenes. Only she knows how much. In the early years this could not have been without it's difficult moments. Apart from having to learn as she went along (which applied to all who contributed as organisers). She had a young family to bring up. The experience of motherhood no doubt helped her cope with many situations. I can imagine a harassed staff member presenting her with an indecipherable batch of match cards. And of course the one from the less than sober match secretary, although legible, expounding on the whirlwind performance of their star batsman as well as their left arm spinner's analysis 9 overs 8 maidens 6 for one. "I hope thee gets that down right luv. That's 6 wickets for woun runn!", his local dialect coming over quite strongly, on the written report. Sadly he failed to include the match result. A problem which to Belinda was a mere bagatelle.

MCC as many will know is considered to be one of the last bastions of male cloistered havens. In a world dominated by the fight for equality of the sexes, those privileged to sport the rhubarb and custard tie will, I suspect go down fighting. They have their traditions and code of conduct, which many a villager attending a final will have learnt to his cost. Showing his red invitation card is not always enough to gain entry to the pavilion. If his sartorial image is unacceptable entry is politely, but firmly refused. There is little point in looking to the chief steward to arbitrate. He will back his steward in upholding tradition. It is for the man himself to rely on his own ingenuity and look to his fellow supporters for assistance. It is often only the loan of a necktie that is required in order for him to gain access. Entry for ladies is taboo, except possibly Her Majesty The Queen. It is a fitting tribute to Belinda therefore that, in recognition of her contribution to the smooth running of the competition, an exception was made. Much to her surprise and joy, she was allowed to see the Long Room escorted by the then President

### The Brocklehurst's Dream

of MCC Maurice •Allom during a Village Final.

The late John Fogg wrote a book on the first year of the competition. More than twenty years on the competition is still going strong. In that time it has done much to enhance and improve the lot of village cricket in many ways. This would not have been possible without the four very generous sponsors, who each have a chapter devoted to their respective period of sponsorship. MCC and Lord's staff have also helped make the Final each year a memorable occasion. But it is to The Cricketer our biggest debt of gratitude is owed. They have organised the competition from day one. Chapter five entitled "The Lean Years" tells the story of those years when a sponsor could not be found. But the staff at the office in Kent soldiered on and kept the competition going without dropping the high standards that were set at the beginning and have been maintained throughout. As a much travelled rustic supporter on the boundary, I say thank you on behalf of the many thousands of villagers in Britain who have had much enjoyment over the years. Some know little about the finer points of cricket. This has not stopped them enjoying many happy hours alongside their more knowledgeable friends and neighbours. Friendships have been made between villagers living many miles apart, who but for the existence of the championships would never have met, or indeed known of the existence of the villages they had visited at all.

Much pressure has been put on often forgotten club secretaries. Bad weather with the resultant chaos to local games as a village competes in the village championships can be a headache to say the least. But this is something village cricket takes in it's stride. Most of our harassed secretaries, like most players and supporters, do not lose sight of the importance of the game being played first and foremost for fun.

In this cherished game that has spanned the centuries, I sincerely hope to see "The National Village Cricket Championships" enter the twenty-first century. With The

Cricketer at the helm and continued sponsorship I firmly believe that to be possible. The dream of Aiden Crawley also became the dream of the Brocklehursts. That dream became a reality. It also afforded village clubs all over the country the dream of playing at Lord's. It would be a great pity if the dream died. So if the director of a large company has started reading this book, read on, you may be surprised, if not I hope amused. Should that be the case next time sponsorship is on your boards agenda, think of this unique competition.

## CHAPTER TWO

# A Tot of Whisky at the Birth

I presume as a fellow cricket lover, you like me look forward to the start of a new season. Lengthening daylight hours, plump daffodil bulbs straining to burst forth into colour and trees laden with buds giving a faint hint of green, are all signs telling us it is time to disgard the heavy winter coat and look forward to summer days. Days of good cricket, good fun and good companionship! It is unlikely therefore such pleasant thoughts could be prompted on a cold wet winter's morning, with dawn struggling to penetrate the stubborn depressing grey clouds.

On such a cold winter morning in 1971, Michael Henderson the managing director of Haig Whisky, was driving to work in central London. Stuck in the usual traffic crawl, which always seems worse in the rain, he was listening to the Jack De-Manio programme on the home service (now Radio 4). Christopher Martin-Jenkins, cricket correspondent for the "Beeb" was interviewing Ben Brocklehusrt chairman of The Cricketer on what plans his magazine had to help promote village cricket, in particular the new experimental national village knockout competition. Ben stressed the need to recognise village cricket for what it was, the grass roots of the game. He went on to say that most of the preliminary work had been done. If response from villages across the country was anything to go by, the project would not fail from lack of enthusiasm. But he emphasised, enthusiasm on its own was not enough, without sponsorship to provide the essential financial support, there was a very real danger of the project being strangled at birth.

Michael Henderson had clearly been impressed by the interview. It appears his busy office schedule took second place that winter morning. His first telephone call was to the BBC and within an hour, a delighted Ben Brocklehurst had secured a sponsor for the first year of the competition. Work could now start in earnest to organise "THE HAIG NATIONAL VILLAGE CRICKET CHAMPIONSHIP." A press conference to announce the sponsorship was held in the Savoy Hotel's River Room. Control was to be in the hands of a committee, consisting of a member of the National Cricket Association, The Cricketer and a member of staff from John Haig and Company, with the NCA chairman to preside. It was appropriate that Aiden Crawley was in the chair, after all it was his original dream, had he not made that chance comment after lunch at the meeting with Jim Swanton and Ben Brocklehurst, there would probably never have been a village competition at all.

**1972** was to be the start of a six year partnership between Haig Whisky and The Cricketer, which was to see the competition become a popular annual event. The Berkshire village of Welford Park had the distinction of becoming the first side to enter the competition. By the end of 1971 794 other villages had been accepted. They were divided into 32 groups, based on their location. The largest of these was Kent with an entry of 58. The seven hundred and fiftieth to enter was Snelling, who received a half gallon bottle of Haig. Appropriately they hailed from Kent. The early games led to a group final, then inter-regional matches leading to a final at Lord's between the Cornish and Worcestershire champions. It is a system, like the rules, that has stood the test of time. Variations have been minor, the change in county boundaries and on occasions variations in the number of clubs made adjustment necessary.

# A Tot of Whisky at the Birth

Many enthusiasts who live in the minor counties, do not have the same opportunity to watch top class cricket without travelling to a First Class county. Their own county ground may host the occasional fixture, but this is the exception rather than the rule. A seat at a test match is, I suspect a rare treat for many. These counties however, still take their local cricket seriously. Anything out of the ordinary seems to attract extra attention and enthusiasm.

This is no more ably demonstrated than in a small village some three miles south of the Cornish town of Camborne. Troon's cricket club was founded in 1875 and they have played on their current village pitch since 1926. Cricket is meat and drink to the village. It has provided twenty players who have played in the minor county league since the war, one of which captained Cornwall in 1961 & '62. M.S.T. Danston went on to play for Gloucestershire in 1973 & '74. And A.L. Penberthy joined Northamptonshire in 1988. He is representative of the strength of their youth team, having played for both the England under 16's & 19's. Also D. Roberts played for the under 16's in 1992.

Troon took part in the first year of the Haig Village Championship. They were delighted by succeeding in beating Evercreech from neighbouring Somerset to become group champions. On the way they overcame four other local village sides. The county final was an exciting affair by all accounts, batting first Troon made 145 for 6. Evercreech were dismissed for 142. Going on to the seventh round they had a comfortable win over Dorset champions Shillingstone who were restricted to the modest total of 83 all out. Troon passed that with the loss of only one wicket. The quarter final was a different matter. Oxford champions Bledlow batted first and had set the Cornishmen a target of more than 5 runs an over when their innings closed at 204 for 4. But Troon rose to the occasion, no doubt spurred on by their enthusiastic supporters, Bledlow's total

## A Village at Lord's

was passed with five wickets to spare. Excitement was mounting with a home tie semi-final against Linton Park champions of Kent, the largest group in the competition.

The day dawned with a buzz of excitement in the air. A crowd of 2000 turned up to see who would make it to the final. It was a keen contest, but the home team were never in any trouble. They scored 171 for 1, while Linton Park were all out for 167. It was a sporting contest of the highest calibre, not only had they booked a place at Lord's, but a firm friendship had been struck up between two village clubs.

Astwood Bank is a village south of Redditch in the heart of Worcestershire. They certainly were rich in talent. John Yoxhall had held the captains role for seven consecutive seasons. His batting ability was beyond question, having passed the 1000 runs in each of the last eight seasons. Another forceful batsman was their all-rounder Colin Robinson, he first played for the village team at the tender age of eight. In 1972 he was a little older, standing at over six foot two in his size thirteen boots, a character of the side. Joe Crompton was a bowler of some repute, he was described as a left handed Dennis Lillie. Frank Morrall their reliable opening bowler, who I understand was a villager by birthright, travelled to play from the village of Horbury Wells near Leamington Spa. They were well pleased with having beaten four local village sides in the early rounds, with some close although low scoring games, before meeting Hockley Heath in the county final. Here they scored a creditable 209 for 7, batting first. A run rate exceeding 5 an over proved too much for Hockley, they finished on 136 for 5.

The sixth round was against Staffordshire champions Swynnerton Park, their score of 124 for 4 was enough, their bowlers did them proud as the opposition were dismissed for 101. Their next game against the village of Horton House was a low scoring affair. The Northamptonshire side were all out for 89, leaving a reasonably easy target, although it has been proved many times, nothing is taken for granted, particularly in this competition. Astwood booked themselves a place in the last eight with a score of 93 for 4. Their quarter final tie against Kimbolton was another low scoring affair. They passed the Hunts. champions' score of 85 all out for the loss of three wickets. In the semi-final they were up against Nottinghamshire champions Collingham, this was to produce a higher scoring game. Astwood booked their place in the final with a score of 137 for 4, Collingham were worthy opponents in a close run game, finishing on 134 for 9, but they were to have their day on another occasion.

The bookmakers had entered into the spirit of the occasion, they were quoting Troon as 5-2 favourite. In truth either side could have won. As history would tell, skill was not the only ingredient needed to win at this stage in the competition. Ask any villager who has played in a final and they will readily tell you, often a slice of luck can turn a game. But the other factor to take into account is nerve. There is a psychological obstacle in playing at such a famous sporting venue, which effects many first class players. Jeffery Stollmeyer, past West Indies captain and honorary life member of MCC is quoted as saying,"Any cricketer who walks on the hallowed turf at Lord's for the first time and does not feel a special thrill, must be made of stone-not flesh and blood." If Lord's has that effect on a world class player of that calibre, how do you think a village cricketer must feel!

Saturday September 9th. 1972 dawned with grey skies and a chilling wind. The Friday had seen almost continual rain, inevitably the start was delayed. Scheduled for twelve noon, play did not get under way 'til one-thirty. None of this managed to dampen spirits among the 3000 spectators. The only ones to be frustrated were the 600 or so Troon supporters who were stranded by a train derailment at Dawlish who never made it. Sharp words to British Rail appeared to fall on deaf ears. Those privileged to be at this unique sporting spectacle were not about to let depressing weather spoil their day. The rustic supporters were in jovial mood. Klaxons and rattles were to cheer every run, wicket, extra or feat in the field.

Troon won the toss and put Astwood Bank into bat. This was partly due to the conditions, but I suspect they hoped the occasion would cause tension and possibly quick wickets. The first two overs were maidens, tension was beginning to tell. Troon's captain Terry Carter must have been well satisfied with his teams start. Astwood's skipper Yoxall had other ideas, proof of his batting ability was about to be demonstrated to the crowd. Unleashing an immaculate cover drive to the boundary, much to the delight of his supporters, he opened his teams account. The fifty came up in the 13th. over. Robinson supported his captain well in helping take the score to 69, before he played across the line once too often and was bowled by Thomas for 30. In the next over Yoxall holed out to be caught by Terry Carter off the bowling of Edwards without the score board moving. They continued without further mishap and the hundred came up in the 26th. over. In celebration, apart from the klaxons and rattles, the band of the Royal Green Jackets, tucked away in the Tavern area struck up a march. The players were however not amused and refused to play until it stopped. It did!

Astwood proceeded with Spittle trying to accelerate, he and Davies took the score to 139 before Spittle, trying once too often for the big hit was bowled by Johns for 36. The partnership of 70 could have provided a platform for a very healthy total, with wickets in hand. Alas it was not to be, as with the opening partnership Spittle's companion departed with the score unchanged. Disaster followed as Troon seized the initiative. They took the next five wickets quickly, only Crumpton showed any resistance and carried his bat for 16 as the innings closed on 165-8.

Troon made a cautious start to their reply. In poor light they

## A Tot of Whisky at the Birth

only managed 23 in the first twelve overs. Losing their opening batsman for two with the score on 14 had not helped. When the fifty came up in the 16th. over the pace was quickening, but Brian Carter was trapped by the guile of Robinson; LBW for 19. Enter captain Terry Carter, he was in no mood to let the initiative slip away. In the next seven overs he and Edwards took the total past the hundred. Yoxall, sensing Troon had seized the initiative, brought back his opening bowler Crumpton, in the hope he could put the brakes on. It was to no avail, Carter was in full cry, first pulling him to the mid-wicket boundary, then thumping him for 6 into the Mound Stand. With eighteen coming off the over Troon were on top, and their supporters in good voice. Edwards tried to match his captain's driving, but played round a ball from Morrall and was bowled for 45 in the twenty-fifth over. He had played his part well, sharing in a partnership of 67 for the third wicket. There was to be no further mishap, Vincent joined his skipper and they brought up the 150 in the thirty-first over. The end came in fine style in the 34th. over. Carter hit the luckless Robinson to square leg for 4 to bring the score to 164 then hoisted him into the Astwood crowd in the tavern for 6! It was all over, Troon were National Champions.

Haig's managing director Michael Henderson presented the £1,000 trophy to a beaming and delighted Terry Carter. Holding the trophy aloft to great cheers from the assembled crowd, must have been a proud moment for him. His contribution to victory had been to score 50 in 42 minutes and carry his bat for a personal score of 79. The winners received a cheque for £250, which went towards improvements to their pavilion. The trophy took pride of place in the local village store. There was much press reaction. John Morgan of the Daily Express summed it up admirably. "Village Cricket has done Lord's proud." The following day in the Sunday Telegraph, Michael Melford commented "Cornwall has played no great part in the history of cricket, but the men of Troon changed that yesterday." There was also comment about the band incident. Ian Peebles expressed his disappointment that the image of village cricket had changed, "immaculate dress and a high degree of professionalism had replaced the cow pat and the cow shot." John Arlott was to have something to say on the subject in 1977. As for the future of the competition? Things were looking promising, already seven hundred and fifty clubs had applied for next years competition.

**1973** Once again Troon were to reach the final, but their first round match against Werrington was a close run affair. They were bowled out for 110. Needing 5 runs to win in the final over, Werrington's last man was bowled trying to finish in style. There were no further scares on the way to securing the group final. They disposed of Somerset's Ruishton then Dorset champions Witchampton, followed by Hampshire champions Steep. Their semi-final opponents Marden from Kent took things seriously, they chartered a jet to take team and supporters to Cornwall. Before a crowd of 3000, Troon set a target of 203 to win. With good bowling and fielding, 5 runs an over proved too much, Marden ended up thirty-seven runs short of victory.

Gowerton is situated a few miles west of Swansea in South Wales. Cricket is the centre of village life in Summer. Rugby appears to dominate in Winter. I understand practice in the nets for the Haig competition early on, met with mock jeering from rugby players, sharing the sports facilities. They changed their tune later and became stalwart supporters, affectionately known as "Renta-crowd." 1972 had seen the team reach the last sixteen. This year they were destined to go all the way to Lord's. En route they beat Avoncroft by 118 runs, having bowled out the opposition for 58. They then defeated Fordham and Milford Hall, before disappointing Collingham for the second time. The Nottingham champions however had their glory to come.

In the final, Troon once again won the toss and elected to

## A Tot of Whisky at the Birth

bat. They were made to struggle for runs. The main stumbling block was not just a pair of hostile fast bowlers, but Gowerton's groundsman Bill Thomas. He was a true character in the early years of the competition. A slow left armer who took just four steps in his delivery, had a see-saw action, which could be most alarming to a batsman. His delivery action was a gentle lob, which cricket writer Tony Huskinson likened to troops lobbing grenades from the trenches. His cricketing apparel too was just as unusual. Dressed in half mast creams. with sleeves buttoned to the wrists and a green sun shade, which it is said was on loan from the local sports editor. No doubt many of the 8000 spectators would remember him. Terry Carter, heroic batsman of the 1972 final will remember him! He was deceived by him. Brother Brian replaced him and batted steadily through the final 26 overs to remain undefeated on 70, which gained him man of the match. Troon eventually finished on a creditable 176 for 6, leaving the Welshmen to score at just over 4.3 an over.

Gowerton started positively, when their 18 year old opener Adrian Daniel crashed three off side boundaries into the Tavern fence. The Welsh crowd immediately lifted their voices, no doubt hoping they could be heard back home in the valleys. Daniel settled down to a more moderate pace, but could not resist reaching his fifty in style. It came with a hook for 6 in the twentieth over. But with Troon's experience of having been there before and conditions becoming darker, later batsmen found it difficult to pierce the field. At 164 for 5 they ran out of overs and Troon retained the title. Their cheque for £250 no doubt helped to further boost the pavilion improvement funds. I suspect the trophy was to remain on display in the local village store.

**1974** With 764 clubs entering the competition this year a headline in The Cricketer read "The Haig; a sturdy two year old-growing fast." The sponsors continued with their generous

## A Village at Lord's

financial support. Eve of match hospitalities, with dinner in the banqueting suite at Lord's had become a regular feature of the competition. Assistance with travelling costs for teams travelling long distances was to continue. In addition Haig announced each team entering the competition would receive a bottle of the company's product. The last sixteen would receive a 40 oz. bottle of Haig, quarter finalists a quarter gallon each and the semi finalists a gallon. As for the finalists, their reward would be a case of Haig whisky each. In addition cash prizes had been increased. The winners receiving a cheque for £500, £250 for the runner up and £125 for each of the beaten semi-finalists.

The additional amber nectar must have been a welcoming bonus to keep out the cold. The season started cold and wet. Despite being littered with a host of rescheduled games, enthusiasm, helped I suspect by a tot of whisky, triumphed over conditions. The programme was tight and some ingenuity was needed to obtain results. But I can safely say there is no truth in the rumour one umpire downed a generous helping of Haig, to help keep out the cold of course. And then proceeded to allow his side 7 ball overs! Neither did he top up with a similar quantity of spirit, having had the error pointed out, and proceed to direct 5 ball overs to the opposition to compensate!

In one semi-final another Welsh side was competing for a place at Lord's. Ynysygerwn must have started favourites, on the way they had defeated both last year's finalists. In Cornwall in front of a crowd in excess of 4000, they restricted Troon to 127 for 6 and passed their total having lost only one wicket with more than five overs to spare. Haig offered to fly the Welshmen to Northumberland, but they declined not wishing to miss the opportunity of a twelve hour coach trip. It was after all an opportunity to practise their singing, without any interruption. They lost to Bomarsund Welfare, batting first they were all out for 99. Admittedly it was a lively pitch, but in their first seven matches they had scored 979 runs having lost only 16 wickets.

## A Tot of Whisky at the Birth

The sun came out and on a drying wicket, with the pace easing Bomarsund passed the modest Welsh total in the twenty-eighth over and won by six wickets. Their opponents were to be the Nottinghamshire champions from Collingham, at last they had made it! Beaten semi-finalists in the first year their determination had paid off. But luck was to dog them even at this late stage, the final at Lord's was washed out without a ball being bowled. As can be appreciated the Mecca of cricket has a heavy fixtures list, so it's not possible just to reschedule the game for another day. Thankfully Warwickshire stepped in and the final was played the following Sunday at Edgbaston, at least both teams had the opportunity of playing the final on another test ground.

There had not been much improvement in the weather when the teams arrived at Ebgbaston. Bomarsund won the toss and put Collingham in to bat on a damp wicket, between the showers they managed a total of 110 all out. The tea interval was extended by twenty minutes as ground staff shuttled the covers back and forth with threatening clouds over-head. Eventually the game restarted. Bomarsund lost a wicket to the first ball of their innings and were lucky not to lose three more in G.Williams' first over. Batting conditions were obviously difficult. Howard Hailey batted patiently for an hour and a half and at the close he was undefeated on 44, and in the thirty-eighth over saw his team to victory. Ben Brocklehurst awarded him the Daily Mirror man of the match. His short speech demonstrated admirably the spirit in which the competition was played. "I got man of the match, but there were eleven men of the match."

**1975** By contrast to the previous year this proved to be a glorious Summer. All 813 matches in the Haig Championships were decided on cricketing skill. Not once did the silver coin appear. This year was to see Gowerton in the final once more, on this occasion their opponents were the Cambridgeshire champions, Isleham. Unlike Gowerton who were located in an industrial area of Wales, this was a village in the rural heart of Cambridgeshire countryside. All players lived within two or three miles of the village green where they played. Their team was truly a family affair, three brothers named Houghton and two sets of brothers the Collens and the Sheldricks, all played for the team.

Gowerton started favourites, lost the toss and were invited to field. On a placid pitch Isleham started nervously, with the tension showing BC Houghton was run out for three early on, similar to his semi-final.

Gowerton however did not take full advantage of the situation in this particular respect, but they still had groundsman Bill Thomas up their sleeve. He came on to bowl with a few noticeable changes from 1973. A fawn coloured Jockey cap had replaced the green eye shade. I never did find out if he had had a disagreement with the local sports editor over the write up on their last Lord's appearance. His run up had been cut in half, he now took two paces, but the lob was still as good as ever. The two bad balls he bowled were to great effect, Cawley was yorked on the second bounce and he had Houghton caught on the long leg boundary. This was all too much for Isleham and they could only manage 120.

Set a run rate of 3 an over they set about the task as if they needed nearer five. Twenty-four came in the first three overs, but they lost their prolific batsman Wayne Jones in the process. With the score on 31 "Dangerous Daniel" was caught for seven. A personal disappointment for a man with two Haig centuries to his credit, he had declined a place in the Glamorgan County side to take part in the championship and help his village get to Lord's again. Bevan 57 not out and RD Evans although bowled by Cole for 46 had steadied the ship. The Welshmen were home and dry at 124 for 4 with more then ten overs to spare. It had been a good game watched by a crowd of 5000 people, some in national costume. This was to be the last year Gowerton were to take part in the competition. They had fallen foul of the inhabitants rule. Gone they may be but not forgotten. Commentator Alan Curtis recalls the occasion in the '73 final, when he had to leave the commentary box for a short period, only to return and find a small band of the rugby rent-a-crowd had commandeered the microphone. Their advice to the team was more suited to the football terraces. A rare incident quickly brought under control by a steward. If anything it will be their singing they will be remembered for, like so many Welsh sides.

**1976** A Summer I well remember as one of the hottest on record. Towards the end of August pitches were bare and outfields parched. Yet my day at the Lord's test match was disappointing — not a ball was bowled all day due to continuous rain! The fine weather had ensured all 835 clubs battling for a place in the final had a good start. This continued with little interruption by weather, although I suspect drink intervals broke all records in '76. Troon were to appear in their third final. The North Yorkshire champions Sessay were to be their opponents this time. A small village of some 400 inhabitants, just five miles from Thirsk, hometown of Thomas Lord.

Cricket has been a way of life in Sessay for almost 150 years. Their most famous son being the Yorkshire and England fast bowler George Freeman. He played against Dr. W.G. who said of him "He is the fastest bowler I have ever come up against." The original pitch of 1860 has long gone. In 1974 they moved to their new home in the middle of the village. The club house is put to good use, as the only pub in the village is closed down. If you wish to visit, don't go on a Monday, particularly if you want a drink, because Sessay sleeps on Monday. Like many villages in the country, they have families who have played for the club from one generation passing on to the next. Today the names Flintoff and Till are well known on the field of play. They

## A Village at Lord's

have a scorer named Clayton. Ask him what contribution his family have made on the field and he will tell you at one time Sessay fielded a full eleven all with the name Clayton. A rare achievement, but what a nightmare for the scorers, perhaps that's why he is todays scorer, secrets are often passed from father to son. I never did find out the name of the twelfth man in those far off days, could his name have been Clayton? If not it would not surprise me to learn the name was Flintoff or Till

Sessay had had little success in the competition in past years. The first year saw them go out in the first round. Their arch rivals Sheriff Hutton Bridge twice knocked them out and they had not progressed beyond the third round until now. But perseverance with more or less the same team had paid dividends. Their first round match was against Londesborough. Batting first Sessay scored a reasonable 140. Just as the home side looked like getting on top, the game was transformed as M Duffield held a one handed catch. That slice of luck referred to earlier had at last gone their way and the Yorkshire side never looked back. Having beaten Cloughton to secure the group final, they were beginning to get noticed locally. As they progressed, defeating Holmesfield (Notts) in the sixth round, then Burnmoor (Northumberland), so interest grew and spread. After securing a semi-final against Isleham, by winning against the Durham village of Etherley, the local TV and Radio gave them star billing.

Glorious sunshine greeted the team and their convoy of coaches as they arrived in the Cambridgeshire village of Isleham. Sessay won the toss and elected to bat. Brian Flintoff and D Harrison came to the wicket to cheers from the 5000 spectators, many of them from Yorkshire. After a steady opening partnership of 41 in 12 overs, two wickets went without any addition to the score. Ian Till and Harrison built a sound platform by taking the score to 82. Isleham brought on their spinner in the hope they could ensure the brakes were applied. It was not to be and the lower order added 52 in the last 10 overs to finish on 159 for

## A Tot of Whisky at the Birth

9. There was a disastrous start to Isleham's reply, Brian Houghton was caught for 3 with the score on 6. Skipper M Collen was bowled without adding to the total. Pope and Les Collen added a further 25 before Pope was stumped. Once again another wicket fell without the scoreboard moving. 31 for 4 was a tight position to escape from, despite a 20 from Barry Houghton and 17 from David Peachey, the Cambridgeshire heroes were all out for 92 in the 30th.over. Sessay were at Lord's and all Yorkshire saluted them.

The local constabularies at Troon and Sessay were to be on full alert on August Bank Holiday Monday. Villains for miles around only had to watch the local news to see the potential for easy pickings. With two empty villages, they hoped for a burglars paradise. But they were to be disappointed. Happy villagers were off to Lord's to see their heroes in action and knew their homes would be safe. Village folk are different to those in urban areas. They do mind their neighbours business, when the need arises.

The weather was overcast when Sessay won the toss, they put the Cornishmen in to bat on the wicket that had been used for England's game against West Indies the previous day. Angrove hit two boundaries in the first over, but at 37 the first wicket fell. Runs had not been easy to come by with the ball being moved about by Ian Till and Jackson. After a delighted Burnett had dismissed Angrove and danger man Terry Carter the Yorkshire team were beginning to get on top. Troon continued to struggle against the bowling. Halfway through the innings they had only reached 48 and the next 10 overs only saw them reach the mid sixties. Opening bowler Jackson was brought back and had Brian Carter well caught at backward short leg. It had been a valuable defensive innings for 34 and Troon were on the rack at 99 for 7. Sessay let the fielding slip and the tail wagged a little with 14 runs coming in the last two overs, to end up on 113 for 7. Ian Till may not have taken a wicket, but with figures of 9-3-12-0 he had done his part in containing the score.

Sessay also found the going hard. In the fifth over the experienced Brian Flintoff was out to a sharp chance at short leg by Brian Carter with the score on six. Tension remained as Harrison and Jackson tried to pierce the field, they looked for the bad ball but it never came. With the score on 36 Jackson was bowled for 19 by Johns. At the half way mark with 43 runs on the board, it was still anybody's game. With eight wickets in hand and opener Harrison still at the crease, only a slight acceleration was all that was needed. In the next ten overs five more wickets fell with only a further 18 runs added to the total. The ninth wicket fell at 81, but still the tension remained. A spirited last wicket stand had developed, which led to further nail biting among the supporters. But with the score on 95 Borthwick was bowled leaving Fred Till unbeaten on 13. There were still fifteen balls left, so the crowd had seen an exciting, if low scoring match. Brian Moyle was awarded man of the match for his splendid figures of 9 − 1 − 23 − 4. Troon took the trophy back to Cornwall along with their two veterans Dunstan and Jim Vincent, both of whom announced their retirement at the end of the match. Troon were to play again at Lord's, but that's another story.

**1977** The weather took its toll once again, with frustration, hastily rearranged fixtures and the tantalising terror of bowling at the stumps, recorded on at least three occasions. These abortive journeys between villages without a ball being bowled, do of course create much frustration for supporters and players alike. But spare a thought for the hard pressed fixtures secretaries. It is they who have to face the wrath of local sides when matches arranged many months earlier have to be rescheduled, or a scratch team has to be drawn from the second eleven to ensure everyone is reasonably happy.

The competition's statistical records had been growing

## A Tot of Whisky at the Birth

steadily over the five years of the competition. Many centuries had been recorded, as well as some notable bowling achievements. But nobody had yet managed a double century. Trevor Botting from the Sussex village of Balcombe was about to change all that. On May 15th. 1977 He opened the batting for his village. At the close he was still there, undefeated on 206. His innings contained no fewer than twenty sixes, having reached his first three landmarks of 50, his century and 150 with a six, the boundary was ringed with fielders as he took strike on 199. A cheeky single brought up his double century. Not content with that he hit a further six to bring the innings to a close at 269 for 4. To put the contribution Botting had made to his sides score into perspective, the next highest score to his was 18. His innings is believed to be a world record in any form of cricket. To date that claim has not been challenged.

Balcombe's luckless Sussex neighbours Chiddingstone had more to contend with. They set about their reply requiring more than six an over, but had not counted on Botting's cousin Albert Constable who took 7 for 34 in restricting the opposition to 151. On the same day Tim Cannon from the village of Cokenach scored 203 not out, his innings included some 13 sixes and 17 fours in a total of 287 for 3. Another bowling achievement worthy of comment is Ian Enters of Alfriston, who in April equalled the Haig record by taking 9 for 14 in his nine overs. No less than five of his victims were clean bowled, and to end a memorable match for him he caught the last man. Alas all three teams went out in the next round.

The final was believed to have drawn the biggest crowd of any final. It was certainly the noisiest! Cookley from Worcestershire were playing Lindal Moor, champions of Cumbria. Both teams had beaten some strong opposition en route to the finals, so an exciting game was expected. I would think Cookley must have started favourites, having deprived Troon of another appearance in the final, winning by two runs off the last ball of

## A Village at Lord's

the match. Lindal Moor had defeated the strong Yorkshire side of East Brierley by two wickets. They were however to have their day on another occasion.

The scene was set. Sunshine, a short boundary to the Tavern stand, and a pitch that looked likely to produce plenty of runs, all pointed to the promise of a high scoring contest. Cookley lost the toss and were put in to bat. With the score on 101 for 3 they were set for a creditable total. It was not to be however, they lost their next seven wickets for just 38 runs. Due in no small part to Lindal's Coulson who finished with figures of 6 for 24 off 6.5 overs. The Cumbrian champions reply was not a good one. They lost their first seven wickets for just 37 runs. There was no wagging from the tail and they were all out for 110. Cookley won by 28 runs, they were worthy winners. Good bowling and fielding had played a major part in their victory. Reg Britton, a brisk medium pace bowler finished with the impressive figures of 6 − 3 − 6 − 3. For the first time a final had been slightly tarnished by a minority of the crowd. Banner waving and clanking beer cans are here to stay. Our West Indian cousins in their enthusiastic exuberance for the game have seen to that. They are after all the undisputed Kings of Carnival. But obscene songs, a pitch invasion and threats of physical violence have no place in any form of cricket. In my experience the mindless disruption which has plagued football over the last two decades, has been prevented from taking a hold in cricket because supporters will not tolerate it. They have their own way of dealing with over exuberant spectators who become a nuisance. They are simply told to sit down and watch the game. In most cases it works, if not ground staff or local police deal with the matter without fuss. Well that is the end of chapter two. It is also the end of John Haig & Company's sponsorship. One that was initially intended to be for only three years, but eventually ran for six. In that time they had aided The Cricketer in firmly establishing the competition's roots. Many villages had been helped to

## A Tot of Whisky at the Birth

improve their game, their finances, and indeed some their very existence. Michael Henderson and his staff could justifiably feel proud. As Tony Huskinson put it, "The purveyors of the amber nectar had given the game at grass roots level a hefty "kick start"- in line with their product."

# CHAPTER THREE

# Cricket Can be a "Bitter Game"

In 1742, some forty-five years before MCC was founded, a new brewing company was established. Its name? Whitbread. 250 years later the corporate name remains intact, while other once famous brand names have disappeared, swallowed up by big fish that have grown bigger in the guise of amalgamation and rationalisation. A rare achievement in this commercial world of ours.

Apart from its reputation for "good ale!", Whitbread is recognised for its contribution to the world of sport. In yachting circles the "Round the World Yacht Race" is synonymous with the name Whitbread. The sport of kings has many famous races, among them the "Whitbread Gold Cup", the first ever sponsored steeplechase.

As with many companies involved in sponsorship, there are periodic reviews. In the late seventies the Whitbread board undertook such a review. On the agenda was an item for them to discuss how best the company could find a sporting event to ensure its name could be advertised at a recognised national sporting venue. At that time John Haig & Company were about to relinquish their sponsorship of the National Village Championships, after six years involvement with the hosts, MCC and The Cricketer magazine, who were the organisers. This seemed to be an ideal opportunity for the company to achieve its marketing objective whilst ensuring continued support for the splendid work that had made the competition the success it undoubtedly was.

# A Village at Lord's

So in 1979 the competition became "THE SAMUEL WHITBREAD VILLAGE CRICKET CHAMPIONSHIP", although it took two years for the competition to be recognised as Whitbread's. It is fortunate that Haig's sponsorship had not been established as long as Whitbread's was for the Gold Cup and Round the World Yacht Race!

It proved to be a happy partnership, spanning a further six years of the competition, a period in which Whitbread brought its own particular style to the competition. Apart from the invaluable financial support, company products and awards, there was a break with tradition for the eve of final dinners. These were held in the company banqueting suite in Chiswell Street. I have seen the hall for myself, with the original architectural features restored. It is an impressive sight, and the exposed queen post roof trusses with heavy black metal straps give just a hint of historical nostalgia from a bygone age, during a banquet. And the modern-day banquets attended by village cricketers became legendary. Transport on the morning of the final was something to behold. Whitbread collected the teams from their hotel and took them to Lord's on their brewer's drays, each pulled by two magnificent shire horses, complete with shining leather and gleaming brasses. A sight which made Londoners sit up and take notice. Each village were of course champions of their respective counties. Here the sponsors added yet another of their own touches. A former England captain from their own county was on each dray. In the first year Sir Leonard Hutton accompanied the East Brierley team from Yorkshire, while Tony Lewis was on the dray pulling Glamorgan's champions Ynysygerwn, the pride of Wales. All went well until they arrived at the Grace Gates.It was here that a rather irate steward refused to allow the horses access to the ground. But Sir Colin Cowdrey came to the rescue, and after a short friendly chat the drays entered the ground to the click of press photographers' cameras.

## Cricket Can be a "Bitter Game"

**1979** 772 village clubs entered the first year of the Whitbread, so The Cricketer must have heaved a sigh of relief, safe in the knowledge they had a sponsor once again. Having had to shoulder all the responsibility the previous year was no picnic, and the thought of having to see it all through a second time with such a large entry was I feel sure a daunting one. By the time inter-group and regional rounds started on July 13th., several familiar names were still in contention. Triple champions Troon, beat Grampound Road in a tight finish for the Cornish crown. Whilst last years champions had an easy nine wicket victory over Kent neighbours Yalding. Toft, runners up to Linton Park, won a cliff hanger to become champions of Cheshire, Clwyd and Merseyside. Set 213 to win by Northrup Hill they finished on 215 for 9 off the last ball of the match. Other teams that had consistently won their group, but not yet made it to the final also won through to the sixth round. Langleybury of Herts. and the Derbyshire village of Quarndon were two who achieved it for the fifth consecutive year. Read of Lancashire playing in their seventh group final out of eight scored 201 for six in their forty overs, then dismissed Woodhouse for 57. G. O'Connor taking 4 for 13 and three catches.

East Brierley of West Yorkshire won their sixth round match against Toft in a tight finish that went to the last over. Round seven was to be an all Yorkshire affair when they took on Stainborough from the north of the county. Chasing a total of 167 for 8 Stainborough had a poor start losing 3 wickets in eleven overs, whilst adding only 17 runs and never recovered. Phil Taylor was man of the match for the second consecutive time, returning a bowling feat of 3 for 8 following his useful knock of 25 runs. In the quarter-final they were up against Burnmoor from Newcastle Tyne and Wear. An opening partnership of 75 between Linsey and Lethard helped Burnmoor off to a fine start. At the end of their forty overs they had set a fair target for their bowlers to aim at with 194 for 4 on the board. East Brierley had it all to do at almost five an over. They were in no mood to allow their north county neighbours get the upper hand, thirty-five came off the first five overs. Then their West Indian Walwyn came to the wicket, and saw them home with a display of batting in true Caribbean style with five overs to spare.

East Brierley were hosts in their semi-final match against Fordham, the champions of East Anglia. Their picturesque small ground had never seen such a sight. Bursting to capacity with some 3000 spectators, they lost the toss and the village from the fen country elected to bat on a fast medium pitch, with a bit of bounce! They had a respectable start, both opening bowlers having completed their allotted nine overs, well almost. In the eighteenth with the score on 54 for 1, Troop bowled his final delivery to Peter Arnold, soundly established on 33. Mindful this was the last ball of the opening attack, he may have lost his concentration for a split second, who knows. But wicket keeper Wilson, who had impressed all, had his just reward with a brilliant stumping down the leg side. With Arnold back in the pavilion the fielders were obviously on their toes, for in the next over a brilliant low catch twixt gulley and third man sent Mims in the same direction as Arnold. The home team had seized the advantage and their supporters let them know it. Heath tried to hold things together with a disciplined defensive innings, while Barry Houghton threw caution to the wind, which paid dividends to some extent. Murphy Walwyn managed to deceive with his change of pace and his 3 for 22 helped restrict Fordham to 145 for 9 at the close. East Brierley made a steady start, Sanderson and Nurse adding 37 for the first wicket, before Nurse was caught by Brown making a fine sprint from deep mid on to take the catch. Enter "Walwyn the Whirlwind", who took charge of the situation. In a spirited 44 he scored all round the wicket with fluency and power. One four took two stumps out of the ground on its way to the boundary. Only a brilliant juggling catch by Rampley stopped the onslaught continuing. Walwyn's shot was

# Cricket Can be a "Bitter Game"

speeding to the leg side boundary, when Rampley sprinting some twenty yards realised the ball was beating him, dived, managed to flick the ball back with his left hand as he fell, then took the rebound with his right. Runs continued to come from one end, whilst opener Sanderson remained as anchor man at the other. On the last ball of the thirtieth over, with five runs needed for victory, Sanderson was facing on forty-nine. There was silence in the crowd as the bowler started his run up, would this be a six to win the match and bring a well deserved half century? No, the ball sped past all to the boundary, four byes! John Decent by name and by nature played out a maiden to give Sanderson the strike. Tension mounted as he played and missed five times. All thoughts of the result were momentarily forgotten as he again took strike for yet another last ball of an over. He swung hard, got a thick outside edge, the ball rose vertically, two fielders homed in on it. No familiar calls of catch it! The situation was too tense. Both fielders arrived at the right spot simultaneously, but so intent were they on keeping their eyes on the ball, neither saw the other approach. The ball fell between them and Sanderson's fifty was greeted with thunderous applause. He had won the award for man of the match. East Brierley were on their way to Lord's.

Llangwm were never on top in the Glamorgan and Dyfed final, they only managed 81 in reply to Ynysygerwn's 203 for 4. In the next round, chasing Gloucestershire champions Frocester's total of 159 for 9, a total of 159 for 6 was on the board at the end of thirty-nine overs. Ynysygerwn then played out the last over as a maiden, to secure victory by having lost fewer wickets. Against Horspath of Oxfordshire only eight overs were needed to pass their target of 55. Curtis took four for four and they won by ten wickets, A. Geogheghan finishing with an unbeated 45 out of a total of 58. Little Durnford were the pride of Wiltshire having toppled the mighty Troon in the previous round. As a result their odds had been cut from 40-1 to 8-1, so they were favourites to win the quarter-final. They certainly started well, dismissing the formidable opening Welsh pair with only twelve on the board. A further scare came when McKay narrowly avoided being run out without scoring, he soon settled down however and proceeded to tear into the bowling, with strokes all round the wicket. With 46 runs coming from the last five overs, Ynysygerwn finished on 190 for 4, with McKay 90 not out. Accurate medium pace bowling tied down the openers with only 11 runs coming from the first eleven overs. When a brilliant stumping from M Davies started the slide, hopes of a Wiltshire side at Lord's were dashed, as Little Durnford were all out for 54.

Langleybury, fresh from an exciting win over Linton Park, travelled to Wales for their semi-final. The facilities impressed them, but not the weather, mist and drizzle were in the air. Despite a wet outfield the pitch was dry and the match started on time, in front of a 3000 crowd. Langlebury lost the toss and were put into bat. Both openers made a careful start, by the time they both departed 84 was on the board. At 138 for 3, the Welsh crowd were worried, with left hander Martin in fine form. One six left a job for the local glazier on Monday morning.

A large total looked on the cards. Much to the relief of the home team he ran out of partners, but there was still a score of 185 to beat.

Ynysygerwn were careful not to lose early wickets. The first two overs were maidens. Alan Geogheghan an experienced batsman who had played for Wales, was out for 12. He was followed almost immediately by Chris Mckay, hero of the previous match. The score had slipped from 93 for 4 to 130 for 7. Tension mounted as the eighth wicket went down with 158 on the board. Jeff Curtis was not overawed by the situation, in true village fashion he hit a breathtaking 26 before being run out off the last ball of the 39th over with the score on 184. If there had been an extra coat of varnish on Terry Hogan's off stump it would have been all over. The second ball was scooped into a deserted

## Cricket Can be a "Bitter Game"

outfield and in the gathering gloom two scampered runs set the Welsh singing for the first time that day. But not I suspect for the last. The luckless Langleybury had it all to do again in 1980.

The late Findlay Rea dubbed Whitbread's first final a glamorous one. It started with the superb eve of final banquet for a hundred and fifty guests at the brewery's headquarters in Chiswell Street. On the morning of the final St. John's Wood was brought to a virtual standstill by the procession of brewer's drays pulled by magnificent shire horses as they travelled from the players hotel to Lord's cricket ground. Inside, a large crowd, which included many of the 10000 cricketers who had set out in earlier rounds, were being entertained by the Band of the Coldstream Guards. All the Tavern boxes were full to capacity, although the weather was overcast there was nothing downcast about the spectators. Nothing could dampen their spirits, particularly the Welsh contingent who were in full song as usual, and a ball hadn't even been bowled yet.

The pitch was easy paced and there was a short boundary to the Tavern. It therefore surprised some of the bucolic cricketing sages in the stands that Ynysygerwn put their opponents in to bat. Sanderson started by nervously missing four of the first five deliveries, one of which had a confident appeal for LBW turned down. Nurse relieved the tension with a six, hooked into the Tavern in the fifth over. He contributed 16 before being bowled, with the first wicket down at 28. Welwyn off drove his first ball majestically, but Geoff Williams read it well at mid off, preventing a certain boundary. The Welsh crowd must have breathed a sigh of relief when he was trapped LBW by Watkins for 19, but not before he confirmed his capabilities by casually flicking a six off his legs to the long boundary over square leg. Enter the second West Indian, Clive Defoe, who immediately flat batted a full toss over mid on. He certainly enjoyed his cricket. When caught out on 61 he was still grinning. Both openers bowled their allotted overs straight through, at

# A Village at Lord's

which point the score board stood at 82 for 2. A good launching platform for the 22 overs yet to come. Sanderson defended while Defoe continued to score freely. With the score on 112 he was run out to a dubious call from Defoe. John Decent joined Defoe and together they put on 40, with Defoe scoring effortlessly before holing out to a skyer at wide mid off, which Geoff Williams judged well in taking a swirling catch. Jones joined Decent and at first found difficulty in getting to grips with things. That didn't last long, he finished on 30 not out while his partner had notched up 45 in an unbroken partnership of 64. The last five overs had produced 61 as the total finished on 216 for four, beating the previous total in a final of 176 for 3 set up by Troon in 1973. Ynysygerwn decided not to stick to their normal batting order. Opener Geoff Williams was replaced by Chris McKay in the hope his forcing left hand prowess would blunt the Yorkshire opening attack. With the total on 13, he was beaten for pace by Pickering and bowled for 10. Wicketkeeper Davies joined Geogheghan and kept the runs coming, but his partner, realising he was bogged down having scored just 9 runs in 12 overs, decided to hit out or get out. Immediately P.Topp bowled him without addition to his score. At 43 for 2 the run rate was starting to creep up. Defoe yorked Davies in his first over for 25. With the score on 49 for 3 in 15 overs things were beginning to look desperate as captain Geoff Williams took strike. He started reasonably well, but was unlucky to play on, off bat and pad for just 13. At this point the Welsh stopped singing, a sign that things were not going well. Free swinging Dave Thomas joined Williams and together they put on 40 for the fifth wicket and with six down for 108 a miracle was needed. It was not to be, the tail showed little resistance as the last four wickets went down for 16 runs. East Brierley were the first Yorkshire village to be champions.

As their skipper held the cup aloft a great cheer went up amongst all the spectators on the ground. It had been an excellent days cricket played in the best of spirit. The Welsh crowd

## Cricket Can be a "Bitter Game"

generous in defeat, didn't stop singing. And in recognition of their opponents' convincing win sang "On Ilkley Moor Bar Tat." MCC president Mr. CH Palmer presented the cup and a cheque for £500 to the victorious Bast Brierley. Their vice captain Clive Defoe was awarded man of the match for his innings of 61.

**1980** The early rounds in May went with little disruption, on firm fast pitches which produced a glut of high scores. Thankfully entries had been reduced to a manageable 128 before the rain set in, bringing a succession of wet weekends from June through to August. Three sides were unceremoniously eliminated by the toss of a coin, a very frustrating outcome at such a late stage in the competition. Humour did still exist however. On one occasion it was suggested that the captain should be awarded man of the match just for winning the toss! To win or lose on such a decision in my view can only be described as a hollow victory. I am sure newcomers Much Markle were better satisfied with losing to Canon Frome in a very one sided affair. Set a target of 10.5 an over, they were all out for 54, losing by 365 runs. Canon Frome's total of 419 for 6 was the competition record. Surprisingly no one scored a hundred, although there were two century partnerships. One hundred and four for two for the second wicket, and one hundred and forty-one for the third. There were sixteen sixes and forty-nine fours, which accounted for 292 of the total. Top scorer Maurice Embrey with ninety-three, followed up with a bowling analysis of 7 for 15.

The final was to see another Welsh side in action, Marchwiel of Clwyd took on the historical Hampshire village of Longparish. To the victor would go the spoils, but in addition the National Champions had another challenge. In September they were to play a match in Rotterdam against an invitation eleven captained by West Indian Clive Lloyd.

Hampshire is a county renowned for cricket and boasts many

# A Village at Lord's

village sides with a long history. None more so than Longparish, so named because it was one long street. It is in a delightful setting in the heart of the county. The picturesque ground with brick and thatched pavilion is set in a conservation area. The present pavilion however is in need of restoration which will cost more than a few thousand pounds to ensure it is in keeping with the environment. Longparish had taken the county title in 1979, beating neighbours Hursley Park in a closely fought contest, only to go out in the sixth round against Oakwood in an equally close game. Needing six from the last ball of the match Luff hooked the ball which fell two yards short of the boundary. They prefer to say they lost by two yards, and not two runs as was shown on the official score card. They beat Ampfield in fine style.

Chasing a total of 163 for 9 they ran out worthy winners at 166 for 1. Luff finishing on 85 not out. In round six, after two abortive journeys totalling more than four hundred miles, the luckless Sussex champions Glynde & Beddingham were beaten by the toss of a coin. Round seven was a similar affair to the game against Ampfield, having bowled Stock of Essex out for 127 they coasted to victory at 135 for 1. Luff was again in the runs finishing on 79 not out. Having started and finished with a six, he had scored four hundred and sixty-eight runs, not out twice, with an average of two hundred and thirty-four.

The semi-final was against the redoubtable Cornishmen of Troon. Batting first Troon scored a highly respectable 211 for 4, J Spry, the Carter brothers and P John were all in the runs. Spry and Carter, having put on 127 for the second wicket, had contributed much to the final total. Troon had started favourites and when Longparish in reply lost their fifth wicket on 111 after 28 overs, and Denis Luff back in the dressing room with a modest total of 42 by his own high standards, they must have fancied their chances of a fourth appearance at Lord's. Andy Jones joined Heagren and together put on eighty runs to tilt the pendulum back. But with eight overs remaining and 140 on the board there

# Cricket Can be a "Bitter Game"

was still some way to go. In the thirty-third over Jones struck the first ball for six and the second for four. The third should have been two, but a fielding error resulted in four over throws. Sixteen off the over, which concluded with a missed catch that broke David Jenkins' finger, preventing him from completing his allotted overs. Longparish survived another dropped catch in the 36th. over, but Jones was out 3 balls later for an agressive 52. John Heagren, with a patient 30 to his name, took charge ably supported by Tony Freeman, he steered his side home at 214 for 6 and 1.4 overs to spare. Heagren carried his bat for 59 and was a worthy winner of man of the match.

Marchwiel defeated Alvanley to become group champions. In round six a score of 125 for 9 was enough to beat Staffordshire champions Enville who could only muster 83. Round seven meant a tie with the strong Derbyshire village of Quarndon, who had an impressive record having played 36 and lost only 6, unfortunately this was to be their seventh. But their day of glory was yet to come. Marchwiel managed a score of 146 for 7 which was not an impossible total to beat, but Quarndon were all out for 118 thanks in no small part to skipper Bell who followed his 40 runs with 2 for 19.

The west Yorkshire village of Kirkburton visited Clwyd for their semi- final. Marchwiel batting first were struggling with 13 for 2 before a record crowd. The partnership of David Jones and captain John Bell brought some respectability to proceedings. When Bell went for 40 Steve Barrett came in to blitz the Kirkburton bowling attack, his 43 in just 30 deliveries included three huge sixes. Seventy-five runs came from the bat in the last ten overs, and the Welshmen finished with a respectable 175 for 6. Kirkburton were never allowed off the hook, against a seamers wicket and superb fielding, they fell behind the clock. Risks had to be taken with the inevitable run outs, two of which were direct hits. At 77 for 5 the task was an impossibility. The tail only managed a further 16 runs and the innings finished at 93. Jones was awarded man of the match for his brilliant undefeated 60.

With a record crowd of 7000, and populations of less than seven hundred and fifty, both Longparish and Marchwiel must have been deserted on Sunday 24th August, together with many other villages from Clwyd and Hampshire. One or two dog collars were in evidence amongst the spectators, so perhaps church services were felt to be pointless in some villages. Then again, for such an important event it would not surprise me if a dawn service had been contemplated with a Lord's Prayer offered for victory. The same eve of match hospitalities took place at Chiswell Street. The drays, shire horses and Coldstream Guards were all there entertaining the crowd on the morning of the final. Although in her seventies and suffering from arthritis, Marchwiel's club president Mary Bell, mother of their captain John Bell, was not about to miss out on her club's finest hour. She didn't feel up to the long coach journey from North Wales, so she flew down on the morning of the match and back again that evening!

Longparish won the toss and on a good pitch of even bounce put Marchwiel in to bat, much to some people's surprise. It seemed to be paying dividends, having taken the early wicket of Roberts, bowled by Sutcliffe without scoring, the front line bowling attack restricted Barret and Jones to just eight runs in the first ten overs. Tension was slowly eased as both batsmen hit a boundary, the smooth acceleration to 42 for 2 saw the opening bowlers complete their allocation. With the score at 69 Bell was bowled by a full toss from Jones, Steve Barrett was also bowled by a delighted Jones next ball. At 69 for 4 it looked as if Longparish's gamble was paying off. Opener Peter Barrett however was playing a discplined innings and punishing anything loose. He was joined by Roy Davies and together they put on a valuable 40 partnership. Davies's 34 included a 6, a rare sight in what was turning out to be a tenacious match before a crowd with appreciable knowledge of cricket.

## Cricket Can be a "Bitter Game"

The score edged on, and when the seventh wicket fell at 135 the seamers had all bowled their quota. The spinning combination of Heagren and Jones bowled the remaining overs. Marchwiel were never given the opportunity to accelerate because of clever fielding placings of an inner and outer ring. Their innings closed at 161 for 8, with Newcombe having the distinction of being caught father bowled son for 4.

Longparish's openers came to the wicket knowing a shade over 4 runs an over was distinctly "gettable". A solid patient start was all that was needed to get them on their way. Knowledgable supporters in the crowd from both sides knew it too. Sutcliffe was bowled by Carson without scoring and a dour battle ensued, with Luff and John Heagren struggling to put on a further eight runs. In the ninth over a delighted Carson had the formidable Luff trapped LBW for five. Shortly afterwards Heagren, trying to release his team from the stranglehold, failed to get to the pitch of the ball and was caught on the short boundary at extra cover. At 13 for 3 the Welshmen were all set to tighten the screws, but Smith had other ideas. He hit two lusty cover drives, but with his score on 25 a brilliant stumping by Edwards sent him back to the pavilion. Freeman was willing to have a go, he stayed 17 overs for his 10 runs, had he connected more than he missed it could have been a different picture. The only other player to reach double figures was Jones, who was caught and bowled for eleven. Eventually Longparish ran out of overs, finishing on 82 for 9. Peter Barrett was awarded the Daily Mirror man of the match for his innings of 47, which was a fine achievement where the ball not the bat dictated terms. The trophy and £250 cheque were presented to Marchwiel captain John Bell, which his mother must have been proud to see before flying back to Clwyd. Both teams had given the crowd an enthralling days cricket. Lord's had not yet seen the last of either team.

**1981** The early rounds in May were frustrating affairs yet again, one of the wettest months on record. Each of the five Sundays were rained off. A third of the first round matches were decided by artificial means, as was a fifth of the second round. This meant that 124 of the scheduled 492 matches did not take place. Thankfully there was a distinct improvement in June, and from the fourth round on every match produced a result, only one having to resort to the faster scoring rate. There were also some group boundary changes, brought about by variations in entries, and in some areas to a greater or lesser degree. This did no harm, in fact it helped widen the fixture horizons of some villages.

Once again familiar names featured highly. Langleybury lost their third semi-final, having won their group for the sixth time in seven years, beaten by the formidable Welsh team of St.Fagans. Collingham, county champions of Nottingham for the seventh time in nine attempts, lost in the sixth round to their bogey team Marchwiel, who went on to fall at the final hurdle against Broad Oak. Had they won it would have been an all Welsh final, between the north and south of the country. Quarndon, East Brierley and Ynysygerwn disappeared in the first round mud bath. Sessay were champions of Yorkshire once again, but lost to Bomarsund in the seventh round, as did Longparish defeated by Langleybury.

St.Fagans, after winning their group final against Ynystawe, disposed of Dafen in round 6, restricting the home team to 107 they safely passed the total for the loss of only three wickets. In round 7 Stapleton finished on 155 for 7, whilst the Welsh side scraped home on 156 for 9. In the quarter finals Perran-a-Worthal's score of 173 for 6 was not enough and St.Fagans went into the semi-final finishing on 175 for 6.

The Reverend William David was vicar of a small village just a few miles from Cardiff from 1857 to 1897. He was a keen sportsman and it did not take him very long to form a village cricket team. So it was that in 1862 St. Fagans CC was born.

## Cricket Can be a "Bitter Game"

Since then it has played a great part in local cricket throughout South Wales and has many achievements to its credit. In entertaining Langleybury in the semi-final, they were about to make their mark at national level. Having won the toss, captain David Painter elected to bat. Seeking to establish the initiative, he altered the batting order by opening with Gareth Jones and Roger Stevens, recognised plunderers of runs. Stevens was back in the pavilion within seven balls, caught by skipper Williams off fast bowler Sean Palmer. So number three came to the wicket — it was Ricky Needham, a batsman with a recognised pedigree in a higher class of cricket. Having played for Harrow at Lord's and a Pro-Am. player, much rested on his shoulders. It was to be an inauspicious start, he ran out a rather disgruntled Jones before he could get into gear. With the Welsh at seven for two Langleybury were not about to let the initiative go. Accurate and intelligent bowling resulted in three wickets down with just fifty-four on the board. Needham however was not a natural defensive player. With two sixes and eight fours he took his personal tally to seventy-five, before running himself out as the innings came to a close. St.Fagans finished on 173 and much was owed to Needham. Only three other batsmen reached double figures, so Langleybury had it all to do.

Opening batsmen Gordon Reddick and Keith Woods applied themselves to maintaining a run rate of four an over. The advantage of a home tie on your own ground can at times pay dividends. With the wicket at St.Fagans broadly in an East-West direction, captain Painter brought himself on. It was late afternoon, and with the sun behind him Langleybury were soon in trouble. From a launching platform of 44 without loss, Painter dismissed all first five batsmen in his nine overs with an impressive analysis of 8 — 6.5 for 4 runs. With Painter off the scene Brian Davey and John Whiteman took the score from 74 for 5 to 108 for 6. The Langleybury tail had the reputation of being able to wag when the occasion arose, so the Hertfordshire

*A Village at Lord's*

contingent of the crowd lived in hope. But Painter had more to contribute, a neat catch from him and two wickets from Needham left Langleybury stranded at 122. St.Fagans had won by the creditable margin of 51 runs, leaving the visitors wondering when they would ever overcome that final hurdle to earn an appearance at Lord's.

West Yorkshire champions Broad Oak had little difficulty in reaching their group final, where they beat Barkisland who were only able to field their second eleven, due to league commitments. In round six they restricted Lancashire champions Thornham to ninety-two, and passed their total with only the loss of one wicket. The match against Tidhoe of Durham was a little tighter, where in reply to a total of 125 they edged home at 127 for 7. Greaves hit a fine unbeaten half century against 1974 champions Bomarsund in round eight, leaving the Northumberlanders to score 177 to win. Bomarsund in reply coasted to 156 for 3 and looked set for a semi-final placing. But disaster struck and seven further wickets fell for just seventeen runs. They were all out for 173.

Broad Oak were certainly not finding the battle to the final an easy one. Their picturesque ground was packed to capacity for their semi-final clash against reigning champions Marchwiel. The 1500 spectators settled back to enjoy the game and a scene was set typifying village cricket. Broad Oak lost the toss and took to the field. Their seam attack backed up by sharp fielding never let the champions get the upper hand.

Opener Peter Barrett was the only batsman to offer any resistance, contributing forty-six before being the fifth wicket down with the score on ninety-three. Marchwiel eventually finished on 129 for 9. This could have been less but for the courageous fifteen from wicket keeper Chris Edwards, who was caught behind by his opposite number.

Captain Dick Horner opened the batting for Broad Oak and immediately let the delighted Yorkshire supporters know his

## Cricket Can be a "Bitter Game"

intention to retain the initiative by hooking the first ball for six! A slight hiccup on losing his fellow opener with the score on seven was the only one. Horner continued to make his intentions clear, and helped by Alan Greaves shared an unbeaten 125 for the second wicket. Horner 61 and Greaves 56, carried their bat to record a memorable nine wicket victory in the Broad Oak records.

The final at Lord's on August 30th. produced a unique record for both sides before a ball was even bowled. Fourteen year old Simon Lewis of St.Fagans, and Simon Hoyle of Broad Oak aged thirteen, became the youngest scorers ever to officiate at headquarters. Whitbread's generous and colourful hospitality was as always in evidence to ensure a memorable final. Rival banners were waving enthusiastically as St.Fagans opening batsmen took to the field, having been invited to bat by Broad Oak's captain.

First blood to Yorkshire came as Lewis was bowled for one with the total on nine. But dangerman Ricky Needham joined Jones, and together they added a brisk fifty-six in what was to be the highest and most elegant partnership of the day. Left armer Wood was brought into the attack and immediately put the brakes on St.Fagans. A maiden over proved too much for Jones who, having swung lucklessly for the third time, had his middle stump uprooted by Wood for thirty-six. Needham followed him next ball after a powerful shot was well caught on the distant third man boundary.

Yorkshire banners heralded an anticipated collapse with St.Fagans going from sixty-five for one to sixty-five for three. A psychological battle ensued between bat and ball. Against good bowling and tight fielding Muir and Toshack played intelligently. Good running between the wickets enabled them to see their team edge closer to three figures. Wood and McCreadie had other ideas. Wood bowled Muir and McCreadie had Toshack trapped LBW. for 17. At 99 for 6 Greaves entered the arena to take a superb caught and bowled capturing the valuable wicket of

Stevens who was starting to flow at 16. Painter and Williams managed to get into double figures, but sadly the tail petered out and St.Fagans were all out for 149 after thirty-eight overs. Broad Oak's Wood's mean analysis of 9 – 4 – 18 – 2 was a major contribution in restricting the Welshmen to less than 150.

Broad Oak could not have had a worse start. Both openers and number four McCreadie were back in the pavilion with only fifteen on the board. Greaves and Wood started to steady things, but were slipping behind the run rate needed. Wood was beaten for pace, and with the total on 47 frustration got the better of him, he was bowled by Jones for 15. Next man in Hey took a quick single to keep his established partner away from Needham, who was to bowl his last over. This backfired on him and he was out off the last ball from Needham, which Greaves would probably have kept out. Painter was bowling an immaculate line and length, which Greaves must have found frustrating, for in desperation he went after James. He didn't quite time the shot and was caught on the extra cover boundary. Welsh voices were tuning up with the score on 69 for 8. The Yorkshire tail however showed signs of wagging. Roberts had been joined by Brooke, and together they took the total past the hundred, which included a six from Roberts. With fifty needed off thirty-nine balls, St.Fagans were forced to bring back Robertson, after Jones had his analysis ruined with 19 off 2 overs. It produced immediate results. With a brilliant diving catch on his follow through he dismissed Brooke for a defiant twenty-one. Wicket keeper Holmes joined Roberts with the score on 108. Forty-two for victory was still possible with Roberts in the groove to hit anything and everything. Robertson bowled Holmes who had stayed for a creditable thirteen, but his luckless partner was left stranded as top scorer on twenty-eight. Broad Oak's innings had closed on 127, 23 short of victory, but a possible eight balls were left when the last wicket went down. Who knows what would have happened had Roberts been afforded the opportunity to face the

## Cricket Can be a "Bitter Game"

fortieth over. Given the rampant mood he was in, I am sure St. Fagans supporters did not wish to dwell on the possibility. The Yorkshire supporters probably felt differently. The trophy returned to Wales for the another year, and Needham made man of the match for his all round performance.

**1982** In chapter two I referred to minor counties taking their cricket seriously. This appears to have been borne out by Wales. With just one first class county, it was to be a Welsh side in the final for the sixth time in eleven years. St.Fagans, champions of Glamorgan, were to take on Collingham of Notts. Both sides had a bye in their first round, and Collingham had an easy eight wicket victory over Whatton and Aslockton in the second. They followed this up by sweeping Thrumpton aside, having amassed a total of 242 for 6 they dismissed the opposition for 41. In the next round Leverton set a target of 180, thanks to D. Loates 94 not out, who shared in a partnership of 83 for the third wicket with his father. At one point Collingham were 58 for 6, but from 162 for 9 they recovered and finished at 183 for 9, winning in the last over. The group final provided plenty of time for a drink in the bar and not because of the weather! Stragglers managed only fifty-five, with England taking four for thirteen. In reply Weeks blitzed a fine thirty not out as Collingham passed the total for the loss of only two wickets. In round six, Treeton Welfare required twelve in the last over, chasing Collingham's total of one hundred and forty-two for eight. However they only managed to make seven, but their day was yet to come. The quarter-final saw Collingham in fine batting form. Weeks, 102, and J. Kirkham, 50, put on 140 for the first wicket. Chasing 176 set by Colwall of Worcestershire, they won in the last over finishing on 164 for 8. The semi-final was a low scoring game yet again. Kirkley from Northumberland were all out for eighty-nine. Norris had fine figures of 3 for 15, and wicket keeper Driscoll held three catches. Collingham were never really in trouble, finishing on 93 for 6.

The reigning champions were never really troubled on their way to the group final. It was only in round four that there was any sign of panic.

Tondu, chasing a target of 131 for victory, were on course when their last six wickets fell for just 31. The group final against Cressely was a low scoring affair. St.Fagans needed to score just 80 to win by six wickets. Gloucestershire champions Sudbrook could only muster 62 to lose by seven wickets. In round seven Winterslow of Wiltshire scored 141, which was passed with only five wickets down. In the quarter-final Lydford from Somerset pushed St.Fagans nearer to four runs an over, finishing on 152 for 9. But the Welsh marched on to the semi-final with the loss of only four wickets. Batting first against Langley of Essex they scored an impressive 202 for 8. Needham was unbeaten on 100, and 97 was put on in the last ten overs. The Essex champions made a gallant effort to reach the final. At one point they were 102 for 2 but ran out of overs, finishing on 185 for 8.

Neither of the teams in the final was a stranger to the big occasion. Last year's champions had eight of their winning side playing, whilst Collingham had but three survivors from their 1974 final. At least the weather on this occasion was set fair, so the village from Northants. could feel confident they would achieve their objective of playing on the hallowed turf at last (no disrespect intended to Warks. CCC.).

St.Fagans won the toss and put Collingham in to bat in what seemed to be ideal conditions. Needham may have been relying on "the nerve tactics" in the hope of quick wickets. Collingham's captain Kirkham set about the task with a sense of purpose, playing strokes right from the start. He put on forty-one for the first wicket with Gavin Driscoll, thus laying the foundations for a reasonable total before being caught by Stevens off Howe for twenty-five. Nigel Weeks failed to capitalise on the situation and

## Cricket Can be a "Bitter Game"

was out for an uncharacteristic three. Had his prolific batting prowess been in evidence the Lord's crowd would have been in for a treat. St. Fagans, sensing an opportunity to seize the advantage following the departure of Weeks, maintained a disciplined field to prevent Driscoll and the new batsman Richard England from getting on top. This may have been in part due to St. Fagans knowing England's capability with a bat, as he had previously played for the Welsh side. They did however take the score from 54 for 2 to 128 before Madley caught England off the bowling of Robertson for 42. After that it was a period of tactics which St. Fagans won. All rounder Needham came on to bowl. Mopping up the tail, he also restricted Driscoll from opening out, which could easily have added a further thirty or so runs. It was not to be, and the innings closed at 148 for 9, leaving Driscoll 63 not out.

Opening bat Gareth Jones had dislocated a finger whilst bowling, so not for the first time St. Fagans changed their order. Graham Lewis found himself as emergency opening bat. He helped his partner Mason to put on 27 in 9 overs before being trapped LBW to Crookes for 15. Most spectators considered this an adequate start as the chairman was applauded out and Needham applauded in. It appears he did not share the supporters' views, as he promptly reduced the rate required by striking five fours from successive deliveries with effortless ease. He was then promptly bowled to a good length ball from Wright for twenty-one. Meanwhile Mason, who had played himself in with the able assistance of Lewis, was in control of the overall situation. Joined by Painter, following the departure of Needham, the pair set about putting the Welsh in a winning but not invincible position. The word invincible is not in the NVCC. dictionary! Mason departed with the score on 125 for 3. Williams was bowled by Smalley for six, with the score on 133. Roger Stevens entered the arena determined to enjoy his moment at the crease in front of Father Time and the assembled crowd. He clouted sixteen off five deliveries to see his side home with more than two overs to spare. Thus St. Fagans had won the crown for a second successive year, the only low point being the luckless Painter being stuck on 39 not out, just eleven short of his half century.

MCC. president Hubert Doggart, considered one of the best presenters of awards, made the losers feel they had won the match and the winners "The Ashes." St. Fagans had retained the trophy to take back to Wales. As for the men from Collingham, they may not have lifted the title, but were not disappointed in being the losing finalists for the second time. After all unlike their conquerors in 1974, they had succeeded in playing at Lord's, which many consider, with no disrespect to sponsors, the greater prize. Unknown to many, St. Fagans had broken another record for the final, which they had set up jointly with the finalists in the previous year. Their scorer on this occasion was Christopher Williams aged eleven.

**1983** The announcement by Lord's that a Test Match against Sri Lanka had been arranged for the last weekend in August meant the Village Final would have to move forward to August 19th. There were however still nine rounds to be played before the final. With our fickle late Spring weather, it was tempting providence to attempt arranging preliminary rounds any earlier than late April. In order to ensure the crowded fixtures programme could be accommodated, rounds 5,6,7 & 8 needed to be scheduled with one week between each. Even with this the possibility of postponement may still have had to be considered as a last resort. The weather in May must have been the worst since the competition began, and decimated the preliminary rounds. An innovation was the seeding of the previous year's group finalists to enter the competition in round three, thus eliminating early mis-matches. The experiment was not wholly popular but was given a trial and reviewed at the end of the season. Despite the frustration of disrupted and non-existent matches, some remarkable feats were achieved on the field. In a match restricted to thirty overs, Middleton Tyas's opening pair put on 216 for the first wicket against Castleton of Yorkshire. M. Rain carried his bat for 139, but had he scored just two more runs, he would have been top of the batting honours list. Another match restricted to thirty-five overs was the game between Staxton and South Milford, again in Yorkshire. This meant that a bowler's allocation was restricted to 8 overs. Despite this, medium pacer Ron Thompson took a wicket in each over for twenty-five in appalling conditions. Had he been permitted his normal allocation he may well have become the first bowler to take all ten wickets in an innings. There was however some consolation, his son David took the remaining two wickets to keep it in the family.

Quarndon of Derbyshire were at last to be rewarded for their consistent fine performance. In the merit table at the end of the 1992 season they had the impressive record of a seventy-nine per cent success rate. En route to the final they were to overcome some stiff opposition such as Sessay and the redoubtable Collingham. In the final however they were to start as under dogs against Troon, who with a ninety per cent success rate were appearing in their fourth final. In the Derbyshire group final they had an easy four wicket win over Old Netherseal. Chasing a total of 138 for 9 they finished on 139 for 6. Wicket keeper Farmer was the main contributor with a fine sixty. In their sixth round match against Addingham (South Yorkshire) J.Morris 10 helped dismiss the home team for 106, with a spell of 3 for 10. In reply Quarndon lost only one wicket in their 109 for 1, with Underwood and Farmer both finishing in their forties. The Midlands clash with past champions Marchwiel was expected to be a memorable battle. Not all memorable battles however mean a glut of runs. Marchwiel were restricted to 81, with wicket keeper Barrett contributing forty-six, and Morris was again among the wickets with an astonishing five for four. They lost seven wickets before overhauling the total, and in securing victory ensured that for the first time a Whitbread final would not be graced with a team from the valleys. In the quarter-final the Worcestershire village of Chaddesley Corbett travelled to Derbyshire, fresh from their victory over the powerful Collingham. The visitors' creditable total of 173 for 8 could have been even more if it had not been for that man Morris returning figures of three for forty. This certainly looked enough at one stage, with the home team losing three wickets before reaching fifty. Andy Acton had other ideas. He enthralled the thousand spectators with a punishing seventy-six in fifty-five minutes, to secure victory at 177 for 5. It was a disappointment for the Worcestershire team and their supporters, having just failed for the second time to reach the semi-final.

Some say the semi-final between Sessay and Quarndon was the best in the competition to date. A superb summer's day set the scene. This coupled with a spirit of good humour and Yorkshire hospitality epitomised what the championships were all about. The wicket was a quick one and Sessay, put in to bat were hoping for a total of two hundred, but lost two quick wickets. A third wicket stand of sixty-four between John Flintoff and father Brian, laid the foundations for a reasonable total. Steady bowling and well held catches helped contain Sessay, but John Flintoff kept the scoreboard ticking over. He was last man out for 89, and the Yorkshire innings closed at 159 for 8. Morris was again among the wickets taking five, but in the process conceding 48 runs.

Quarndon required exactly four runs an over for victory. The home team were not going to give anything away, and just before the half way stage most of the batting was back in the pavilion at sixty-four for four. Memories of 1976 may well have come flooding back to the minds of the Yorkshire supporters at this stage. Andy Acton however brought them back to reality with a quick fire 36 before departing and leaving wicket keeper Steve

## Cricket Can be a "Bitter Game"

Hollis to take centre stage. A painful blow to the face did nothing to disturb his concentration. Just as the run rate looked like flagging and with only the tail in support he struck a superb six. He ensured the Derbyshire supporters had some nails left to bite at Lord's by making the winning hit off the third ball of the fortieth over. He finished with a creditable sixty-eight, and deservedly took the man of the match award. Troon had few problems on their way to Lord's, with a comfortable victory over Beacon in the group final. In round six Werrington finished 33 runs short of victory. Their seventh round tie against Goatacre was a low scoring match. The Wiltshire side's 104 was never enough, and a six wicket victory left them with a tie against Carew, the one remaining Welsh side in the competition. Scoring 166 for 8 they disposed of the opposition for 116, no mean achievement for it contained several members of the Welsh Eleven. Once again Langleybury were in the sem-final. In recognition of their past efforts Whitbread flew the Hertfordshire team and officials to Cornwall. Supporters left by coach at three a.m. on Sunday morning.

Having succeeded in winning the toss Troon batted first. Gale force winds caused problems, and in the early stages extras exceeded runs from the bat. Sean Palmer achieved a great breakthrough by dismissing the Carter brothers, who between them only contributed one to the score. At thirteen for two the Cornishmen were in all sorts of trouble. Palmer was in full cry, He may not have taken any more wickets, but at the end of his nine overs only ten runs had been conceded. This contributed much to a total of 85 for 4 after 29 overs. But a village team of this calibre could not be written off so easily. Scot Pedlar was joined by seventeen year old Jonathan Warren and together they put on 86 in 10 overs. Pedlar finished undefeated on sixty-five having hit a huge six and four fours as the innings closed on 171 for 5. The start of Langleybury's reply was confident, but at fifteen in the seventh over hesitation left Keith Wood stranded. Next ball Gordon Riddick was bowled. Middle order batting swung hard and high, but the Cornish fielding held on. Veteran Peter Johns, who had played in the first final in 1972, came on to bowl and finished with five for seventeen as Langleybury ran out of batsmen on 143.

It had been a see-saw match, but sympathy has to be extended to the pride of Hertfordshire. They had failed to get past the final barrier yet again. For the fourth time their supporters travelled home from a semi-final, this time arriving back at five a.m. on Monday morning. On a personal note I would hope to see them make it one day, and if they do I suspect it could be the biggest crowd of any final. Many who have witnessed their graciousness in defeat will no doubt wish to be there to see one of the finest village sides play at Lord's.

The final was to see two of the strongest village teams in the country contest the Whitbread National Trophy. Troon in their fourth final had never been beaten at Lord's, and were hoping to take the title again. Quarndon were knocked out in the first round when they entered the competition in 1974. Since then they had won the Derbyshire group title eight times from a possible nine, and twice reached the national quarter-finals. As under dogs they had it all to do in their first appearance at cricket's Mecca.

Winning the toss, Quarndon put Troon in to bat on a firm wicket. Carter and Spry made a controlled start with thirty in eight overs. Once again a good launching platform had been set. Underwood had to retire from bowling due to a slight strain, and slow left arm spinner Butcher joined Tunaley in the bowling attack, who was bowling faster with every over. Between them they had removed both openers by the time the score reached forty-four. Brian Carter entered but found difficulty in piercing the field. Just sixteen more runs had been added by the end of the twentieth over. Kitchen departed with the score on 95. The

## Cricket Can be a "Bitter Game"

batting order was changed in the hope of boosting the scoring rate. It didn't work and Pedlar went for six, followed by Warren and Johns for a single apiece.

With the score on 117 for 6 much rested on Carter's shoulders, with only the tail to come. Williams supported him well with a spirited twenty- two. This enabled Carter to get his half century and finish on 55 not out. The last wicket partnership had added an invaluable 38, to give the score line respectability at 155 for 6. But was it defendable?

Underwood and Morris shared in a brisk opening partnership of 52 in reply. Both openers having done all the hard work were soon back in the pavilion. Underwood was first, bowled after an injudicious slash at Kitchen. Morris's full blooded drive should have been a boundary, but Spry snapped up the catch from Kitchen's bowling. Farmer and Hibberd came together with four runs an over needed. Quarndon were up with the clock but were not about to sail home at their leisure by picking off the bad ball. Steady bowling and keen fielding under Terry Carter's experienced captaincy, pushed the run rate towards six an over. The natives were beginning to get restless. Murmuring speculation as to the likely outcome came from both sets of supporters. With ten overs to go the rate had crept up to 6.3 an over. These two great sides had set the scene for a nail biting climax.

Hibberd started to play strokes, quick intelligent running between the wickets soon brought the rate down to five an over by the thirty-sixth. An uncharacteristic heave-ho from Hibberd to the boundary over mid-on left eleven runs from the last two overs. The excitement was mounting, probably more in the Derbyshire camp than Cornwall's. With his personal half century as well as victory in sight, Hibberd had crossed the psychological barrier into that rare state of batting infallibility. Quarndon wrenched only three runs from the thirty-ninth. Troon however were not letting go without a struggle. In the next over Hibberd, feeling he could walk on water, accomplished four things. After hooking the first ball to the distant Grandstand boundary he took guard to receive the second, and promptly repeated the shot. In so doing he completed his own half century (53), brought up the hundred partnership, secured for himself the man of the match award, and ensured the Whitbread Trophy went to Derbyshire for the first time.

Quarndon had set another record, which probably went unnoticed at the time, they were the first side to beat Troon in a final. The Cornishmen however were magnanimous in defeat, their veteran quartet comprising the Carter brothers, John Spry and Peter Jones, knew what it was like to win. Presentations were made by M.C.C. treasurer David Clark, who apart from congratulating both teams on an excellent match, complimented them on the exemplary spirit in which it had been played.

**1984** Sadly this was to be the last year of Whitbread's sponsorship. Once again a Welsh side would reach the final, with Marchwiel of Clwyd taking on Hursley Park, champions of Hampshire. During the six years of their sponsorship, only in 1983 did a team from the valleys not grace Lord's with its singing and banner waving.

On April 29th. over six hundred villages began the preliminary rounds of the competition. Those who had won their group final in 1983 were exempt from the first two rounds. The idea being by seeding in this way, it was hoped to avoid mismatching and afford the less prolific village an opportunity to advance further in the competition. It is not possible to cater for every eventuality however. Milford for example, having scored 314 for 8, promptly dismissed Huby for 47, to win by the impressive margin of 267 runs. Canon Frome's record against Much Markle still remained unbeaten. Another fine performance was from West Yorkshire champions Outwood, who beat Shamley Green from Surrey by 220 runs.

## Cricket Can be a "Bitter Game"

There were some notable performances with both bat and ball. The Cornish village of Roche scored 287 for 1 against Stoke Climsland in the early rounds and beat Chumliegh of North Devon with an impressive 271 for 7. They also set a new partnership record of 274 for the second wicket, with C.Libby on 132 not out, also D.Hollyoak scored 130. Although their most notable achievement must have been the victory over triple champions Troon in the seventh round. Quarndon of Derbyshire, last year's champions went out in the sixth.

The season's highest individual score went to J.Lightfoot of Copley (Bedfordshire) with 158 not out. Close on his heels was P.Flynn from the Oxfordshire village of Hanborough with 147 not out. Also from Oxfordshire G. Hamilton of Horspath had the impressive bowling figures of 9 for 34, which was the fourth best bowling in the whole competition to date. Ian Bailey of Gretton also enters the record books with his eight for five and R.Gibson of Cloughton with eight for eighteen. The spirit in which the competition is played is no better illustrated than in the preliminary round match between two Warwickshire villages. The players left the field at the end of the match with the scoreboard showing Fillongley on 120 for 9 and Tanworth-in-Arden on 120 for 7. After the umpires had completed their check with the scorers it transpired Fillongley had not included one vital run which would have secured victory. The Fillongley committee had this to say :- "We came off the field knowing we had lost. We do not want to win on a technicality. We have had several good runs in this competition and are therefore happy to concede to our good friends Tanworth. It's their turn now and we wish them Good Luck in subsequent rounds."

Lord's was bathed in sunshine, a perfect day for cricket. Marchwiel elected to bat. Darryl Wallis and David Jones started steadily putting on 28 before Bryan Loveridge struck, bowling Jones for seven. Trefor Roberts joined Wallis to share in an aggressive partnership of forty-two before Hursley's captain brought Wallis's exciting innings to a close, bowling him for thirty-eight. Skipper Bell and Roberts shared a fifty partnership before departing in quick succession, Bell (27) and Wallis (55). All was set for the final onslaught, but Hursley held their nerve. Barrett was the only other batsman to reach double figures as they ran out of overs on 159 for 7, leaving Hursley exactly four runs an over for victory.

Hursley Park may not have started the match as favourites, but this did not affect their opening pair Adrian Aymes and Paul Wright. Together they brought up the fifty against an all pace attack, with the score in the nineties they appeared to be coasting to victory. Off spinner Wallis came in to the attack immediately deceiving Wright, bowling him for thirty-nine with the score on ninety-seven. Medium pacer Arwell Morris then took centre stage quickly disposing of Aymes, caught by Hancock for a superb 56. Thow was trapped by Morris LBW for one and Kellaway fell to his guile for one. Suddenly the complexion of the game had changed as Hursley fell behind the clock. A spirited innings by Davis ended when he was run out for sixteen chasing the runs. Only Bunney succeeded in getting into double figures. The September issue of Whitbread News carried the headline "Welsh Wizards Cast A Spell". They certainly did, Hampshire's almost certain victory a few overs before turned into defeat, as their innings close for 151 for 8. Marchwiel had won the title by the narrowest margin on record for a final. For the fourth time in Whitbread's sixth and last year of sponsorship the trophy was returning to Wales.

So it was that an era had come to an end. There would of course be future sponsorship, but the village finals at Lord's would no longer see the impressive spectacle of the brewer's drays pulled by magnificent shire horses. Chiswell Street would no longer echo to the banter and laughter from after dinner speeches. Finance is only one side of the equation in sponsoring an event of this nature. Manpower is another. Whitbread had always striven to

## Cricket Can be a "Bitter Game"

provide a high personnel profile at as many matches as possible. This was proving difficult to maintain as staff services were given freely and willingly. So it was that Whitbread decided to quit whilst they were ahead.

The competition had certainly continued to grow in popularity and stature. It's notoriety was evident for all to see. The finals had attracted increasing national TV coverage. The 1984 final for example saw outside broadcast services from HTV, BBC. Wales, STV and BBC South. Interest in the final meant that a press box at Lord's, designed for twenty-four journalists, had at times to cater for more than forty! Local radio up and down the country had also been seized by local village participation in the contest. There is a story of one local radio's director attempting to keep listeners updated with half hour bulletins from St.John's Wood. Eventually his switchboard was so jammed with callers that he quickly rescheduled programmes and went over to Lord's for live commentary on the remainder of the match.

Sadly four days after this memorable final Findlay Rea died of a heart attack. He had a great love for the competition and his contributions to it's success are immeasurable. His sterling work as editor of The Cricketer Annual each year was unique. Gordon Ross, who was to take over his editorial role, said of him that he and Whitbread were synonymous.

CHAPTER FOUR

# Fertilizer as a Growing Agent

In 1974 The Haig was described as a sturdy two year old growing fast. At the end of their sponsorship in 1977, John Haig and Company had given the competition a hefty kick start. Whitbread took over the reins from 1979 to 1984. An appropriate partnership, for many a Whitbread country inn was not far from the boundary of a village green. A green which in summer saw the local cricketers enjoy their game, with a jar of ale at the inn afterwards. Sometimes accompanied by a smiling apology for the six that meant a job for the local glazier after the weekend. The Whitbread sponsorship ensured the kick start provided by Haig was not wasted. After six years they left an efficient reliable machine in the capable hands of those stalwart organisers at The Cricketer.

Soon it was the turn of another ideal partner to take over sponsorship. Norsk Hydro, one of the largest fertilizer suppliers in Britain, had been helping the rural community improve their crops and harvest. A harvest to help provide an income for the village farmer. Which would also enable him to keep both his plough and tractor efficient running machines. At first glance the company may appear to be a spring chicken, in the eyes of those who might query their place in the historical league table when compared with John Haig, Samuel Whitbread and even village cricket itself. That is not strictly the case.

It is true the company was not heard of before 1982. But their parent company Hydro of Norway were pioneers in fertilizer at the turn of the century. Norsk Hydro was formed to acquire the Fertilizer Division of Fisons, which was the oldest remaining agricultural business in the country, dating back to the middle of the last century. As a new name on the agricultural scene it was desirable to firmly establish that name in the agricultural community. Sponsoring a national sporting event that had a direct relationship with rural life seemed the best way to achieve their objective. To take on the vacant role of sponsors for the National Village Cricket Championships seemed the logical solution.

So in 1986 The Cricketer had a new sponsor, after two years of having had to run the competition virtually single handed. The only support coming from Lord's for the finals. With the generosity of Norsk Hydro, the championships could continue as an efficient reliable machine, along with the village mowers and rollers. As with previous sponsors, financial assistance for villages travelling long distances was of great benefit. Trophies and other useful prizes were awarded for individual and team performances. Many of those splendid unique engraved plaques hang proudly in village clubhouses, reminding all of their achievements during the "Hydro Village Cricket Era." A welcome return was the eve of final banquet at Lord's, which always helped establish friendly cordiality between the teams ahead of the Big Day. Then the spotlight is on them, so time for introductions is limited. Although village cricket is played for the fun it gives, it is still a serious matter when the whites are donned.

**1986** No it wasn't raining in May, but it snowed in April! With the final scheduled a week earlier than normal, round one of the competition coincided with the first Sunday of the season. For the groundsmen it was a nightmare. On the outfield of one pitch it was a little slow, with grass nine inches high. Both Vency and Winterbourne spurned the silver coin in favour of a darts match

## Fertilizer as a Growing Agent

to decide their first round ties. Unfortunately for them the weather in the second round was set fair, so bat and ball replaced the silver arrows and they lost.

There were some memorable individual and team performances in that year. David Dixon of Swarkeston was top scorer with 158 in their win over Old Netherseal. Hard on his heels was Nick Meed of Ightham with a sparkling 156 against Weald. One hundred and twenty-four of Meed's runs came in boundaries, with ten sixes and sixteen fours. C. Cockerton of Tuddenham secured a place in the record books by becoming the sixth bowler to take four wickets in four balls. He finished with an analysis of five for three, as the luckless Stansfield were dismissed for just twelve. Les Smith of Cuckney took eight for sixteen, including a hat trick against Moreton Hampstead. A. Witton of Feniton took eight for five as Halwill were dismissed for ten, top score was extras with four byes to the boundary. Probably the best bowling performance came from P. Redshaw of Stillington, when they beat Bolton Percy. Bolton struggled for runs only managing a total of fifteen in 14.4 overs, as Redshaw took seven wickets whilst only yielding six runs.

Many sides scored in excess of two hundred runs in 1986. Top of the list was Lydford who hit 332 for 9 against Fitzhead, with a magnificent 145 from Max Foote. Feckenham amassed 328 for 4 in their demolition of Warren by 260 runs. David Baylis scored 134 in a partnership of 131 with Paul Teskey, followed by another of 161 with Paul's brother Adam. But by far the most remarkable team performance must have been by Carlton in their match against Stones. Having struggled to 57 for 4 in 20 overs G. Cooper hit 127 and K. Barnett 102 in an unbroken fourth wicket partnership. They finished on 298 for 3, with an incredible 195 runs off the last 15 overs. Carlton were eventually beaten by Forge Valley in the quarter-finals, as the Yorkshire side progressed into the final for a battle with yet another Welsh side. Ynysygerwn, beaten finalists in 1979, were to keep the Welsh banners flying and the crowds singing at headquarters once again.

Mike Almond was secretary at Forge Valley C.C. as well as groundsman, second team captain, the man who looked after the bats and so on. Linseed oil ran in the Almond family's veins. Mike's mum Betty had a strong pair of wrists for a pensioner, being able to carry one twelve pint teapot in each hand with nonchalant ease. Wife Pat is the official scribe. If you ask Pat what she was doing on Sunday August 24th. 1986 — the greatest day in Forge Valley's one hundred and ten year history — she will tell you through gritted teeth "At home, looking after our twelve week old labrador puppy." Why you may ask? The family had arranged to collect their pooch on return from a summer holiday in Cyprus earlier in the month. A holiday which coincided with the semi-final. Mike however managed to keep up with progress from the Mediterranean which added a £27. telephone bill to their hotel account. This story is typical of many which demonstrate how a team's progress to the later rounds can cause chaos when it coincides with advance committed events such as holidays and weddings. Often cricket comes first!

Cricket is a serious business. In many rural communities throughout the Summer months it is the most important aspect of village life. According to John Glavin, president of Forge Valley at that time, it is a second religion. When interviewed by the press he advised "The whole village is cricket barmy!" Not content with five teams there were plans afoot for a nursery side and a ladies team, because the women were feeling deprived. In round one Forge travelled to Cloughton, chalked up 200 for 5 and dismissed the home team for 70. Playing hosts to Alne in the next round, the visitors ran out of batsmen at 122 chasing 176 for 7. Ingleby Greenhow had no answer to a total of 199 for 6 and caved in on 38. At home again 213 for 4 was more than enough to brush aside Bedale who only managed 88. Cayton in round 5 made a spirited attempt chasing 131, but only managed 118. Excitement was mounting after their sixth round visitors

## Fertilizer as a Growing Agent

Kirkley could only manage 156, against an impressive 207 with the loss of just one wicket. Forge appeared to be stepping up a gear with three further ties left before Lord's, all to be played at home. The game against Woodhouses was a close affair with the visitors scoring 189 for 7, but Forge managed a six wicket victory with 193 for 4. In the quarter-final they played host to Carlton. Fresh from their victory over reigning champions Freuchie and with that formidable 298 for 3 against Stones still in their minds, they must have fancied their chances when the home team were struggling at seven for three after seven overs. Skipper Martin Shepherdson with 61 and John Sowdon put on 104 to finish with a respectable, but not unassailable 164. Carlton were always behind the clock. Despite a valiant innings from M.Schofield (40) and K.Taylor's 23, they couldn't match the bowling attack of Sowdon (3 for 25) and gamekeeper Stephen Glaves 4 for 23. They were eventually all out for 144.

Chaddesley Corbett were a strong side, having won fifty-two of their sixty-six matches in the competition to date. Forge Valley therefore knew they had a tough match ahead of them. This small Yorkshire village had never known anything like it. The village hall had received a fresh coat of paint for the occasion. Betty Almond had been at the ground since breakfast supervising the catering corps., who had probably been baking all week. By lunch time banners were in evidence carrying the simple slogan "EAR WIG O".

The match was to prove a nail biting affair, even for John Glaves who had never before bitten his nails in fifty-five years. Chaddesley batted first and captain Martin Shepherdson captured the wicket of Blundon in the first over. One for One! With the score on 43 Shepherdson struck again capturing the valuable wicket of Rentch (alias Spanner). This must have been a relief as he had scored an unbeaten 103 in the previous round when they scored 246 for 3 in defeating Toft. Tight bowling restricted the Worcestershire champions, it took 19 overs before the fifty

## A Village at Lord's

came up. Seven wickets were down when the score reached one hundred in the thirty-third over. Truswell had been there from the beginning, contributing much to the total with his innings of 67 which included four sixes. Unfortunately he was run out trying to increase the scoring. Chaddesley finished on a creditable 157 for 9.

Forge Valley were off to a confident start. In an opening stand of 63 Martin Wall was out just two short of his fifty, but they were finding it difficult to keep up with the run rate. At the end of the thirty-second over forty-eight runs were still needed for victory. By the time they reached the end of the thirty-seventh the rate had been reduced to five an over. Sowden hoisted Forge's first six out of the ground to disturb the sheep and settle the nerves a little. The scores were level at the end of the thirty-ninth over, 157 for 5. Hartley faced Bond for the first ball of the final over, and was promptly bowled — 157 for 6! Nigel Pettit played and missed to the next three balls, connected with the fifth and scampered the most important single of his life, to see Forge Valley into the final.

There was much celebration following the victory, which went on well into the night. Among the revellers were the banner boys, who after much ale and merriment hoisted their banner on to the clubhouse roof. This now read "FORGE HAMMER CHADDESLEY EAR WIG O EAR WIG O EAR WIG O!" But a firm friendship had been established between two villages, and Chaddesley Corbett were to be seen at Lord's cheering their conquerors on. Forge Valley were the toast of Yorkshire, and the fortnight leading up to the final was a hectic time. Messages of Good Luck came from all quarters, including their Yorkshire rivals Sessay who knew what it was like to play at headquarters. Mike Almond was in great demand on his return from Cyprus, giving interviews to local newspapers and radio stations. The banner boys were also busy, determined to make their mark on the big day.

## Fertilizer as a Growing Agent

The Welsh have a passion for rugby, cricket, music and life! Ynysygerwn of West Glamorgan undoubtedly had a reputation as a strong village side, proved beyond doubt by their 1986 passage to the final. Following a bye in the first round, they swept aside Cloughton who were beaten by 105 runs, having no answer to Ynysygerwn's 220 for 6. They made a brave effort but at 115 for 8 ran out of overs. I would like to have been present at their next match against Ynystawe. I suspect the low scoring result between two Welsh sides led to a contest of another sort in the clubhouse afterwards. I never did find out who won the singing contest, perhaps they called it a draw? St. Fagans were only able to muster 152 in the next round, which was passed with the loss of just three wickets. In the group final a four wicket victory over Narbeth secured them a place in the regional rounds.

Their next opponents were Gloucester and Gwent champions Witcombe, fresh from their seven wicket victory over Frocester. In reply to Witcombe's 157 they recovered from 22 for 7 to 159 for 9! J.James obviously held the side together with a valuable 78 not out. Against the Oxfordshire village of Aston Rowant they scored a creditable 182 for 8, but Aston Rowant could only manage 159 before running out of batsmen. The quarter final provided a home tie against the mighty Troon, who scored a respectable 151. The Welshmen had no real trouble, starting with an opening partnership of 103 in 27 overs. Their captain Royston Williams hit 67 with the stolid Harris achieving his half century. The rest was a formality as the Welshmen finished on 155 for 4, with a boundary in the thirty-eighth over.

The semi-final was to see them play hosts to the ever-wandering Langleybury. The Welshmen were marvellous hosts and well aware of their opponents formidable reputation. The Hertfordshire champions were tied down by David Evans, who took the wicket of Simon Palmer with his second ball. He also disposed of Graham Reid and Gordon Reddick to finish with the superb figures of 9 − 6 − 10 − 3. Veteran Jeff Curtis took three late wickets and the innings closed at 109. In reply Ynysygerwn had some stiff opposition from young Sean Palmer, who bowled his nine overs for just thirteen runs. This no doubt had a bearing on the Welsh reply at 44 for 2 in the twenty-second over. But when skipper Royston Williams joined his prolific partner Wayne Harris, for the first time all day bat dominated ball. Putting on an unbeaten 76 run partnership they saw their team home for a second bite of the cherry at Lord's.

It was indeed a sad disappointment for Langleybury to have lost their fifth semi-final. As I said earlier the Welsh were good hosts, and one hell of a party followed! The Welshmen felt for their Hertfordshire colleagues, they were both true village sides and the main victor that day had been village cricket. The Cricketer's editor, Tony Huskinson, felt moved to quote from the poet Crahaw:-

> "Eyes are vocal, tears have tongues
> And there be words not made with lungs ..."

No doubt, like showers, they are just passing and sometime, without doubt, Langleybury and Chaddesley Corbett will grace the ground at Lord's.

Norsk Hydro's first final was to be a fitting accolade for village cricket played between fine players and gentlemen. The four thousand strong crowd basked in sunshine. Armed with picnic hampers and ale they were to see an exciting game go to the very last ball. Players, wives and officials from both villages had enjoyed a splendid banquet the previous evening. They had rubbed shoulders with some famous cricketing personalities such as Sir Leonard Hutton and son Richard, Colin Cowdrey, Tom Graveney, not to mention Brian Johnston and guest speaker Christopher Martin-Jenkins.

Forge Valley were put in on a wicket with some lift and had to earn every run. A quarter way through their overs saw just

## Fertilizer as a Growing Agent

a dozen runs on the board. At the half way stage the Welsh had their first breakthrough when Jeff Curtis trapped Martin Wall LBW for twenty-four with the score on sixty. Andy Grayson helped boost the run rate by scoring twelve off one over, sharing a useful partnership of forty-six with opener Ridsdale before being caught by Prout for twenty-nine. Captain Shepherdson sent the first ball he received to the boundary, as he and Ridsdale set about accelerating, however he then became Curtis's third victim, bowled for ten. Ridsdale was run out for forty-one whilst trying to keep things moving. But wickets were falling steadily, 4 — 138, 5 — 139, 6 — 142 and 7 — 142. Pettit, wagging the tail with thirteen, fell to Curtis, and T. S. Glaves who was run out for fifteen helped their side to a useful total of 170 for 9 at the close. It was first blood to "The Tykes", as the Welsh set about their task. Shepherdson bowled Harris for nine, with the total on twenty. He claimed his second wicket when he bowled opener Williams for twenty-three leaving the total at forty-six. Hick was starting to feel his feet when he was run out for twenty-two. At the half way stage six an over was needed. However while Thomas was still at the crease Ynysygerwn were still in the hunt. Steven Glaves' maiden in the thirtieth heightened tension. With three overs to go twenty-six were needed for victory. It was at this point Thomas set the Welsh supporters alight, with a six and a four. But when Glaves bowled him for a superb fifty-five Forge had once again seized the initiative, as twelve was needed off nine balls. The next eight produced six, leaving a six needed off the last ball to secure victory. It would have been a thrilling way to win, but it was not to be, the innings closed on 165 for 9. Chris Prout was run out on his second run having struck the ball to third man.

    A marvellous game had been enjoyed by all. Yorkshire cricket had something to celebrate at last. The Welsh, gracious in defeat, lifted their voices in tribute to the new national champions, as the strains of "On Ilkley Moor Ba Tat" echoed around Lord's. Only one sad note tinged the day. One of Ynysygerwn's most valued club members, Cyril Jenkins, died at the ground. He was one of the club's greatest characters, doing a great deal to maintain the high standards both on and off the field, which had been much in evidence at Lord's that day. He is sadly missed.

Celebrations continued long into the night. Next day the Forge Valley team arrived back at Scarborough to be greeted by a crowd of more than three hundred. An open topped bus had been laid on for their return journey to the village. Unfortunately it broke down! Alternative transport was found and the team returned to a heroes' welcome. More celebrations were enjoyed, as a party had been laid on for the evening. As if that wasn't enough, the mayor of Scarborough invited them to a civic reception, followed by a meal laid on by a local restaurateur in recognition of the village's finest hour.

**1987** The weather played it's usual part in the preliminary rounds. At Crakehall hailstones had to be brushed from the pitch before the mower could be brought into action. Little Harrowden beat Pytchley by 140 runs between hail and snow storms. Marchwiel and Northop Hall were determined to beat the weather, but at what cost? Chasing Marchwiel's total of 156 for 5 Northop eventually started their innings at six forty p.m. They were all out for 139, losing the match in total darkness after the village clock had struck nine.

Treeton Welfare won the South Yorkshire group final against Addingham, and Longparish beat Sparsholt by 103 runs to take the Hampshire crown.

Both were to go all the way to the final. For Longparish it was their second opportunity to gain the title, having been runners-up to Marchwiel in 1980. While Treeton Welfare were hoping to keep the title in Yorkshire. Forge Valley the holders, lost their re-match in the group final against Bedale, who had their revenge for defeat in 1986 with a tense finish.

## Fertilizer as a Growing Agent

In round six Poynings had a respectable score of 176 for 4, but it was not enough to beat Longparish, who won by five wickets. Their next match was an enthralling home tie against Winchmore Hill, who grafted for a total of 119 for 8. Longparish had a struggle, after 30 overs they had only accrued 77 runs. John Hibberd was the hero of the hour, hitting two sixes and the winning run off the first ball of the final over, to earn a six wicket victory. The quarter-final was another home tie, this time against Surrey champions Rowledge. It was a relatively low scoring match on a seamers wicket in overcast conditions. Keith Sutcliffe tore the heart out of Rowledge's top order by taking all five wickets, and had them reeling at 22 for 5. They were 49 for 6 when Chris Yates and Robert Simpson came together to lead a recovery, but Longparish still restricted them to 115 for 9. Rowledge's left arm spinner caused havoc to the Hampshire side's reply. He took four for twenty-five and held three catches. As the overs started to run out they began the last over needing six to win. The last pair were at the wicket and all was hushed. Nothing off the first ball, Simon Mundy struck the second to the boundary. Two to win, four balls to go. Two more scoreless deliveries and two runs still needed, or one wicket for victory to go the other way. Mundy scrambled off the fifth. Scores level. Somehow Barry Smith kept the last ball out. Both sides finished on 115 for 9, but Longparish won having scored more at the twenty over mark. They had taken one more step nearer to Lord's, but before the evening celebrations were too well established they learnt St.Fagans had beaten Tiddington. So a hard fought battle was on to topple the strongly fancied Welsh side.

The weather was hot, the crowd large and many new friends were made the day the Taffs of St.Fagans came to Longparish for the semi-final. A wicket that looked full of runs greeted Welsh opener Gareth Jones. And he took full advantage of it. Carrying his bat he scored 101 off 114 deliveries, hitting three sixes and ten fours. He also shared a fourth wicket partnership with Roger Stevens. There was no doubt about it his contribution was the main reason his side finished on an accreditable 197 for 4. This was only the second century in a semi-final, the other having been scored by St.Fagans skipper Needham when they beat Langley in 1982. Longparish could not afford mistakes. Keith Sutcliffe (67) and Kelvan Finch who was still there at the death on 75, shared a third wicket partnership of 120. However a run rate of almost five an over is hard to maintain. It had not been plain sailing. In the thirty-eighth over Bob Sturt sealed St.Fagans fate with two huge sixes. He hit the winning boundary in the thirty-ninth to see his side home at 201 for 3. So Treeton Welfare carried the Yorkshire flag into the sixth round along with Bedale, Hesleden and Barkishead.

Yorkshire is a big county particularly when it comes to village cricket, hence the county made up four of the thirty-two groups in the preliminary rounds. Hesleden were playing Barkishead and won through to the seventh round, to be beaten by Scottish champions Freuchie. They had defeated North Yorkshire's Bedale in the previous round. Having beaten Gretton in a Midlands clash and Old Netherseal in round seven, Treeton took on the mighty Toft in the quarter-final. The Cheshire champions came with an impressive record in the competition, they had won fifty-five of their sixty-nine matches, but today was not to be their fifty-sixth. A rare batting collapse left them shell shocked at 35 for 7, although the tail wagged valiantly they were all out for 90. Treeton breezed to a seven wicket win, scoring 91 for 3 in the twenty-sixth. Even an early finish in the village championships is turned to full advantage, more time is left for socialising and making new friends.

Treeton played hosts to Cleator, fresh from their victory over 1985 champions Freuchie. The village club had never seen such a sight, or experienced such a day in it's 66 year history. Two thousand spectators ringed the ground on a sweltering day. They ran out of beer twice, but still managed to find enough to celebrate well into the night. Cleator were soon in trouble and by the half way stage only thirty-five runs were on the board. Two of their main batsmen were back in the clubhouse, no doubt

## Fertilizer as a Growing Agent

helping to find some beer, in between keeping an eye on the scoreboard. Although wickets fell steadily the last twenty overs produced 127 runs, with the innings closing on 164 for 9. Cummings could feel proud of his forty runs and Cumbrians would not forget L. Morritt Esquire's five for fifty-seven. Treeton started steadily, with Andrew Jones at the crease and wickets in hand they were never in serious trouble. Finishing on an undefeated 69 he saw his side home by hitting the winning boundary with four balls to spare.

It was August Bank Holiday Monday. What better way to spend it than watching a village cricket match? Some four thousand people thought so, as they took their seats at Lord's to see if "The Cricketer Trophy" would go to Hampshire or stay in Yorkshire. The toss was completed at the appropriate time appointed by law. But Longparish captain John Heagren invoked his prerogative to deliberate, and deliberate he did, before electing to bat. The umpires followed by the players came down the pavilion steps to applause and cheers. At the same time the sun decided to come out from behind a cloud to watch proceedings, it must have found them interesting, for it stayed all day.

J. D. Heagren may have taken his time in deciding on the toss, but he had made the right decision. His innings was the backbone of Longparish's total.In the second over he cracked two boundaries off "Quickie" Harris. When he departed in the thirty-fifth over, stumped by Meadows off the bowling of Thorpe, he had hit five more in his innings of sixty-nine. As wickets fell steadily only three other batsmen made double figures. One of these was Simon Paine, he joined his captain, promptly hit his first ball for four and went on to share an invaluable partnership of forty-two. Big hitter Sturt had the Yorkshire crowd worried when he hit twenty-two runs off eighteen balls, before needlessly running himself out. There was little resistance from the tail except Hibberd who also ran himself out trying to emulate Strut. Seventeen off twenty-one deliveries however was most helpful to Longparish's total of 166. Deliberations in the crowd were earnest during the tea interval, "was it enough?"

Treeton started their reply well aware that only in the first year of the competition had a side batting second won. It was also the fourth highest total in a final. Sturt helped by Sutcliffe, never let them get started. The first four batsmen went cheaply and Treeton were in real trouble at 21 for 5 after fourteen overs. Young Nigel Jacobs however batted superbly for his twenty-one, and when Barry Smith bowled him the crowd rose to applaud him all the way from the wicket. Anyone who may have been asleep (if that was possible) would have awakened to the applause thinking he had scored a century. Only skipper Allsopp managed double figures. When he was caught brilliantly by his opposite number on eighteen, it was all over and the trophy was to go to Hampshire. It was all smiles at the presentation by Hubert Doggart, treasurer and acting MCC president. Norsk Hydro personnel were there in force as usual, including managing director Geoffrey Richards who presented the cheques, medallions and prizes. There was much celebrating in Hampshire well into the early hours of Sunday morning. As Treeton and their supporters made the long journey home to Yorkshire, they may have deliberated what might have been. But they were assured of a warm welcome in the village on their return.

**1988** The third year of Norsk Hydro's sponsorship was to see some new records. Canon Frome's was to remain intact at least for the time being. Himley however jumped into third place with 343 for 0. This put the Staffordshire team firmly at the top of two other statistical tables. The partnership was to beat Roche's 274 in 1984. Andy Shorter's contribution was a real captain's, scoring 221 not out he beat M.Hopkins individual score of 214 made in 1978. This impressive feat stood Himley in good stead as newcomers to the competition, as they went on to the final. Kevin Iles, Goatacre's captain, made 133 in the match against

Oxford Downs. This put him on his own as the first player to have scored five centuries in the competition. Goatacre had been in the competition since year one and were also to go on to the final as the first Wiltshire side to do so.

There were also some new records at the other end of the table. The most incredible in my view was Great Eccleston's visit to The Forest of Boland, where they played the village of Chipping. It was a picturesque ground with some extraordinary bounce. Eccleston were all out for 39, the home team's reply was even more unusual as they were dismissed for fifteen. In anticipation of a joint entry in the record books the teams improvised between 5 pm. (close of play) and 7 pm. (when the bar opened). The celebrations then started in earnest. They had had a marvellous tea and seen twenty wickets go down for fifty-four runs. It had been a day for both villages to remember and treasure.

Himley's group final against Woore was a high scoring affair. The former batted first making 251 for 8. S. Walker top scored with an impressive 111. Woore of 212 for 8 in reply, which would have won many a game. Sadly they could not keep up with the clock. The next round match against Kington was decided by bowling at the stumps, which they won by 3-2. Round seven saw them take on Marchwiel in a close game, winning by the narrowest of margins, Himley 147 for 7 Marchwiel 143 for 9. The quarter-final was against last year's beaten finalists. Treeton batted first and were all out for a creditable 154. Steve Rogers top scored with 59, but Himley helped them a little with nineteen wides. John Day however had a good game with 4 for 24, clean bowling three Treeton victims in his seventh over. Himley's batting record stood them in good stead, scoring 155 with the loss of only six wickets they won with five overs to spare.

The Yorkshire village of Harome were relative newcomers to the competition, but on the way to the semi-final they had beaten last year's group champions Bedale. There were almost a thousand spectators to see the match against their Staffordshire guests. Himley didn't start well in the field, giving four wides in the first five balls of the match. They continued in that vein throughout contributing seventeen extras to Harome's total. Harome looked well set for a sizeable total on 121 for 3. They then lost wickets needlessly by all accounts, and slumped to 155 for 9, before their young batsman Johnathan Marwood steadied the tail. He saw his side home to 179 before being run out on the last ball for 23. Andy Shorter started Himley's reply briskly. He hit three cavalier fours in one over before being stopped in his tracks by a brilliant catch from wicketkeeper David Collier. His cousin Darren was next in and set about building an innings of class before he was sixth wicket down, having scored 59. He had taken his side to within sight of victory on 161 in the thirty-sixth. At the end of the thirty-seventh they needed twelve with four wickets in hand. Andy Bowes came on and had Soley brilliantly caught at long off by Chris Marwood. This must have been a relief for Harome, after Soley had smashed three towering sixes in one over. Eight was needed from two overs when Johnathan Marwood was brought on to bowl bowl for the first time. After conceding just two singles Chris Norris struck his final ball for a straight four. With four balls to go, a leg bye tied the scores. It must have been agony for Harome as Norris played out the last four balls to leave the scores level and victory by two wickets. It was all too much for skipper Peter Collier, he sat in the dressing room with tears rolling down his cheeks. Not because his team had lost a game of cricket, but that his village had been within a whisker of Lord's. He need not have worried, the dream was to come true.

Goatacre's victory over Cattistock left them a sixth round tie against Oxford Downs. This was to be a most amazing game with a four wicket victory for Goatacre. In the next round batting first, a score of 114 for 7 was just enough to beat Werrington who were all out for 108. The quarter-final against Ynystawe was a memorable occasion which will live long in the minds of

## Fertilizer as a Growing Agent

Goatacre. They had their first taste of Welsh hospitality. Despite having lost by six wickets the Glamorgan village made many firm friends from Wiltshire. The semi-final against Hampshire champions Hursley Park turned the whole village of Goatacre upside down and inside out, as well as confusing many motorists just passing through. You can read all about how Goatacre's dream came true in chapter seven. The 1988 final went down in the record books as the longest in the competition — it took 121 overs before one side was declared the victors! Leslie Crowther was the guest speaker at the splendid banquet on the eve of the final. Keith Iles, president of Goatacre was presented with Hydro's copper beer jug for the team's memorable victory over Oxford Downs in July. Keith was so overwhelmed at the presentation being made by his idol Sir Leonard Hutton, that both he and Sir Leonard gave impromptu speeches. The weather as we left Goatacre on the morning of the final heralded definite signs of Autumn. Lord's ground staff had accomplished a magnificent job against daunting odds. Miraculously the sun came out and play started promptly at two thirty. Himley batted first, and as the opening overs progressed I thought of the article I had read in The Daily Telegraph, on the coach journey from Wiltshire. Himley had been tipped favourites. The openers never really looked in trouble as they notched up a first wicket partnership of 49, followed by a second of 56. Goatacre had some respite from a potential onslaught taking Soley's wicket for one, but Himley still achieved the second highest total in a final as they closed on 207 for 6. The only winner at Lord's that day turned out to be the rain.

John Turner played out a maiden in the first over after tea, but poor Alan Walters never lifted his bat to strike a ball. A monumental black cloud had come from behind the pavilion and the heavens opened. By the time we managed to scurry for shelter at the rear of The Mound stand a lake had appeared on the pitch in front of The Tavern. It was clear no further cricket would be played at Lord's that day.

The coach journey home was a subdued affair. It felt just like having celebrated Christmas without opening presents! All had to be done again at the Midland Bank ground at Beckenham the following day. The next morning did not herald confidence, as umbrellas, mackintoshes and blankets accompanied the picnic hampers. At breakfast on the M4 services, a discussion about our destination resulted in the coach drivers' spokesman saying "Beckenham — Beckenham? I don't know where the hell Beckenham is!" Luckily my twelve years experience driving around London proved useful. Accompanying the lead coach in our convoy, reduced from the previous day, I only managed to lose one, who made it eventually.

Tina and Ken Slater had received just nineteen hours notice for the rescheduled fixture at their ground. Despite this the organisation had been handled with effortless ease. The only people to be put out were the Beckenham first eleven, who had been demoted to the second team pitch. They didn't particularly approve of "Mel's Bell", which heralded wickets and boundaries, in Goatacre's favour of course! The bar was open and the covers off. So suitably sustained with picnic and ale, we sat back to watch the whole proceedings start again.

Himley set about building a score on similar lines to their abortive efforts of the previous day. Steve Walker looked particularly menacing when scoring seventy-five off ninety-two balls, in thirty-three overs. With just three wickets down and 150 on the board, it looked like Goatacre were going to need much more than the 208 they had been set the previous day. Turner's guile however was still in evidence, as he had Shorter caught behind for 24 and Hughes for 30. Kevin Iles meanwhile had brought himself on, and things started to change drastically. From 150 for 3 Himley were all out for 192 in the thirty-ninth over. After Hughes had gone for thirty top score was extras on 17. No other batsman made double figures.

Goatacre's start was to be an inauspicious one, Darren Shorter

## Fertilizer as a Growing Agent

caught Turner off the first ball of the innings. Reliable Mark Hunt (Bunter to his village chums), joined Walters and together they took the score to 36. Walters who was finding the conditions particularly trying, was caught by Meagen off the bowling of Shorter for nine. Kevin Iles took his guard with Himley continuing their tight bowling and even tighter fielding. Two steady batsmen at the wicket, and Goatacre were hoping for consolidation rather than heroics. Iles obliged by playing himself in, scoring just seven off his first thirteen balls. He tugged at his cap after peering beyond the long leg boundary to the tennis courts, where ball and racket were much in evidence — but not for long. One mighty six startled those in white shorts and skirts and the bell clanged loudly. Goatacre supporters stirred themselves, knowing glances were passed from one to the other. Iles had touched his cap! Before long another six heralded Iles taking the game to Himley. A four followed, then another huge six back into the tennis courts. When the third six went in that general direction the asphalt courts were deserted.

Tension mounted, no time to go to the bar, thankfully somebody had a hip flask which steadied the nerves. The light was failing, a damp misty atmosphere meant bowlers were having problems keeping the ball dry. A rueful Andy Shorter patrolled the boundary in front of the supporters as Iles continued his surge. "While he's at the crease" Shorter mumbled "anything can happen." One ball left in the penultimate over, 179 on the board and Iles to face. This was to be his last scoring stroke as he hammered his sixth six into the gathering gloom. Veteran Kenny Butler faced the first ball of the final over. In all his twenty-one seasons with the club he had never played a more important innings. The first ball came off his bat handle beating fine leg and went to the boundary. The second was struck confidently off the middle of the bat behind square leg. Iles had played a true captain's innings. His ninety-one not out was the highest in a final. That, together with his 4 for 46, also earned him the

## A Village at Lord's

record for best all round performance in a final. Tony Huskinson, editor of The Cricketer Annual referred to Goatacre as "The Escapegoats!"

There was great jubilation as stalwart supporters rushed to carry their skipper shoulder high to receive "The Cricketer Cup". Andy Shorter, his team and supporters were just as enthusiastic in their applause. Presentations over, it was time for the celebrations. The Cricketer magazine were so pleased that things had turned out so well, after the disappointment of Saturday, they put £250 behind the bar in order that festivities continued. This coach trip home around midnight was a vastly different affair. Many motorists on the M4 between London and Wiltshire might well have learnt from the singing that there was only one Kevin Iles.

We arrived back in the village after midnight, but the celebrations hadn't finished yet. My elder daughter, who had stayed behind to run the kennels, joined the party in farmer Fred Jennings barn. The cup had pride of place atop some bales of hay, while Wiltshire songs and local rhymes went on until first light.

We wandered home to grab an hours sleep before starting the days work. At lunchtime many gathered on the pitch to await the arrival of Hydro's helicopter. This was to take some on a brief airborne trip to announce The Cricketer Cup had come to Wiltshire. But everyone knew that, HTV and BBC TV as well as the local radio station had seen to that, before we had finished our first celebratory pint at Beckenham.

**1989** It was the opinion of some that village cricket had changed considerably since 1972. Many sides were competing in local league and cup competitions. Tea ladies were more overworked than usual, had it not been for the fine weather laundry would have been another headache. In a third round match on May Bank Holiday, one village were playing one game

## Fertilizer as a Growing Agent

in an uninterupted ten days of solid cricket. We must not forget the problems success brings to the poor fixtures secretary. However the added strain often brings rewards of good cricket, good companionship and good fun. Some things never change. In all walks of life voluntary work is essential to keep things going, it is the willing handful that do most of the work. So it is only fair they should have their say.

Canon Frome were toppled from the top of the record table. Barkisland scored 440 for 5 against Old Sharlston. An opening stand of 217 between J.Ball and Craig Longbottom was broken when J.Ball was bowled E.Ball for 136. Longbottom carried his bat for 164, making one mistake in an otherwise faultless innings. He edged his first ball but was dropped! All rounder Tony Skyes helped with 81. Fifty-nine boundaries were scored and a herd of cows in an adjacent field moved away to less dangerous quarters. Old Sharlston had tried nine bowlers and two wicket keepers to try and stem the run flow, but it was all in vain. They did however score a creditable 130 in reply, thus ensuring they shared in the records with a match aggregate of 570. This nudged Feckenham and Bramshill into second place.

Local newspapers up and down the country had certainly been bitten by the village cricket bug, even in the early rounds. Local rivalries obviously had an historical record to go by. The Hereford Times for example heralded with great excitement Canon Frome's thrilling one run victory over local rivals Stones. Two villages that had given their supporters much to talk about over the years. There was also some admirable coverage in the second round. The Dursley Gazette carried the headline "MAY-TIME FIREWORKS AS FROCESTER GO IN TO THE FOURTH ROUND." This recorded Pat Field and Ian Smith's stand of 136 in just twelve overs. I smiled when reading an article in The Burton Mail of April 19th., which referred to "Hydro Village Cricket debutantes Dunstall" having to wait until May 14th. for their first round match in what the reporter referred to as "this prestigious competition." No it wasn't the weather that frustrated them, merely a bye in the first round. Their coverage and headlines in August 1990 was to be far greater, as Dunstall were to reach the final at their second attempt.

The northern semi-final produced a clash between two previous finalists. Northumberland champs. Bomarsund and Toft from Cheshire had their original fixture rained off. In their rescheduled match weather was still a threat. Toft scored 155 for 5 in their forty overs. Bomarsund had nearly matched the run rate when bad light brought a halt to proceedings. Rule eight (i) came into force, and the home team had lost by the narrowest of margins on a slower scoring rate of just 0.2 runs per over. Bomarsund had been deprived of an appearance at Lord's in 1974, because not a ball was bowled in the scheduled final. Yet again the weather had dealt the hand of fate. If there was to be a statistical record of the unluckiest villages, they would certainly be jostling for top position with Langleybury.

What, you may wonder, happened to my own village. You can read of our demise in the quarter-final tie against St.Fagans in chapter seven. After beating us, they travelled to Hampshire for a semi-final against a village that had played at the hallowed ground more than a hundred years before the Glamorgan club was founded. Before a crowd of more than two thousand spectators Hambledon stopped cricket history in it's tracks for one afternoon. They also stopped the traffic and caused the Hampshire constabulary a headache in having to direct the local bus through leafy lanes blocked by cars.

Hambledon won the toss and elected to bat. St.Fagans bowlers were not to get things all their own way, runs were steady in coming but there were no sensations. Colin Pay scored thirty-two and captain Mike Donaldson had contributed eighteen when the innings closed at 139 for 9. Not for the first time the Welsh were off to a flying start, with 36 from the first four overs. It all changed after that, the guile of Robert Turner's off spin,

## Fertilizer as a Growing Agent

returning figures of two for fourteen, and McDonald's two for nine, was too much for the Welshmen. They only managed thirty-four in the next sixteen overs. From 70 for 5 they were all out for 131. Gareth Jones was top score for St. Fagans with 34, but Hambledon were next highest, having conceded twenty extras.

The national press had a field day heralding 1989's village final. In The Daily Telegraph John Fogg's article carried the headline "Hambledon qualify at last for a Lord's final." Pat Gibson's World of Cricket article was headed "Hambledon's happy return to Lord's," he referred to the village as "the fabled cradle of cricket." For Ben Brocklehurst it must have been a particularly satisfying turn of events. The Cricketer had done much to help village cricket since 1972. Their sterling work had now brought the most famous village cricket team out of relative obscurity into the spotlight, albeit for only a day.

The men of Hambledon were going to enjoy their day to the full. Their best performance until now had been to reach the last sixteen in 1977. One survivor from that year was their legendary "Topsy Turner". He had played for the village for thirty-five years, in that time he had scored more than 35,000 runs and taken over 350 wickets. Born and bred in the village, he had always dreamed of following in the footsteps of his eighteenth century contemporaries, who had played on Broad Halfpenny Down. After their semi- final victory over St.Fagans this modest bricklayer said "I've never seen anything like it!"

Hambledon batted first at Lord's, but it was not to be a notable day to record as far as the cricket was concerned. Struggling at 72 for 5 off 29 overs, the rains came and brought an abrupt halt to proceedings. A repeat of the frustration in the 1988 final unfolded, with both teams having to travel to the Midland Bank ground at Beckenham to start all over again the following day.

Toft won the toss and Hambledon again batted first. Runs were hard to come by against an all spin attack. Slow off spinners

## A Village at Lord's

Locke and Burtenshaw each bowled through their allotted nine overs. At the end of this they had conceded just twenty-eight runs between them, and Locke had captured the first three wickets. S. James and J. Brindley were the only two batsmen to reach double figures. Their partnership never took off and when Stimpson caught Brindley on the square leg boundary, the writing was on the wall. The score was on eighty-nine for eight when "Topsy Turner" had injury problems. With the aid of a runner he was stranded at three not out when Hambledon's last wicket fell at the end of the thirty-seventh, with the score on 104.

Pay gave Hambledon hope by dismissing both openers cheaply, Stimpson for three and his partner without scoring. Caro and Stiles pushed the score to 31 before Pay struck again, when he had Stiles caught by Faithful for ten. Ashley joined Caro and together they batted sensibly before Ashley was caught by Barrett with the score on 65. There were no further mishaps as Toft passed the Hambledon total with five overs to spare. The fairytale ending had received a double blow. First the rained off final at Lord's, to be followed by Cheshire champions Toft preventing The Cricketer Cup from resting in the cradle of cricket. I still fancy there was much celebration at The Bat and Ball Inn on Broad Halfpenny Down. Hambledon had come out of the wilderness. The descendants of John Neyrn and company had graced Lord's once more. Would they manage it again? Only history will tell.

Norsk Hydro had shared a happy and purposeful relationship since 1986. A relationship which had benefited village cricket. Sadly this fourth year was to be Hydro's last. Malcolm Lukey told me he has many fond memories of the championships. Particularly the marvellous spirit that shone through both on and off the field in villages all over the country. You can rest assured Malcolm, your company did put something back into the grass roots of the game, Ben Brocklehurst was quick to point that out. Although a new sponsor had not been found for 1990 the competition would continue.

# CHAPTER FIVE

# The Lean Years

1978 was to see the first of four years when the competition would be run without sponsorship from a commercial company. The Cricketer's organisational skills were just as efficient as ever. They could competently handle any matter which may crop up in relation to rules, conditions or administration. So in the absence of outside financial support they took on that responsibility also. Under the circumstances the eve of final banquets were not feasible, but a more modest welcoming reception still enabled the two villages to get acquainted. Awards for team and individual achievements also had to be scaled down. The competition however did not suffer. It was still as popular as ever, thanks to The Cricketer's tenacity. When the need arose, local benefactors in the local communities stepped in to help.

On the statistical front, Canon Frome scored an impressive 331 for 6 against Flyford Flavell to go top of the table with a win by 305 runs. This spot had been held by Sutton-On-the-Hill with their 318 for 5 against Hilton in 1973. Cookley equalled that score in 1978, with 318 for 6 against Woolhope (57). The most notable individual batting performance also went to Cookley, M.Hopkins score of 214 beat Tim Botting's 206 for Balcombe in 1977. With the ball, L.Macfarlane of Abthorpe became the fifth bowler to take four wickets in four balls. The best all round performance was from M.Copplestone of Abinger who scored 88 and five for thirteen. M.Fowler of Wilby also did well with 63 and 6 for 61. The match between Grampound Road and Ladcock produced 468 runs. Grampound hit 236 for 2 and Ladcock managed an impressive 232 for 8 in reply.

Toft of Cheshire were celebrating their golden jubilee that year. They were to celebrate it in fine style by reaching the final. Their opponents were the strong village side of Linton Park. This Kent village had an impressive record, having won twenty of their previous twenty- five matches in the competition. Each side had some close games in their preliminary rounds. Although both had convincing wins to reach their respective group final, Toft with a victory over Cholmondeley by 106 and Linton beat Leigh by 42 runs.

The group final for Toft could have gone either way. They ran out winners at 118 for 7 against an Alvanley total of 110 for 9 In round six, 141 for 8 was always too much for Normanby of South Yorkshire, who only scored 77 in reply. Next they played Durham champions Tudhoe, who had only lost six of their previous thirty-two matches. This was to be their seventh. Toft's 184 for 6 left them chasing a run rate of more than 4.5 an over. They tried hard but were eventually dismissed for 151. In the quarter-final the match was decided on a faster scoring rate at the fifteen over mark. Toft (180 for 9) were on 63 at fifteen overs, whereas their opponents Bomarsund (98 for 7) were on thirty-six at the same stage.

Fillongley had home advantage in the semi-final, but their skipper was in Spain. What a strange fellow, I could have understood if he had been getting married, or would I?!! It was glorious weather and the Warwickshire ground had been suitably prepared to receive it's fifteen hundred spectators, who were to see a tense match. Toft batted first, and apart from a scare when opener Butler was dropped at slip when on seven, he and Stimpson laid the foundations with a fifty-three partnership in eleven overs. Fillongley were not going to wilt and Tony Davis's nine overs conceded only seventeen runs. He took four for thirty-two, although three deliveries were struck for six. Stimpson was

## The Lean Years

still there, and on reaching his fifty started to attack, hitting twenty-four off one over from Jackman. His side's total of 186 all out owed much to Stimpson's spirited 77. Toft gave Fillongley a good start, with the first six on the board consisting of a wide, a no ball and four byes. The young seventeen year old opener Harris played a mature innings which earnt him man of the match. He started with cautious defence, building his innings. At the twenty over mark he was still there with his side on 75 for 3. It was not all over yet as there was plenty of batting to come. Phillips and Smallwood were both capable of scoring freely, but today it was not to be. With them out much rested on the youthful shoulders of Harris. As his confidence grew he took what runs he could against tight fielding and experienced team work. Forty-nine were needed off the last seven overs, but six wickets had fallen. It was a tall order as the young Harris played some flourishing strokes, but was last out as his team finished on 159 all out in the thirty-ninth. Butler had returned an impressive 3 for 27.

In the Kent group final Linton Park dismissed Marden for 97 and were never in trouble finishing on 98 for 5. Round six was a low scoring affair when Langleybury struggled to 101 for 9. A five wicket victory was secured at 102 for 5. Havering of Essex scored 157, but it was never enough and Linton were worthy winners on 160 for 3. Their quarter-final match against Hursley Park saw the Hampshire champions restrict them to 122 for 5, but Hursley were never allowed off the hook, and finished on 89 for 8.

Aston Rowant brought plenty of supporters from Oxfordshire for the semi- final against Linton Park. The match was played in front of more than 2000 spectators. Aston lost opener John Pearson in Gauna's first over. Shortly afterwards McQueen, scorer of many memorable innings, departed. Against a well disciplined fielding side they never really reached their full potential, as a large part of the innings was one of recovery. A spirited 46 from

Lambourne however gave their bowlers something to aim at in their total of 151. Openers Brattle and Bowles set about building a partnership rather than building an innings. They reached fifty with relevant ease before Brattle was eventually run out with the score on 73. When Thirklell came in he immediately took charge of proceedings by hitting two sixes, and shared in a partnership of 62 with Bowles. When Bowles departed with the score on 135 for 3, he had scored a solid 62 to ensure his team was safely through to the final, finishing 152 for 3.

The big occasion was not going to unnerve these strong village sides. The crowd were in for a thrilling tactical game. Linton invited Toft to bat (which they would have elected to do anyway by all accounts). Immediately opening bat Alan Stimpson and Tony Gauna, with his left arm seamers were testing each other. First blood to Gauna who bowled Butler for one, with the score on three. That may be the only wicket Gauna took in the match, but he bowled three maidens and conceded just sixteen runs in bowling straight through. Stimpson, uncharacteristically, had been tied down only managing three singles in the first thirteen overs. Mulholland had done most of the scoring with 26. When at the half way stage only 54 had been scored, this pair needed to accelerate. Mulholland tried, but holed out to Pay at short leg, who took the catch at his second attempt. The pair had added an invaluable 64, but Stimpson was not allowed to play his natural game. Nigel Thirkell had been brought into the bowling attack, and his final figures of 9 − 2 − 36 − 3 ably demonstrated the effect he had on proceedings. A frustrated Stimpson was eventually caught and bowled by Black. Not his best day, it had taken 34 overs to achieve his 41 runs. The lower order had too much to do. With wicket keeper Hall's fine agility running out Holland for 15, the tail could only muster a few, as Toft's innings closed at 130 for 8.

Bowles and Brattle decided to see off the opening attack, after an early scare with a catch from a no ball in the first over. They

## The Lean Years

scored at one an over for the first six, but gained confidence by adding another thirty in the next six. Bailey decided to bring himself back on and bowled Brattle almost immediately, with the score on 39. Bowles was missed off a difficult chance in the gulley with the score on forty. Bailey however bowled him next ball. A captain's strategy appeared to have paid off. Thirkell and Piper advanced the score to 67 before Coutts had the latter brilliantly caught by Mulholland for fifteen. But Thirkell was feeling his feet and started scoring more freely than any batsman had done all day. Toft still kept the screws on as Black and Hall fell cheaply. The total was on 90 for 5. The Kent supporters may well have been starting to bite their nails as Tim Thirkell joined brother Nigel. A near run out when the hundred came up must have set a few hearts racing. After that the brothers kept their heads and took the score to 125 before Tim was out for 10. Brother Nigel got his desired half century, being undefeated on 51, as Linton ran out victors by six wickets.

The Cricketer must have felt justly proud, having sponsored and organised the competition, to see such a final. It was one of cricketing skill and knowledgeable tactics even Brearley and Close would have been delighted to see. Both teams had demonstrated the quality of cricket villagers were capable of producing, while still not losing the spirit in which the game is played.

**1985**   Once again The Cricketer was to take full responsibility for the competition. Thankfully MCC and Lord's ground staff were still there to provide much needed and appreciated support for the final.

Top honours with the bat went to St.Fagans' captain Ricky Needham. He hit 201 not out, in a total of 307 for 4 against Wenvoe. Some other notable achievements were K.Hill of Blythe who scored 172, R.F.Floyd of Bledlow was third with his 137, while W.Taylor of Nassington was unbeaten on 135. J.Patel returned the best bowling figures of the season with 8 for 6. Two fine all round performances came from J.Lowe of Oxford Downs who hit 51 and returned bowling figures of 5 for 13. D.Pitt followed his 80 with 5 for 23. The highest partnership of the season was 209 for the first, by J.Irvine 105 not out and S.Poulter 101 for Mainsforth. The spectators who watched the match between Roxwell and Great Burstead saw a glut of runs, 485 in all, as Roxwell 244 for 8 beat Burstead by a narrow margin of 3 runs. The most convincing win of the competition in '85 was Outwood's demolition of Bletchley, who could only muster 45 in chasing a total of 253 for 9. Warren would probably prefer to forget their claim for inclusion in the records with the lowest total for the season, an unlucky 13.

Two Surrey villages met on May 10th. 1981. Rowledge were away to Shere, a small village nestling under the North Downs. The ground was straight out of an English Tourist Board calendar. A watery sun greeted the Rowledge team as they arrived, looking forward to their first encounter in the competition with great interest. As the players and officials alighted from the coach misty rain began to fall. The hearty band of supporters, well protected with gloves and scarves, patiently waited for the start of this very special match.

The umpires appeared, looking just a shade hesitant. Perhaps the uncertain conditions were affecting their gait to the wicket? It was rumoured however that the visiting team's umpire was wearing two pairs of trousers and six jumpers! He also carried more than an umpire's normal equipment in his top pocket. The rain soon turned to sleet as Rowledge set about building an innings. Their skipper didn't feel keen to field that day. The overs slipped by, with the visiting umpire being seen to take more than card and pencil from his top pocket. As his hand regularly passed his face, it was rumoured he had replenished his flask before taking the field. The sleet was now turning to snow, so no one blamed

## The Lean Years

him. As the eighteenth over started the snow became heavier, and the hip flask no doubt emptier.

Consultation led to agreement on suspending proceedings and repairing to the pavilion. Supporters had taken refuge in their cars with heaters on. Conditions failed to improve, in fact they became worse. After a brief discussion it was mutually agreed to abandon play and replay the following Sunday, provided the snow wasn't too deep. The flask was passed around, and Rowledge's 89 for 3 off 18 overs was considered a memorable start to their village cup games. Who said cricket was dead? Not these twenty-two players. As an afterthought, much later, it was muted that if this was what the competition was all about, then the sooner we were out of it the better. I wonder if they recalled this match and those words when they appeared in the 1985 final?

Just a wee few miles north from Glen Rothes is the hamlet of Freuchie (no not Frookie, Freuchie!). It was 1985, Scottish cricket's bi- centenary year, and Freuchie were preparing to win their fourth consecutive group final. They readily admitted to not being the best batting side in Fife. But their bowling and fielding, well that was another matter. Their captain/chairman Dave Christie, affectionately known as "Dad", would tell you "We find it easier to give away money than runs!" When the team batted first, no matter what the total, their "mean machine" of bowlers and fielders went into action. Given the thousands of pounds the club has raised for charity, I am convinced "dad's" pragmatic view of the team was correct.

Defending a total of 175 for 8 the mean machine restricted Meigle to 134 for 9, thus becoming champions of Scotland once again. Four English villages crossed over the border during the next couple of months, all failed. In the semi-finals, Leicestershire champions Billesdon arrived in the pouring rain. Despite the weather, more than a thousand spectators ringed the boundary. They saw the Scottish champions dismissed for 117. A run rate of less than 3 an over is comfortable by many standards. But this

## A Village at Lord's

is village cricket, and it's raining. Freuchie's strength won through as Billesdon were all out for 105. In all cases, as villages succeed in the long road to Lord's, so their following grows. This was to be no exception. "The Tartan Army" had two weeks of preparation before they crossed the border to invade the home of cricket in St. John's Wood. Only the Surrey village of Rowledge stood between them and their chance to take The Cricketer Trophy home in their country's bi-centennial year.

It was a busy fortnight. Letters and cards of congratulations flooded into the village. Local sponsorship offers also poured in. P.C. Ian Gordon had to organise extra police patrols to protect the deserted village. Dad Christie and secretary Alan Wilkie were guests of honour at the Scottish Bi-Centenary dinner on the Wednesday before the final. The following evening they also attended a hastily arranged sponsors night function at the club. This was to enable the players to say thanks for all the help that had been given. Everything possible had been done to ensure the Scottish invasion of London was afforded the best opportunity to inflict the greatest defeat on the English since Bannockburn in 1314.

On Friday afternoon Alan Wilkie checked his list :- ten coaches fully booked, "Hamish Mac Haggis", match report telephone number for ball by ball coverage passed on to the few guardians left behind. Oh yes, 'plane. booked for Pipe Major Alistair Pirnie to fly down tomorrow after the Highland Games. No point in preparing a special anthem for the occasion, if you haven't got the piper there to play it.

So the players, their wives and girlfriends, set off that Friday night to enjoy a day in London before the Big Match. All Scotland wished them well, and just for good measure, another team were on board the coach. This was a Scottish TV. crew who had become part of the village during the preceding fortnight.

In Whitbread times the occasion of the final had made

## The Lean Years

St. John's Wood take notice with shire horses and drays. At 11 a.m. on Sunday September 1st., any resident hoping for a lie in could forget it. Pipe Major Pirnie saw to that. He piped the team from the Westmorland Hotel and through the Grace Gates, to the strains of their specially composed anthem "Freuchie's March To Lord's." Dave Christie was by his side, like the team following behind he wore full Highland dress. As he surveyed the ecstatic Scottish supporters waving their various banners, he couldn't help smiling. Then one which simply said "DAD'S ARMY" brought a lump to his throat.

As the official photographs were taken, so the supporters soaked up the atmosphere. As I said in my introduction, the main achievement was to play at Lord's, to win was the icing on the cake. For the first time the passion was a little more intense, in the Scottish camp that is. The 1400 inhabitants of Freuchie were representing their country, so they had an added responsibility thrust upon their shoulders. Press and TV. interviewers received the same reply — "We're here to win". One photograph epitomises their harmless audacity. A young supporter viewed the pavilion from the mid tier of the New Mound Stand before the start of play. The Daily Record's photographer could not resist capturing the slogan on the back of a tartan rug draped across his shoulders "Freuchie Cricket Club The Flower of Scotland".

Rowledge won the toss, I believe before lunch, but their captain Alan Prior delayed his decision to bat until fifteen minutes before the start of play. This did not worry the Scots at all. With three off the first over and a maiden in the second, the mean machine were starting to get into gear. Opener Tony Hook hit the first of five fours in his innings of 28. When Cowan had Simpson caught by Crichton in the fifth the score was fifteen. The tartan army began to roar. Neil Dunbar, who became top scorer of the day with 33, walked on to the hallowed turf to the strains of ere we go. Together with Tony Hook he saw the fifty up. When the partnership reached 41 in the seventeenth, Niven

## A Village at Lord's

McNaughton uprooted Hook's middle stump. His 28 was the second highest score of the day. The stage had been set for the Rowledge run machine, Chris Yates, to take centre stage. He already had three centuries under his belt from previous rounds. He opened his account with a boundary. At the half way stage the Surrey village's total stood at 68 for 2. Yates was never allowed to settle, when Dave Christie bowled him for ten, the total was on 73. Dunbar and Cooper scored a dozen each, but the mean machine ensured wickets fell steadily. Field was stranded with ten to his name, as Rowledge finished on 134.

Both Mark Wilkie and Alan Duncan found the boundary at the start of Freuchie's reply, before Wilkie was bowled by Field for ten. He followed up by deceiving Andy Crichton, trapping him LBW without scoring. George Wilson soon found the boundary, but Yates caught opener Duncan off Silver for sixteen. Forty-seven for three. Dave Cowan brought up the fifty in the nineteenth, Wilson had been dismissed for fourteen, which brought Stewart Irvine to the crease. Freuchie's two youngsters then put on 33 off four overs, before Silver bowled Cowan for sixteen. Irvine, in an attempt to maintain the momentum, had hit the only six in the match, when Prior snapped up a smart caught and bowled, to dismiss him for twenty-four. Terry Trewartha and George Crichton saw the hundred up in the twenty-ninth, before Riffold bowled Trewartha for a single. This brought the Scottish side's captain to the wicket. The pair kept their heads and saw the team to within one run of victory, before Dad Christie was run out for eleven at the end of the penultimate over.

Rowledge's captain, Alan Prior, bowled the last over, Crichton was facing. He managed a single off the first ball to bring the scores level. The Freuchie captain's son Brian was adjudged not to have played at a ball which brushed his pad. The leg bye was disallowed, and he was sent back, as was the premature pitch invasion of the tartan army. But Christie the

## The Lean Years

younger held out, Freuchie had won the tightest final in the history of the competition, by having lost fewer wickets.

The celebrations "north of the border" were incredible. The men from Fife were hailed national heroes. Arriving home in torrential rain did nothing to dampen anyone's spirits. Banners, tartans, flags and balloons decked the hamlet of Freuchie from end to end. A great cheer went up as the team coach approached from the west. Captain Dave Christie politely refused an umbrella as he stepped from the coach. His first duty was to hold the trophy aloft, and no one was going to be prevented from seeing it. A huge roar went up from the crowd.

Back at the clubhouse there was no room to move inside whilst the welcoming speeches were given. After the team took to the roof of the clubhouse to salute those standing in the pouring rain. Freuchie then set about a second night of celebrations, the like of which Scotland had probably never seen before.

Newspaper reporters had a field day, with banner headlines such as "Fabulous Freuchie", "A Freuchie Freak-Out!" and "Tartan Army Sees Fifers Hit Lord's For Six." I suppose the best way to put this justifiable national euphoria into perspective, is to look at what it means to win the title of Skol Scottish Sports Team Of The Year. In winning the award this small hamlet joined previous winners. Who were they you may ask? Aberdeen Football Club, European Cup winning side and the Scottish Rugby Union's "Grand Slam" team of 1984.

In the latter stages of my research, I had reason to telephone Dave Christie to check on a small point. "He was na in," said his father, "Can I take a message?" When he knew who I was and what I was on about, I could hear the emotion in his voice as he recalled that weekend of over seven years ago. Wee Freuchie were the Pride of Scotland, not I suspect for just a week or so.

**1990** Following the departure of Norsk Hydro, The Cricketer found themselves at the helm once again, this time for two consecutive seasons. The group finals were to see some regular strong contenders appearing once again. Freuchie of Scotland beat St. Boswell by 78 runs in their group final. What a surprise, their original fixture had to be cancelled due to bad weather. Treeton Welfare beat Whitley Hall in a close exciting finish. Treeton had scored 166 for 9 and Whitley, needing four to win, had their last man caught on the boundary, Ow Zat! Toft beat Northrop Hill by 15 runs, Quarndon beat Swarkestone by 34 runs to become champions of Derbyshire yet again. The Glamorgan group final was a clash of the gladiators, between Ynysygerwn and St.Fagans, and what a battle it was. The scheduled date was washed out and the second looked just as suspect, however they did play 25 overs a side. Ynysygerwn still managed 168 for 6 and St.Fagans rose to the occasion. With 30 needed off the last three overs they charged on, running out winners by 1 run off the penultimate ball of the day, at 169 for 9. I fancy however Ynysygerwn won the singing contest afterwards.

Those old stalwarts Langleybury had an impressive 110 run victory over Copley, scoring 234 for 4, the second highest total in the group finals. Could it be their year at last? Regrettably not, although they beat 1985 finalists Rowledge in the next round, Essex champions Hornden on the Hill beat them by four wickets in round seven. They scored a respectable 157 for 8, which could have been more had it not been for D.Towler's miserly bowling of 2 for 28. Despite S.Walford's 2 for 18 in his nine overs and Rice's 3 for 24, Hornden's Stitson jnr. stole the show with an unbeaten 85, to see his side home on 158 for 6.

Two of Hampshire's oldest and finest village teams contested their group final. A large crowd saw Hursley Park (203 for 5) beat Longparish (127 ) by 76 runs. Rowledge won a cliff hanger against Farley Hill by 2 runs, in an absorbing 4 runs an over contest. Kent champions Linton Park hoisted their total from 151 for 9

## The Lean Years

at the end of the thirty-ninth, to 175 at the end of the fortieth. Croucham Hill made a valiant effort, but ran out of overs at 166 for 9.

The tiny village of Dunstall, near Burton-On-Trent, first entered the competition "just for fun" in 1989, and didn't get beyond the first round. Their committee decided to have another go in 1990, but this time felt they must take it seriously. And so they did. Batting first in their opening match against Woore they expected to score at least 200 on a good batting track. They finished on 255 for 5 with a fine undefeated contribution of 121 from Colin Boulton. Woore attacked from the start of their innings. The front line batsmen looked capable, but in losing a few quick wickets they fell behind the clock. Dunstall won by an impressive margin in excess of 100 runs. In the second round tie they again topped 250. Their opponents Oakmore, although getting off to a rapid start, were hampered by Dunstall's improved bowling and fielding. Teamwork was inspiring and Dunstall had an easy win.

The next game was at home to old friends and neighbours Marchington. There were more than a few spectators to see the visitors bowled out for 136. The team felt they were becoming a solid unit by now. Helped no doubt by the band of supporters that were becoming an integral part of proceedings. After their previous two comprehensive victories, a win over Marchington was possibly considered a formality. At 83 for 6 they soon learnt nothing should ever be taken as a formality in this competition. It was then they realised just what it meant to be a unit. Their lower order batting saw them safely past their target. Marchington's umpire was heard to comment "You were in a bit of trouble there, did you have much batting to come?"

A visit to Enville near Stourbridge was the venue for their area final. The ground was set in a private park, where cricket was prohibited on Sunday. But the owner made an exception for such an important match. Worcestershire CCC. may have been refused had they asked, but the village of Enville was a different matter. Dunstall struggled to 146 on a rain affected wicket, but their bowlers and fielders once again did what was required. At the end of the match Enville's secretary announced his team's congratulations to the new area champions over the loud speakers.

Everyone in Burton-On-Trent was starting to talk about the little village of Dunstall, including the local press. Off they went to the Malvern Hills to take on Colwall. It was here they realised things were getting tougher. They had to fight for every run, managing a total of 147. Helped by Tony Higgott in the lower order, who hit three enormous sixes. In the field Dunstall dished out the same medicine to their opponents, who could only muster 90 against some excellent fielding. This included three brilliant run outs, one of which featured Phil Wallbank hitting the one stump he had to aim at from twenty yards or more. The buzz was growing back at Burton-On-Trent, as were the headlines, one read "Lord's Beckons". The closer they got to Lord's, the closer the team and their supporters (now known as The Dunstall Army) were becoming.

Their seventh round tie was away to Isleham who had previously done Cambridgeshire village cricket proud. This match was to be no exception. The Dunstall contingent travelled to the match in a convoy of coaches. They were greeted by a banner in the pavilion which read "Welcome to Dunstall CC". Batting first again, Colin Boulton carried his bat for 91, with several other useful contributions. Isleham had been set 229 to win. They made a brave attempt at it. Good bowling, fine fielding and wicket keeping however restricted the home team to 196 for 8 at the close.

The quarter-final was a home tie against the formidable Treeton Welfare. All pitched in to make the ground fit for such an important match. It must have impressed the neutral umpires, for they even took callipers to the ball after measuring the stumps.

## The Lean Years

Dunstall chairman, Tim Ward, commented that the volume of traffic around the ground reminded him of the Normandy Invasion. Apparently Phil Wallbank's mythical double headed coin did the trick once more, as yet again Dunstall batted first! The openers set off at a brisk and confident pace, which Rob Cooper capitalised on with his six sixes in a quick fire sixty-five. Under normal circumstances 258 for 4 is a total with which to be well satisfied. But would it be enough against the power of Treeton? It did not appear to perturb the opening pair. As they set about their task, Dunstall supporters could be seen to have caught "the walk-about syndrome". This was a disease many a supporter had contracted since the competition began. Mine started in 1988.

Two hours of nail biting tension left Treeton needing eleven to win off the last over. Charlie Crossland was to bowl to Shackleton who was well settled. Walkabouts were too much to bear at this stage. The run up for each ball was in dead silence. Five to win off the last ball. More than twenty sixes had already been hit in the match, was this to be another? No! Just a single. Treeton's hero Shackleton was left stranded on 87 and Dunstall were through to the semi-final. So it was that Dunstall travelled to Yorkshire where cricket is, as I have said previously, a religion more than a game. The weather was not up to its normal standard, and there was to be one brief interruption for rain. Nevertheless this did not prevent Colton from making their visitors welcome with a grand barbecue. Phil Wallbank's "coin" did the trick again and Dunstall set about building a score for their bowlers to aim at. It was another struggle against experienced fielding, but a respectable 149 for 7 was something for their bowlers to get their teeth into. Colton began well but were not finding it as easy to score as they would have liked. Stuart Scrimshaw had a superb spell, and contained the best Yorkshire batsmen in conceding just 21 runs for his 9 overs. With Scrimshaw finished, Colton started to score and tilt the game back. Then a good catch from Abid

# A Village at Lord's

Ali on the long on boundary dismissed Colton's danger man. This was followed by two more fine catches which sharpened the fielding. In the last over Colton needed eight to win. But David Shipton had Lord's in sight, and was not about to let go. Dunstall won by four runs. They had two weeks in which to prepare for the greatest match in their club's history of ninety-two years.

I owed a favour to a friend of mine who lived in Cherhill, a village about five miles from Goatacre. Peter was a keen cricket fan, so what better way to repay him than inviting him to spend a day at Lord's watching the village final. Little did he, or any of us for that matter, realise what a final it was to be. We waited for our fleet of coaches in brilliant early morning sunshine. It was to stay that way all day. We had an unhurried journey, with breakfast en route at Heston services on the M4. This still left plenty of time to wander round Lord's soaking up the atmosphere and swapping stories with the Dunstall Army. Alan Curtis's dulcet tones over the public address system reminded us that the main business of the day was not too far off. We took our seats armed with a pint, and settled back to see Pete Leavy and Mark "Bunter" Hunt descend the steps to loud applause.

Shipton marked out his run up from the pavilion end. Silence as Leavy took guard, the dull thud of Shipton's footsteps were all that could be heard around the hushed ground. A gasp went out from The New Mound Stand, and cheers from The Tavern. Because the next sound was a click as the unfortunate Leavey's off stump was knocked drunkenly to one side. My wife, who knew little of the laws of cricket, asked what all the fuss was about. She was fully convinced they were just "knocking up". Tennis is much more her game! John Spencer joined Hunt and helped edge the score to 23 before Shipton struck again, having him caught behind by Higgott. Hunt was joined by John (JT) Turner, who in his days of minor county cricket had taken a ton off the Pakistanis when Imran Khan was starting to flex his muscles on the World stage. J.T. hit an aggressive 53 whilst his solid partner

## The Lean Years

played anchorman, but never failed to punish the bad ball. When JT departed in the twenty-third the score was exactly one hundred.

Captain Kevin Iles was next man in. Goatacre supporters were well aware of his all round capabilities, but none could have foretold what was to follow. Before another hour had passed there was to be what I consider the finest display of powerful batting ever seen at Lord's. I had been watching cricket there at all levels for almost thirty years and have never heard of the like. Iles hit a blistering 123, four of his ten sixes were dispatched out of the ground. On the way to his century he hit the luckless Shipton for four consecutive sixes. Delays in retrieving the ball did not disturb his concentration. Amid all the excitement Hunt was bowled by Crossland for 39. The score by then however read 220! Once again Bunter had done his job well. Iles continued to plunder. When on 123 he slightly mis-timed a drive that may well have been over the pavilion, and back into St.John's Wood Road where it had been ten minutes previously. Instead it hung in the air for what seemed like an age. Dunstall had their first piece of luck since the first ball of the innings. In the deep stood ex Derby County goalkeeper Colin Boulton, what safer pair of hands. Iles tucked his lethal willow blade under his arm, and set off on the long journey back to the England dressing room. The crowd stood as one man to applaud him. MCC members stood either side of the pavilion steps forming an impromptu guard of honour. Iles had long disappeared from sight before the crowd settled. Andy Dawson and John Wilkins added the last seven runs. Goatacre had broken their own record set in 1988. Dunstall were faced with a total of 268 to win.

To sustain 6.7 runs an over for forty overs is a tall order indeed. Geoff Shilton and Phil Wallbank set about the task purposefully and intelligently. Together they put on 67 for the first wicket, before Paul Rose struck in the sixteenth. He had Shilton caught for an accreditable 35. Turner's slow left armers

## A Village at Lord's

were brought into play, and he quickly bowled Cooper for a single. From 73 for 2 Wallbank and Keith Shilton took the score to 114, before Jon Angell uprooted Shilton's middle stump. Wallbank played a captain's innings, but when he was out for fifty-one the run rate was approaching ten an over. Iles eased the bowling attack and gave several of the team an opportunity to bowl at Lord's. Boulton and Ingles enjoyed themselves scoring 21 and 24 respectively. Abid Ali and Scrimshaw put on 29 for the ninth wicket, but by this time everyone knew a win was a forlorn hope. Dunstall finished on 217 for 8. In so doing they had scored the second highest total in a final behind Goatacre in this match, and had beaten East Brierley's 216 for 4 made way back in 1979.

I find it almost impossible to conclude this report on the 1990 final without appearing arrogant or condescending to the reader. I will therefore refer to Nick Stewart's concluding paragraph in The Cricketer annual:- "The two sides had given of their best, and had entertained a large crowd to great effect. In the end though, the day belonged to a quiet, modest, undeniably talented cricketer whose loyalty to his club, and whose devotion to the game should prove inspiration to all cricketers, great and small. For that one hot August day at Lord's belonged to Kevin Iles."

**1991** Lack of commercial sponsorship did not prevent the twentieth year of the competition being another resounding success. It was a season which saw 638 villages enter. Each one hoping the club secretary would have to postpone their scheduled fixture for August 31st. They would explain they had an unexpected fixture in London that day, and apologise for the short notice. No, the second eleven could not possibly stand in, and where appropriate the third, fourth or fifth. The tea ladies and ground staff would be busy as well. In fact so would the whole village. They were however welcome to come and watch the

## The Lean Years

London match if they wanted to, it was quite a big ground, so there would be plenty of room. 636 of them would not be making such excuses, but two would have to.

Plumtree had an impressive 317 run victory over the luckless Leverton, who could only manage 98 against the season's top score of 415 for 5. Harome also had an impressive 235 run victory over Middleham. They scored 293 for 2, thanks in no small part to a first wicket partnership of 186 between Peter Collier and Tom Marwood. Collier's innings of 166 was the highest of the season. S.Williams of Bledlow hammered twelve sixes in his 145 against Bradenham. With the ball M.Robinson of Cumberworth had the best bowling figures of 8 for 16. There were also eight hat tricks during the season.

Harome is a tiny village a few miles south of the Yorkshire town of Helmsley. It had but one claim to fame — the local thatched village pub "The Star" was pub of the year in 1982. In 1988 they lost their semi-final to Himley, which was the furthest they had advanced in the competition. Last year they won their group final and were to do so again. They beat Barton convincingly by 131 runs. This year however they were to be one of the two teams asking the fixtures secretary to postpone their scheduled match of August 31st. In round six they beat Durham and Cleveland champions Mainsforth by 26 runs. A marginally closer contest in the next round, saw them beat Warkworth by 16 runs. It is just not possible to include the achievements of all villages who have taken part in the competition. Had I done so the book would have been as big as, if not bigger than Tolstoy's War and Peace. Many have been great ambassadors for their village and county, indeed village cricket as a whole, but have never been in the spotlight. One such place was Sheriff Hutton Bridge of South Yorkshire. They were to contest the all Yorkshire quarter-final against Harome. In so doing they were to show the typical tenacity of village cricket in a thrilling match.

Harome batted first and scored 144 for 7, with Dowson just

missing out on his fifty, being stranded on 46 not out when the innings closed. Their opponents had made them fight for every run. When Sutton batted they were reeling at 41 for 6 in the thirty-first. But when T. Wilford and C. Clark came together things became altogether different. They put on one hundred and one before Clark was unfortunately out, just before the end for 41. Wilford tried in vain finishing top scorer of the match, unbeaten on 55. Regrettably Sheriff Hutton Bridge had run out of overs on 142 for 8, leaving Harome victors by just two runs.

In the semi-final against Colwall (Herefordshire & Powys), more than a thousand spectators saw Harome make a respectable 193 for 7. P.Collier top scored with 45, B.Dowson (28), C.Marwood (27) and J.Marwood (21) all made useful contributions. A.Mackie was Colwall's best bowler returning figures of 3 for 39. In reply P.Williams matched Collier's top score and Wood made a useful 28. Harome's bowling and tight fielding however prevented Colwall from maintaining a run rate close to five an over. P.Collier was miserly with 2 for 26. Dowson and A.Bowes also returned creditable figures of 3 for 30 and 3 for 34 respectively. David Collier behind the stumps, was razor sharp in taking four catches and one stumping. It was a spirited effort by Colwall, but they were all out for 167, leaving the Yorkshire village victors by 26 runs. Harome were to be the twenty-seventh village side to reach the final.

So who was the other side to reach the final I hear you ask? That man Needham was at it again. In the group final he hit an unbeaten 118 in St.Fagans' demolition of Hopkinstown. Their total of 244 for 4 included an unbeaten 106 run partnership between Needham and Martin Powell (55). Pember hit an unbeaten 53 in Hopkinstown's reply, but Lawlor's 3 for 26 helped restrict the score to 131 for 9 at the end of the forty overs. Their South-West regional round against Somerset and Avon champions Chew Magna was a very close affair, which the Welsh won by two runs. The scores were 131 for 8 and 129 for 9. In

## The Lean Years

round seven Werrington scored 181 for 4 with Kristian Bell scoring a sparkling 80 runs. St.Fagans ran it close to the line again, with a win in the last over.

In the quarter-final they scored 241 for 3, with Needham again in top form scoring 92. The Dyfed champions Carew could only manage 102 against the impressive bowling of Hardwick with 5 for 10. The semi-final saw Needham out just three short of his century, but he had done enough to see his side to a comfortable total of 228 for 7. The Essex champions Stock made a spirited effort in reply, but Davies's 4 for 29 was too much for them. An accreditable 173 was not enough to prevent the Glamorgan champions going through to their third final.

There was to be good news to announce at the final. Rothmans were to be the new sponsors in 1992. It was clear they meant business, they were very much in evidence at Lord's that day. We heard that they intended to continue much in the same vein as previous sponsors had, and leave the day to day management to The Cricketer. It added a touch of welcome relief and satisfaction before the serious matter of an important village cricket match got underway. There was sun to greet us as well, so the scene was set for the twenty-first final.

Needham and Bell strode to the wicket. Neither looked overawed by the occasion. No small wonder, they were no strangers to the situation. Needham confirmed my observation by opening his account with two fours. They were powerful strokes indeed. Harome were aware of his reputation, but held their nerve, his next scoring stroke was a single. That was to be his last. To the delight, and no doubt relief of the whole Yorkshire contingent, Charles Marwood bowled him comprehensively, as he played across the line. If the Harome supporters were to consider this a prize scalp to stop the Welsh in their tracks, they were in for a disappointment. Two of their younger batsmen were at the crease, and together they set about building an innings. When the second wicket went down on 84 Jamie Sylvester and his

## A Village at Lord's

partner Kristian Bell had put together an intelligent 69 run partnership. They had punished the bad ball and demonstrated a mature understanding of running between the wickets. That was until Bell took a calculated risk which didn't pay off, he was run out for 35. But with 15 overs to go there was still the chance of a sizable total. Harome however stuck to their task. Dowson bowled Davies with the score on 98. Bowes then deceived Sylvester by bowling him when he had scored a stylish 38. St.Fagans were now however looking shaky on 110 for 5, with Powell also back in the pavilion for just 3. Williams was stumped for 13, and the sixth wicket went down at 124. By now Bowes and Dowson had completed their allocation and the captain had no option but to return to a pace attack. Rosser and Mitchell took full advantage. Their strokes may not have been as elegant, but they still put together an unbeaten 45, to bring some respectability to the final total of 169 for 6.

Harome's reply started on a positive note, as Collier hit the first ball of the innings for four. Needham however read the situation, and before long had brought in the all spin attack of Hardwick and Lawlor. This had the desired effect, bowling to a strategic field left the Yorkshiremen fighting for every run. At 28 for 2 in the sixteenth the rate was creeping towards six an over. By the thirtieth this had reached nine. Strickland was obviously a man with true Yorkshire grit, as he was not about to go down without a fight. In the thirty-fifth he struck Mackinson for three huge sixes. Marwood was ably supporting him, and suddenly Harome were back in the match. Needham took a gamble on youth by bringing back his off spinner Sylvester. It paid dividends when he yorked Strickland, who was in such an aggressive mood he may well have won the match on his own. Marwood was hitting out but was regrettably caught in the deep. Thirty-one was needed off 18 balls. St.Fagans' fielders ringed the boundary and the tail could only scamper singles, which they did with the result that Bowes and Ellis were both run out. Sylvester

## The Lean Years

bowled the last over with nineteen needed for victory. The young Glamorgan colt did not let his team down, he yielded only two runs and had Greenlay stumped for good measure. St.Fagans had received a bit of a shock from Strickland and Marwood, but experience won the day. The cup was going back to Wales, this was the third and last time it would sit in the St.Fagans' trophy cupboard. 1992 was to be their last year in the competition, and their victory against Goatacre, you can read about in chapter seven.

# CHAPTER SIX

# A Cavalier's Return

My first experience of cricket at Lord's, was watching a match between Middlesex and Surrey in August 1961. The days of Parfitt, Titmus and John Murray, the finest wicket keeper I have ever seen. In those days first class cricket was definitely going through the doldrums. Indeed concern had been expressed about the falling level of spectators at the gate throughout the fifties.

After a special meeting of the advisory county cricket committee in December 1961, the word came from Lord's that a one day knockout competition was to be inaugurated in 1963. From this "The Gillette Cup" heralded the introduction of limited overs cricket. At the same meeting the first steps were taken to amend the Lord's Day Observance Act. Thus allowing cricket to be played before paying spectators on Sundays. This made way in later years for the John Player League, which we now know as the Refuge Assurance. The Benson and Hedges Cup also came into existence. When Gillette relinquished responsibility for what many consider the premier first class limited overs competition, the world of banking stepped in with the Nat. West Trophy.

With the aid of sponsorship much was done to improve interest in the game. It must be said some purists did not agree with limited over cricket at all. They argued that skill and technique would suffer. The arguments in the pavilion, and at the bar, will no doubt continue. No one can deny however limited overs cricket has given pleasure to many.

Let us not forget the fore-runners to Gillette and Company "The Cavaliers", who while the Gillette Cup was feeling it's feet in the early sixties, were touring places like South Africa, New Zealand and the West Indies.

They too needed sponsorship, and this was provided by Rothmans. So it was good news to learn at the end of the 1991 season that they were to make a welcome return to the cricket arena by sponsoring the National Village Cricket Championships for 1992.

The prize structure was quite impressive, as can be seen below:-

| | |
|---|---|
| Losers in round 5 | Framed gold certificate |
| Losers in round 6 | Framed gold certificate; magnum of champagne |
| Losers in round 7 | Cheque for £100; framed certificate |
| Losing quarter-finalists | Cheque for £150; framed certificate |
| Losing semi-finalists | Cheque for £200; framed certificate |
| Runner-up | Cheque for £500; framed certificate; magnum of champagne; medals |
| Winner | Cheque for £1000; magnum of champagne; framed certificate; medals; The Cricketer Trophy. |

Each of the sponsors has brought their own individual style to the competition. A corporate hallmark if you like. Rothmans looked at many options when considering their sponsorship support. They settled on developing a pub quiz to take place in the local pubs of villages who entered the competition. This, along with the specially designed "Howzat Competition", meant they were able to support the Championship and the village community as a whole. No doubt as Rothmans sponsorship continues, more innovative ideas will emerge.

## A Cavalier's Return

The first year under new sponsorship saw over 620 villages set out on the road to Lord's. The first round was contested by 266 teams, all hoping for a place in round two. In West Cornwall one team, Goldsithley, were to demonstrate their determination when visiting Cornish neighbours Ruan and Philleigh. Their total of 404 for 1 was the highest of the season. It also took them into fifth place in the record books. Their opening batsman Wade overhauled Andy Shorter's unbeaten 221 for Himley in 1988, to go top of the batting honours with an incredible 239 not out. His partner Kitchen also did well, scoring 118 to share a first wicket partnership of 373. This became the highest partnership in the history of the competition. Again it was Himley who were toppled from top spot, when Shorter and Walker's unbroken first wicket partnership of 343 was passed. Ruan and Philleigh's reply of 52 resulted in a comprehensive 352 run victory. However, Canon Frome's record against Much Markle, way back in 1980, remains intact.

Two games produced match aggregates in excess of 500 runs. By coincidence they both totalled 507. Barkisland's 296 for 6 was responded to well by Blackley with 218 for 5. St.Buryan's total of 302 for 2 was always too much for Butleigh, who were all out for 205, but what a run feast both crowds must have enjoyed.

The best bowling performance of the season came from D.Fenton for South Weald, who returned figures of 9 for 15 in the match against Hornden On the Hill. It was still not enough to better Steve James's 9 for 7 in 1990. Sixteen bowlers in all took six or more wickets in an innings. There were also five hat tricks recorded throughout the year. Armitage Bridge's wicket keeper joined two others in the "seven victims club", with six catches and one stumping against Whiteley Hall. Finally the best all round performance was C.Knightley of Dumbleton, with an unbeaten 113 and five for 50, against Stone. It is interesting to note that no out fielder has succeeded in taking six wickets in the field throughout the championships, except N.Somerton of Hathersage in 1989.

## A Village at Lord's

Several familiar sides were still in contention at group final stage. Marchwiel beat Oakmere by 22 runs, to become champions of Cheshire and Clwyd. They had a good run in their efforts to make it a triple appearance at headquarters, but in their quarter-final match they lost to the Yorkshire village of Methley. Bourne, with 3 for 18, and Waite 3 for 46, helped restrict Marchwiel to 139 for 9 at the close. Methley were never in trouble, as Graham Boothroyd and Keith Rich carried their bats with 69 and 43 respectively, to see their side home to an eight wicket victory.

George Clinton had been a staunch Methley supporter for more years than he cared to remember. He was one of the coach party that travelled to Fife for the semi-final "We were in for a shock, I can tell ee laddie," he said to me, "You'd a thought all Scotland had turned out ta watch, there were bagpipes, sporrans and tartans everywhere." Despite this true Yorkshire grit was to triumph over Scottish determination.

In not ideal conditions for cricket, but typical for Freuchie cricket, it was the ball which dominated. The Scots batted first and lost half their side for just sixteen runs. Boundaries that day were hard to come by, and at the end of 40 overs the home team finished on 96 for 9. M.Smart returned bowling figures of 3 for 11. The Freuchie mean machine was soon in action, which saw Methley struggling on 11 for 3. But Jones and Jarvis saw them safely through to victory in an unbroken partnership of 85. Once again a Yorkshire village were in the final.

Last year's beaten finalists Harome, won the North Yorkshire (North) group. Hovingham, batting first, were all out for 165, thanks to fine bowling from Collier (5 for 42) and Dowson (3 for 21). Neil Elliott gave his side something to bowl at, striking a spirited 52. A useful contribution of 35 was made by John Anderson. Graham Strickland's purposeful innings of 60 helped Harome achieve a six wicket victory. Anderson, although on the losing side will have a match to remember. He took 3 Yorkshire wickets in his nine overs, to add to his impressive innings.

## A Cavalier's Return

Unfortunately they came up against Freuchie in the next round.

Buckinghamshire champions Bledlow beat Kimble by 42 runs, but lost to the strong Essex village of Stock by a similar margin. Stock had previously beaten Audley End by nine wickets, to become champions of their group. 1985 finalists Rowledge had a comfortable win over Moreton to become Surrey and Berkshire group winners. In round six they won an exciting game against Crookham Hall by one wicket. Their quarter-final tie against Hursley Park saw their demise. Adrian Small scored a fine 104, while L.Rogers returned figures of 4 for 39, to help restrict the Hampshire total to 202 for 8. Lloyd made a spirited attempt, top scoring for Rowledge with 64 out of their total of 171. The semi-final saw two of the most prolific teams in the country contest a place in the final. It was Hursley Park against St.Fagans. The Welsh champions lost their final match in the competition, they leave a gap that will be taken up by other villages wishing to follow the same path they have — to Lord's.

The Bedfordshire and Hertfordshire final was between two stalwarts of the competition. The tenacious Langleybury played hosts to the redoubtable Reed. Colin Spinks did not let the home side down, he carried his bat for 120 as the innings closed on 232 for 6. How many were at the game? I don't know, but probably more than would have been at a minor county fixture. Baldwin was in determined mood, his 3 for 18 was too much for the opposition, who were all out for 122. Would it be Langleybury's turn to tread the boards at Lord's? Sadly it was not to be, in the following round they lost to Suffolk champions Abberton by four wickets, on what was clearly a difficult wicket. What they will do in 1993 is anybody's guess, but they haven't given up. They are now preparing for their first round tie against the village of Sampfords.

Our small band of Wiltshire supporters who went to see the final at Lord's, were greeted by grey skies and the ever present threat of rain. We surveyed the scene of joyful supporters setting

## A Village at Lord's

up camp, and decided to mix with the Methley supporters in The New Mound Stand. I of course was hoping to get a few more Yorkshire tales. They were a friendly crowd. I was soon in earnest conversation with a few supporters who recalled exploits in the competition. The memory of the battle against the Scots, a fortnight earlier, was clearly fresh in their minds. George Clinton from Castleford felt no matter how good a side you were, a bit of luck was needed to get to the finals. He said to me "You've got to seize the advantage whenever it's presented. Methley rely on an old Yorkshire saying." When asked what this was, a mischievous smile lit up his craggy features. In a broad Yorkshire brogue he retold his philosophy of life:-

> "Hear all, see all, and say nowt,
> Eat all, sup all, and pay nowt,
> If thou dost owt for nowt,
> Make sure ye does it for thee sen."

It is difficult to understand just what this had to do with Methley reaching the final, but there again I'm not a Yorkshireman!

I also met club secretary Dave Clegg, who had been through a hectic season. He said he was pleased to sit back and relax now, having done all that is necessary to organise getting a team safely to H.Q. A point that would not go unnoticed by our own secretary, Eddie Jenkinson. But the match was to prove such an enthralling tussle, that he like everybody else was not able to relax much. I was disappointed not to have met club president Ron Wolfesdon, he apparently was in the area of The Tavern shaking Hursley supporters warmly by the hand. Still, I have been assured of a warm welcome if I am ever in the Castleford area. I may well take Dave Clegg up on his offer one day, in which case I'll take my wife along, provided the club president can get her a seat at Castleford Rugby Club. She's not just a tennis buff, and one day she may understand a bit about cricket!

# A Cavalier's Return

Hursley won the toss and had no hesitation in inviting Methley to bat. Partly I suspect because this was the Yorkshire sides first appearance in a final. The occasion therefore could perhaps cause nerves and result in mistakes. Also the wicket was evidently damp, so the outfield would be slow. True, there was the threat of rain, which could well mean they also faced the same problem. Probably the most important point of all, was the 20 overs rule, which if brought into play definitely favoured the team batting second.

Frank Thow looked thoughtful as he finely tuned his fielding positions. Obviously he was hoping for an early breakthrough, but he wasn't about to give runs away either. Bourne and skipper Graham Boothroyd made a cautious and thoughtful start. The crowd were disappointed with stoppage for rain in the fourth over. Memories of the 1988 final came flooding back to me. I need not have worried, it only lasted twenty minutes. There were to be no further stoppages, despite the occasional few drops of rain that did fall.

Fox and Oliver bowled intelligently, pitching the ball up and rarely straying in line and length. That, together with keen fielding, ensured Methley had to fight for every run. Boothroyd was caught behind by Kellaway for 11, when the score was on 17. David Jones looked confident right from the start, he was ever watchful for the mis-field to keep the scoreboard ticking over. Bourne was out for 16, when Thow caught him off the bowling of Westbrook. The score was then on 45, but with the half way mark looming the Yorkshire grit did not appear to be enough — acceleration was called for.

Keith Rich recognised this when he joined Jones, who was starting to show signs of taking the game to Hursley. Encouraged by his partners determination he hoisted a rare six to the boundary. He was third wicket down, with the score on 95, when Fox bowled him for a useful 19. Next man in was Andrew Jarvis. Alan Curtis left the crowd in no doubt as to his pedigree, as he advised over the P.A. that Andrew's brother Paul played a bit of cricket too. He was England's fast bowler! Andrew helped lift the run rate with some straight driving. Methley saw up the 150, but ran out of overs. This was in no small way due to their wicket keeper Jones, who although punishing the bad ball, owed much of his 57 runs to intelligent quick thinking between the wickets.

It is often felt by some that 160 is a fair bench mark. It is something for the bowlers to aim at, and the opposition have to score at 4 an over. I would prefer to keep my own council on that point. Hursley may have only needed to score at the rate of 3.7 an over, but runs were not easy to come by on this wicket. You don't get this far without fielding and bowling talent. It was a similar beginning in many ways. At the start of the tenth Methley had managed to force the rate up to 4.3 an over. Their fortunes were further improved when Mills bowled Adrian Small for 10, when the total was on 19. I was deafened, being sat in the middle of the Yorkshire crowd. They were aware of Small's capabilities with the bat, he had scored 104 in the quarter-final against Rowledge and top scored with 69, in the semi-final against St.Fagans.

Clive Surry joined Mike Oliver to put on 49, before Oliver was caught by Jones off the bowling of Waite, for a painstaking 27. By now thirty overs had gone, and with 68 on the board Methley had stuck to their task well. The rate was now more than eight an over. Kellaway was bowled by Waite for eleven, and Thow was caught by Graham Boothroyd off the bowling of his brother Allan. He sacrificed his wicket for 4 in the quest for runs. Thirty-four needed off three overs — almost twelve an over! The atmosphere was a mixture of tension, excitement and anticipation. Methley had a whiff of victory in their nostrils, but Surry was still there with 50 to his name. He gave Hursley hope with fifteen off one over. This only heightened the tension and quickened the heart rate. Against a grey menacing background, Allan Boothroyd bowled the first ball of the last over to Arnold

# A Cavalier's Return

who was on 9. He was in no doubt about what to do, and scampered a quick single to give his more aggressive partner the strike. A sensible move indeed, Surry promptly hoisted the next ball into the rear of The Tavern for six.

The pressure was becoming unbearable, both on and off the field, following two leg byes and a wide. Surry skied one, which the Methley supporters hoped would see a repeat of the Boothroyd double act that disposed of Frank Thow. It was a spiralling difficult chance in wet conditions. The Methley skipper slipped on the wet outfield, and Keith Rich anxiously backing up, collided with his captain as the ball rolled over the boundary.

The scores were level, with one ball to go. Hursley had lost fewer wickets, so Surry only had to block the final ball to secure victory. He was in no mood to do so, he hammered the luckless Boothroyd to the boundary. Hursley had won the title at their second attempt, and in what was to be their final appearance in the competition. They had come to Lord's fresh from victory over Bournemouth the previous day, when they secured the Southern League title. In so doing they had declined their invitation to the superb Rothmans banquet that evening.

M.C.C. president Michael Melluish had hardly finished the presentations when the heavens opened, just as had happened in 1988. By now though the weather could do nothing to dampen the spirits. It was all over, (barring the celebrations), until May 2nd. 1993, when it would all start again. The 1993 competition saw twenty villages exit. Some no longer qualified under the population rule. Others had grown in stature to such an extent that it was time to make way for less prolific, but equally dedicated villages to enter. Seventy-five more did enter. Who knows, maybe one of them will lift that silver cup on August 29th. 1993. I hope I'll be there to see if they do. Meanwhile I've booked a place for my deckchair at Goatacre on May 2nd., when they play hosts to the Dorset village of Paulton.

# CHAPTER SEVEN

# A Villager on the Boundary

On a cold crisp morning in March 1987, after two years searching, we found our ideal boarding kennel. It was in the tiny hamlet of Goatacre in the heart of rural Wiltshire. I telephoned the selling agent that morning to check on final viewing details. I was amused by his parting comments, "Don't blink when you get past the village nameplate, or you'll be through it, look out for the 'phone. box on your left and you'll be O.K. If you reach Hilmarton then you've gone too far."

On leaving the M4 at junction 16, we checked each landmark along the A3102 for the next six miles. Sure enough, a little way past R.A.F. Lyneham we found the nameplate for Goatacre. Nobody blinked, but within two minutes we were in Hilmarton! We turned round in the car park of a rather impressive looking stone building. This was The Duke Hotel, which I found out later was the nearest public house to Goatacre. When passing the nameplate from the other side of the village we rounded a double bend. Low and behold, there on our left was a bright red 'phone. box. We turned up the single track road, and the rest was easy.

We moved into Corton House on 27th.July 1987, at the height of the boarding season. With a licence for 116 animals and our own menagerie of 12 pedigree dogs and 6 felines, together with a pet shop it truly was a baptism by fire! The removal men by the way had no trouble finding the kennels. Unlike the agent, my wife Pauline knew her left from her right.

Down Goatacre Lane is where you will find the hub of the

village. There is no pub., village store or garage. Much speculation and estimates of the population have varied widely. The press have quoted between 350 and 650. My advice to the reader is to rely on our senior tea lady, Pauline Matthews. In an interview with Dudley Doust of the Sunday Correspondent, on the occasion of the 1990 final, she reliably informed him the residents of Goatacre numbered but 172.

Half way down the lane the compact cricket green nestles next to the clubhouse. Between there and the main road are the dozen or so bungalows that make up Iles Court. Sandwiched between the two are a couple of houses which I hope have shatter proof windows. At the other end of the ground stands Goatacre Nursing Home. Many an elderly resident can be seen watching cricket on a summer afternoon. They particularly enjoy the atmosphere in the latter stages of the village championships. Several have been to Lord's and thoroughly enjoyed the experience. A few years ago the ground was enhanced with a view across rambling Wiltshire countryside, including the famous White Horse near Marlborough. Regrettably this has now been obscured by extensions to the nursing home.

Although moved to a tranquil village setting we hadn't a minute to breathe. The demands business made on the family allowed us to see little of village life that first year. I have always been an avid cricket lover, but lately had only been able to catch the occasional half hour highlights of test matches on late night television. That was until one Friday evening in August 1988, when everything changed.

I was returning from a trip to Swindon at about seven p.m. On entering the village I saw the one word "CRICKET" in red letters on a white card pointing down Goatacre Lane. Arriving home I explained the strange phenomenon to my wife, and set off to take the dogs for a walk! I saw several other signs of a similar nature, one read "DIVERSION CRICKET TRAFFIC ONLY." This was all too much for me. So I went home, speedily fed the dogs then went down to the club to find out what it was all about.

Approaching the ground a scene of frantic activity greeted me. Scaffold poles were everywhere, boundary ropes were being checked, the rollers and mowers were busy also. Then I spotted the poster that revealed all:-

NORSK HYDRO NATIONAL VILLAGE CRICKET CHAMPIONSHIPS
GOATACRE (WILTSHIRE CHAMPIONS)
versus
HURSLEY PARK (HAMPSHIRE CHAMPIONS)
SUNDAY 7th. AUGUST 1988 AT 2 P.M.

Walking round the ground I saw a very professional bank of temporary seating being erected in the practice net area adjacent to the hall. On the other side of the ground, arrangements were in hand for a large covered trailer to straddle the tiny girth of Goatacre Lane. Now I understood the reason for the diversion signs. When I entered the bar I was greeted by Tony Twigg. I'd seen "Twiggy" before on the odd occasion I'd managed to steal a few minutes from kennel duty to visit the club. Like everyone around he wore a justifiably proud smile, after all no other Wiltshire village had come this far in the competition.

You would I suppose describe Twiggy as the self-appointed sage of the village team! A jovial chap, never far from the bar, the wicket, the umpire's coat, or the scoreboard. He knew everything there was to know. Well he set about telling me of Goatacre's exploits in having reached this stage. There were helpful corrections to detail from others at the bar. I soon realised what an amazing experience this season had been for the village, which I had missed! We replenished our glasses as Twiggy began telling me about the unbelievable cricket polo match against Oxford Downs. It took longer than necessary, probably because wicket keeper John Wilkins quietly corrected him on one or two

## A Village at Lord's

statistical inaccuracies. "Wilkie", I was later to learn, could take the field, keep tabs on his own score, that of the other batsman at the crease, as well as those who had come and gone before. He was also not averse to raising an eyebrow and touching his cap if an umpire mis-counted the over.

There was no way I was going to miss Sunday's semi-final. A hastily re-arranged staff rota, enabled me to enjoy most of the match, although I still arrived late. The ground was packed to overflowing and I had to watch from the entrance gate, which although obscuring a little of the activities, did not prevent me from seeing everything that mattered. This was apart from one incident right at the end of the match, to which I refer later.

Under a cloudless sky, on the hottest day of 1988, John Turner and Alan Walters strode to the wicket to open Goatacre's account. With the total on fourteen Alan was bowled. This brought Mark Hunt to the wicket. He was in determined mood, no doubt spurred on by team mate Pete Dolman's promise of a pint for every run he scored above twenty-six. Together with JT he saw the fifty up in the fourteenth. When his partner was out for a spirited thirty-eight, Bunter was joined by skipper Kevin Iles. The pair stepped up a gear and passed the hundred in the twenty-fifth. Hursley must have breathed a sigh of relief as Iles became the first of Paul Mead's six victims, when he had scored just twenty-five. Bunter kept the score ticking over, and when he was finally out for sixty-one he had assured himself of ample free beer for a while, courtesy of Pete Dolman. Goatacre's lower order kept chipping away, and when Kevin's brother Graham was caught off the last ball of the innings the visitors had been set 204 to win. Paul Mead had finished with the impressive figures of 6 for 48.

Hursley's reply was disrupted by Paul Rose, who had both openers caught. With the total on 44 for 2 Kevin came on to bowl. Hursley's third wicket partnership between Surry and King looked ominous until the skipper bowled Surry for 22. He followed up soon afterwards by having Thow caught at the wicket

## A Villager on the Boundary

for two. They were to be his only two victims that afternoon, but his nine overs yielded only 17 runs. King was still there leading from the front. While he was at the wicket Hampshire were still in with a chance of getting to Lord's, even though tight bowling and fielding had pushed the run rate to almost eight an over in the thirtieth.

Goatacre and Paul Rose kept their cool. Rosie charged in to bowl at King, who was on 67 and looked set to punish anything Goatacre had to throw at him. A mighty roar went up as Mel clanged his bell, King's wicket had disintegrated. The Hursley supporters became a little subdued now. They weren't dead yet, their bowling hero Paul Mead struck a mighty blow to the furthest part of the ground. I, along with the other supporters hemmed in around the entrance, lost sight of the ball. We were all sure this was the six that would seal our fate and let Hursley march on. Suddenly that Wiltshire roar and Mel's bell heralded a superb diving catch from Graham Iles. A thousand spectators leapt to their feet and applauded both teams off the field. This was a double reward for the Goatacre team, it was their diamond jubilee year as well.

There was much celebration after the presentations. Our Hampshire friends stayed until well after dark. Nobody wanted to let the festivities finish. During the course of the evening I was introduced to a local roofer named David Strange. He turned out to be the phantom sign writer. Among his other talents was the ability to wrench every spare penny from even the tightest supporter, for raffle tickets. I had an early appointment in town the following morning, when I passed Dave's house I found he had been busy during the night. A huge white board proclaimed "Good Luck Goatacre at Lord's."

The main topic of conversation in the village for the next two weeks was to be cricket. Some of our customers travelled many miles to board their animals with us. Even they had heard of the team's achievement, and wished them luck without prompting. I spent some time in the bar during the evenings leading up to the final, learning more of the earlier exploits, mostly from Twiggy. Some of the incredible facts he reported were no doubt true, as Wilkie didn't correct him much. Some of these stories are to be found in chapter eight.

The report on the marathon final against Himley, and the celebrations afterwards, was covered in chapter four. What I omitted to mention was our "strange" sign writer had been at it again on Sunday night. The original sign in front of his house on Monday morning now read "Goatacre CC. National Village Champions...OWZAT!!"

In 1989 Goatacre found themselves promoted to the first division of the Wiltshire league. Everyone was waiting for the National Champions first match against NALGO., who were a strong league side. Goatacre started in fine style, winning by 110 runs. Having scored 189 they skittled the opposition out for 79.

I had a busy start to the boarding season, so saw little of the early round matches. Even with home ties it was impossible to see the complete game. In the unlikely event we ever acquire another boarding kennels, it will have to be where no village cricket team exists! Animal boarding and cricket don't mix.

There appears to have been only one moment of panic leading up to the county final. It was in our first round match against Great Durnford. Wilkie was in good form with the bat, helping Goatacre to a total of 222 for 7. One of his huge sixes struck Ken Butler's car windscreen. By coincidence Ken's insurance broker was a spectator at the match. Our opening bats Turner and Walters became bowlers, taking three wickets apiece, reducing Great Durnford's reply to 115.

The National Village Champions' visit to Steeple Langford appears to have moved a professional photographer to record the occasion. I was browsing through a copy of "Country Life" in a waiting room, when I spotted some shots of the game. It quite brightened an otherwise miserable Winter's day. Paul Rose stood out in one shot, despite his back view, those long curly locks gave the game away. He didn't however, his two for twenty-one helped restrict the home side to 114 for 9. This was passed without trouble, producing a six wicket win, leaving plenty of time for the hospitalities.

Our last defeat in the championships was in the 1987 group final against Redlynch. 1989 was to see them visit Goatacre to contest that crown once again. I was given the whole afternoon off to enjoy the game, which I did, as much as the residents of Goatacre House who had also joined the expectant crowd. Redlynch won the toss and elected to bat. There was an early vociferous appeal from pace man Paul Rose, as he rapped opener Savage's pads before he could open his account. That was sufficient for the umpire to hold up his finger, and Mel to clang his bell. "He's in one of they moods", prophesied Twiggy. "I tell yer Rosie ain't gonna give nuthin away today." When Twiggy's right, he's right! Rosie conceded but two runs in his first five overs, one wide and a no ball. Sarton and Matthews then settled down to graft a second wicket partnership of 102. But keen fielding with three run outs, accurate bowling from Rosie, JT and Spencer restricted the visitors to 170. JT and Alan Walters put on a fine opening partnership for 88, then the skipper and John Spencer saw Goatacre home, with more than eight overs to spare.

Our total of 159 all out, off the penultimate ball of the innings against Bredon, caused some discussion during the tea interval. One pessimistic spectator found it difficult to make inroads into his picnic hamper. He felt our total wasn't enough. Ever helpful Twiggy assisted him on both counts. Accepting a sandwich, he said between mouthfuls — "They gotta get 'em mate, we got the runs on the board, but they've gotta match it. Ours may be a small ground, but the lads know every inch of it, and the traps. Hey you wait an see, ta for the sandwich, time for a pint I think."

He was right, despite a positive start our Gloucestershire

## A Village at Lord's

visitors found it difficult to keep up with the run rate. They didn't quite make it, thanks largely to Jon Angell who tore into the middle order taking 4 for 32.

We had a narrow 13 run victory over Oxford champions Tiddington. It was good training for absorbing pressure, preparing us for the quarter-final tie against the Welsh dragons of St.Fagans. The village bush telegraph has been in use since 1972, and many villages had it's communicative capabilities tuned to perfection. So much talk of tactics took place both sides of the Bristol Channel during the next fortnight.

If we beat the Welsh we would have a good drink to celebrate. Should we lose we would drink to commiserate. We felt it safer therefore to travel there by coach. Our journey was pleasantly interrupted by lunch at a pre- arranged hostelry. Several thirsty supporters panicked, thinking we were going into a "dry" county. They need not have worried, as I recall the bar was open for most of the match.

There was tension in the air for all supporters, as time drew near for the five minute bell. The wicket looked impressive and the boundaries long as the game got under way. Even though John Spencer struck early, when Pete Dolman snapped up a catch to dismiss captain Needham for seven, the tension did not ease. There was much evidence of the "walkabout syndrome." At one stage the Welsh went clockwise, and the English anti-clockwise, (what am I talking about, this isn't a test match — or is it?).

At tea we faced a total of 192 to equal St.Fagans' score. If we lost less than five wickets at that stage, victory would be ours. It was viewed that way by the statistical pundits in both camps. We did not bat well — not my opinion, but Goatacre's, that is team, officials and supporters. I can smile now, but was not able to at the time. When I realised the writing was on the wall it was time to visit the bar. As I ordered a drink a roar went up, another English wicket down. One Welsh voice said "Perhaps it's time we booked the coach for Lord's." Was it the drink, or the relief of tension? I didn't ask him, they still had one more obstacle before a date at the hallowed ground. It was a little village in Hampshire called Hambledon. I was cheered by the pragmatic headlines in our local press a few days later "GOATACRE LOSE VILLAGE CHAMPIONSHIP – BUT LEAD THE LEAGUE TITLE RACE."

The nursing home had grown during the closed season, and so had the netting to protect the new extension. We had a new fast bowler in the side too. Andy Dawson was distinguishable by his short cropped blond hair and natural exuberance. He had posted his credentials by demolishing local league side Bradford, returning figures of seven wickets for nine runs in 9.5 overs. When this was the subject of discussion before the start of play in one game, a regular supporter said " Ay, I believe he can bat abit too."

Our first round tie in 1990 meant we played hosts to Steeple Langford. Little did we know it was to be the first of ten straight victories that would see the national trophy come back to Goatacre. But this time our famous mascot "Googlie", the stuffed goat, would be staying in the local museum. In 1988 he stunk the place out. Not only were Lord's staff relieved, our local coach company were as well. Cyril Thomas keeps his vehicles very clean, but drew the line at a triple valet service of the luggage area, to get rid of the smell a second time.

The team's championship run also helped raise morale in my own home. Our elder daughter Julie was in a wheelchair all Summer, following a road accident. This meant she was virtually housebound. Every other Sunday she looked forward to watching the team play, and the socialising afterwards! I recall her receiving a telephone call from a friend wishing to visit her one Sunday, just to keep her spirits up he said. "Hang on a minute while I check my diary" said Julie, "Sorry can't make it that Sunday, I'm in Cornwall watching cricket, but the next week's OK." I could hear her friend laughing at the other end of the 'phone. In

## A Village at Lord's

between chuckles he spluttered "Cricket? Cricket? But you don't like cricket!" "Ah yes, but this is a bit special" she replied.

Our preliminary rounds saw the team's performance steadily improve, and the crowds grow with each match. Round three was a repeat of last year's county final against Redlynch. A fair sized crowd turned up, this was inter-county rivalry at it's best. The sun came out, but not the beer — no one had arranged for a licence extension! Still, there was always the pint bet on the side, for when the bar did open. Dave Strange and Twiggy had started betting on what our final total would be when we reached fifteen overs. That's when we batted first of course.

They lost out heavily that day I fancy. Following captain Kevin's 122, we settled back to see a comfortable total amassing. Enter Wilkie, with the score on 294 for 6 and three balls of the innings to face. He dispatched the first for six to see out the 300, then came a cut for four. For good measure his text book follow through yielded another six, as the last ball went sailing into the car park. 310 was always too much for our Dorset cousins, and a comfortable 183 run victory heralded the bar opening just a little early.

Bunter kept filling Sir Len.'s Whitbread copper jug, as Wiltshire songs competed with Dorset ballads. The sun had long gone as the last visitor set off home to Redlynch. Walking back to the kennels I recalled a conversation with Kenny Butler at last years dinner. It was before the Royal Toast, so we were both sober. Ken was remembering when he hit the six to win against Oxford Downs in 1988. "You know" he said "I said to myself then, we were going to win through to Lord's. Don't ask me why, I can't explain it — but I just knew." I was beginning to see what he meant. The match against Grampound Road in Cornwall made me realise it even more.

It had been many years since I had experienced real Cornish hospitality. Having secured the county final against Cattistock, we visited Kington Bagpuize in Oxfordshire. In a cold biting East

## A Villager on the Boundary

wind JT. switched bowling from "the pig farm end" at just the right moment. Frocester travelled from Gloucester, in the hope of halting The Goats. Strong batting and good bowling ensured our victory. Dawson's warning at Bradford came to mind, as he and our other opening bowler John Spencer took seven Frocester wickets between them. So the quarter-final saw a coach trip to Grampound Road.

It was a pleasant ground, and the club had obviously made great efforts to make it a memorable occasion. I don't think they expected such a large Wiltshire contingent. Having a wheelchair to contend with meant we were almost the last of our spectators to enter the ground. I recall the steward on the gate saying in a broad Cornish accent "Blimey how many more of ye!". I retorted as mischievously as I could, and with as straight a face as possible "Not many, only two more coach loads, but they've got some scrumpy drinkers on board. So they stopped in the last village we passed through, to wet their whistles!" His face paled momentarily then he smiled, told us to enjoy our day and made sure two young colts settled the wheelchair out of the cold wind.

We certainly seemed to have caught our Cornish hosts unawares with our larger than expected crowd, which outnumbered them three to one. Their home made food was delicious, several picnic hampers returned only half consumed. I tried to buy my third pastie just before tea, only to find they had sold out. The game was under way a little earlier than scheduled. We had some distance to travel and wished to leave time after the match for socialising.

Batting first, we continued in the same vein as previous rounds. Several batsmen had creditable scores, including John Spencer with 52 and John Turner with 49. Skipper Kevin Iles scored fifty-two of his sixty-five in boundaries. One home supporter was standing by me when a six from Kevin's bat soared up to the far end of the ground. "Oh no, not again" said the supporter, "that bloomin' house is in for it, more broken glass!"

## A Village at Lord's

He need not have feared, the ball sailed over the house by several feet. It appears the owner was used to an occasional six reaching his property, and considered the odd pane of glass a small price to pay for living so conveniently close to the ground. Never, it appears, had a ball passed over the roof tiles. It transpired later the old Cornish supporters could not ever recall a ball travelling so far outside the ground. Goatacre finished on 245 for 7.

Grampound started in fine style, with a four off the first ball. One experienced supporter could be heard to say from the bar "Hold yer hosses, one swaller don't make a summer." It didn't, they were soon struggling against some inspired bowling and fielding. One Cornishman could not bear to watch his team's dream disappear, so he retired to the bar. As he placed the empty mug on the counter and held his head in his hands, the barmaid quipped "Same again, Tony?" "No" came the desperate reply, "a pint of cyanide would be more appropriate." "Sorry" came the mock sympathetic response "we're fresh out of that, you'll have to make do with cider!" JT's inspired bowling of six for twenty-nine, and Wilkie's performance behind the stumps (two catches, two stumpings and no byes) ensured a 110 run victory and a place in the semi-final against Kent champions Linton Park.

Following our victory we had a brief but jovial exchange with our hosts, before departing for Wiltshire. At one point during the afternoon, an independent spectator from Devon struck up a conversation with me. He remarked on the uncanny resemblance between Mark Hunt and a chap he used to play with in Chumleigh back in '47. "Yon kiddy of yorn", pointing to Bunter as he struck his first boundary, "be he an all rounder?" "No I replied, but he's no mean fielder when the occasion arises." This was to prompt a very unusual story. But you'll have to wait for chapter eight to hear old Jake's tale. I hope to return to Grampound Road one day, I enjoyed it, and also experienced that Kenny Butler feeling.

It was a fortnight of frenzied activity, at the end of which

## A Villager on the Boundary

we had a ground fit for such an important match. Dave Strange had trebled his order of raffle books, whilst Pauline Matthews and the ladies of the village worked round the clock. She obviously wanted to ensure there was more than five loaves and three fishes to feed the expected multitude. The match was not due to start until two-thirty. I went over not long after breakfast to stake our claim for a position on the boundary, but already found my selection limited. By 2 p.m. the ground was full.

Mark Hunt and Pete Leavey opened Goatacre's innings under a cloudless sky. Despite the early departure of Pete, Goatacre scored steadily. A big score looked distinctly possible, with the ever reliable Bunter continuing his purple patch. He scored an invaluable fifty-three to set the side on course for a total in excess of 200. I recall a conversation between two Kent supporters, commenting on his undoubted batting ability. One remarked that he seemed a little overweight to be much use in the field. Useful contributions from JT., Spencer and Dawson plus a ferocious 75 from the captain gave us a satisfactory 252 for 7 at tea.

Linton's reply began purposefully. Our two Kent supporters were taken aback to see Bunter sprint some twenty-five yards round the boundary, snap up and return the ball, for Piper to be run out for eleven. They graciously withdrew their previous observations. Nigel Thirkell was another batsman with a formidable reputation in the competition. As he and Gibson set about building a three figure partnership, the Wiltshire crowd were not at all complacent. When Iles brought himself on we saw what was probably the turning point in the match. Thirkell was on 44 as Kevin came in to bowl. It was well pitched up and hammered back down the wicket. In anyone's book it was four the second it left the bat, but in the blink of an eye we witnessed a superb caught and bowled. The adrenalin was now running high, fielding was tight, catches were held and Goatacre had Lord's in view once again. Despite a fine 67 from Gibson, and spirited innings from Hatcher (34) and Whyte (20), Linton were all out for 197.

# A Village at Lord's

The next fortnight was to see a repeat of the pre-final hype of 1988. There were many letters and cards from well-wishers, as well as the media coverage. One letter I think was very special to the lads, it was from John Corns, treasurer of Himley CC., to secretary Pete Dolman. Dated 13th. August, it simply read:-

"Dear Peter,
Please extend to all members of Goatacre Cricket Club the warmest congratulations of Himley Cricket Club on again getting to Lord's in the National Village Knock-Out.
We all think it is unfortunate that our Group Winners are playing and it is not Himley!!!
I am coming down to Lord's for the Final (I know it starts at 11 a.m.) and can feel that I will not be disappointed whoever wins.
Kindest Regards,
Yours Ever,
John."

Sufficient coverage has been given to the 1990 final, so I will not go over old ground. Before leaving that momentous year in Goatacre's history, I would like to highlight one item which turned up during the course of my research. Unfortunately it brings to mind Pete Leavey's dismissal at Lord's, but I'm sure Pete will forgive me as it is a typical example of sporting spirit.

Dunstall's chairman Tim Ward, who sadly died in January 1993, kept a diary of his team's greatest year. Their secretary Frank Clewley sent me a copy of his notes for which I am eternally grateful. So I will leave the last word on 1990 to the late Tim Ward, and some of his recollections of the final:-

"And so to the game; the first ball and we had a wicket. Dave Shipton bounded 22 yards in three leaps and we were all in heaven. But then came the realisation that a young Goatacre lad was walking back to the pavilion. I found myself wishing that the umpire would call him back but this was for real; there was nothing we could do about it. He was out first ball.".......

"We had not won the trophy but we had won a lot of friends and had a truly wonderful day in every way. Unfortunately, our stay with the Goatacre party was very brief after the game but our friendships will last and we shall do our best to play them again.

Once again our team had been a credit and we had a happy journey home. We had arranged to go back to the club at Dunstall and have a party, and my highlight came when we reached the club. We were met at the door by our 92 year-old president, a beaming Sir Robert Douglas, a truly wonderful man. What an appropriate end to the day."

Our first round match in defence of the title was away to Southwick. A reasonable crowd was there to watch the national champions in action. One family whose house overlooked the ground, had heard of the hard hitting Goats. So they took the precaution of moving their precious caravan from the side of the house to a neighbour's drive, out of range.

Our 154 total was largely due to opening bat Mark Hunt's invaluable 85. Tony Donegan was well pleased with his teenage son, Andrew, who had entered the first team that season. Batting at number ten, he defended sensibly and patiently, but punished the bad ball. He finished second top score with 14. Southwick were well satisfied at tea, having dismissed our lads in less than the allotted forty overs. But they had no answer to Jon Angell, who returned figures of 7.5 – 5 – 2 – 5, folding for 59 in less than thirty overs.

Next we met Spye Park, where we had an initial hiccup when both openers were back in the pavilion with only twenty-four on the board. John Spencer and Paul Rose then set about the bowling with devastating effect. They shared in a third wicket partnership of 134. The skipper weighed in with 45, and Rosie was unlucky not to get his hundred. He was out for 97 having faced just 98 balls. We finished on 256 for 7. Talking to one Spye supporter during the tea interval, he said his team looked on this match as their final. The general view appeared to be that they didn't expect to get into treble figures. Young Andrew (Donnie) Donegan had earnt his place in the side. Sharing the opening attack with Jon Angell, he took the first three wickets. They never recovered from 35 for 3, and Goatacre ran out convincing winners by 153 runs.

Our first home tie saw Fonthill chasing a total of 204. They made a brave effort but Wilkie was magic behind the stumps. He caught three, and stumped Scott-Gall as he started to look settled with 25 to his name. Twiggy had been gazing into his crystal ball in the fifteenth over of our innings. We were 56 for 3 when he said "Two hundred plus — easy." When Fonthill were on 67 for 3 at the same point, he went walkabout in an anti-clockwise direction. Tony Donegan went clockwise, they met by the side screen at the far end. As they waited for the bowler to finish his over they could be seen in earnest conversation. By the time they returned to base, the half way stage had been reached. Twiggy, trying to look casual, asked me for a comparison. To which I replied we were 64 for 4 at the 20 over mark. The score board read 102 for 6. "Ah yes" said Twiggy, ever the optimist, "But JT's not finished yet." When he had finished, his figures of 4 for 26 reinforced the optimism. The brief stoppage for rain towards the end of Fonthill's innings coincided with the bar opening. So some of our lads took the opportunity of downing a presumptuous pint before the last wicket went down in the thirty-sixth at 162.

Another match against Redlynch was looked forward to with great relish. Earlier in the day I travelled to Dorset under my own steam, to look at some pedigree puppies in a village a few miles on. I had left Wiltshire in reasonable sunshine, but by 1 p.m., when I left Blashford, a huge black cloud scrolled ominously from the west. It got to the ground before I did! We sat in the

## A Villager on the Boundary

bar for an hour or so, but the deluge clearly ruled out any possibility of play that day. After a chat over old battles, it was back home to pencil in a re-scheduled home tie for the following Sunday.

Flaming June, what flaming June?! On Sunday 23rd. it was raining cats and dogs. The crowd were good humoured, with the wicket covered we lived in hope. Occasionally it showed signs of relenting, but as the afternoon wore on it became increasingly obvious we would have to make alternative arrangements for a result. So at 6.15 p.m. we had the spectacle of "bowling at the stumps." It was my first nerve racking experience of this contest. A word of warning to the enthusiastic supporter with a weak heart. Don't watch, go away and hide in the bar until it is all over! The covers were removed and all was in place just as if a game was about to commence.

Redlynch won the toss, a hollow advantage to the successful skipper in such a situation, for the decision is his to start or offer it to the opposing captain. Ian Souter decided his team would have first crack. It seems simple doesn't it? Three stumps, two bails and no batsman to protect them. Don't believe a word of it; Blake opened for Redlynch and missed. Paul Rose next for Goatacre, he missed too. So did the next pair, and the third Dorset bowler also. After five balls it was Redlynch nil Goatacre nil (I said it was the equivalent to a penalty shoot out). Adam Iles was our third bowler, and it was first strike to the home team. Donnie, Dawson and Wilkie followed Adam's success and did likewise, while the opposition still hadn't scored. With twelve balls gone, and Goatacre four nil up, you may be forgiven for thinking we could relax a little. No way! With five balls aside left, a five four victory to Redlynch was still possible. Our next five bowlers all missed, thankfully so did three of the Dorset side. The official result in the score book read:- Goatacre won four two. Not really cricket, more like Russian roulette, but it was better than tossing a coin.

# A Village at Lord's

As I did my last round in the kennels, just after nine p.m., the sun started to shine. By the time I had finished my inspection there wasn't a cloud in the sky. Perfect weather for cricket I thought. As I closed the gates and looked down towards the house I thought again. The umpires would uphold an appeal against the light if we tried again, or would they? You never know with village cricket what is going to happen next.

The county final away to Witchampton was very much a stop go affair for both teams. It was overcast all day, and not long after we arrived it started to drizzle, but not enough to prevent the game starting on time. We won the toss and Kevin elected to bat. It was slow scoring with wickets falling. After twenty-five overs we were 73 for 6. With Kevin Iles and John Haines at the wicket they did start to accelerate, putting on 71 for the seventh wicket. Kevin had just brought up his fifty with the second of only three sixes in the match, when he was bowled by Wayman for 56. John went next for a well grafted 37. With the score on 149 in the thirty-eighth, Turner and Angell prevented any further mishaps, and the innings closed on 161. It had lasted a shade over two and one half hours.

A reasonably well satisfied group of supporters discussed the situation at tea. We were fairly confident, but the threat of rain could well upset the situation if Witchampton got off to a flyer. We readily agreed our early struggle may well be our downfall. Mel Wilkins glanced at the brass bell by his chair and remarked "That's the quietest that bloomin' thing's been for a long while."

The home team's reply was marginally better than our start. Three of our first overs had been maidens. They had scored off the first three of theirs. Dawson then struck in the fourth. With the score on seven he had opener Tubbs caught by Donegan without scoring, having suffered for fourteen minutes and faced thirteen balls. This demonstrated just what conditions were like. Two balls later, he bowled Bailey without the total moving. Mel's bell made one of it's rare appearances at that point. Conditions did not improve as time went on. The light was poor and the ball at times damp. It was slow progress indeed, by the half way stage eight wickets were down with just 37 runs on the board. Bennett stayed with skipper Froud for fourteen overs in a dour partnership of 45. But with six overs to go, and a run rate of twelve an over, the game simply petered out. There was one bright spot right at the end in the final over, Witchampton scored ten runs to take them into treble figures. Out of a total of 103 for 9, which included 31 extras, Froud had grafted for almost two hours and faced 90 balls in his 37 not out. A true captain's innings of a different style. He was applauded to the pavilion in the gathering gloom as the hands of the clock edged towards eight o'clock.

You may have found the last few paragraphs heavy going. I suspect so did the teams who contested the match in not ideal conditions. In the bar after however, things were much livelier. Thankfully the weather cannot interfere there.

On the Wednesday before the sixth round home tie against Tiddington, JT came into our shop for pet food. He looked dreadful, clearly trying to shake off a heavy cold. When asked would he be fit for the match, he replied that he had no worries on that score, but was worried about some South African kiddie called Lock. He appeared to have posted his credentials around Oxfordshire. The village bush telegraph had been in action.

How different things looked on the same ground a week later. No rain clouds or covers, not an umbrella in sight, just sunshine, shorts and sunglasses. I arrived early, as I suspected a reasonable crowd, and it was. Right I said to myself, first things first, a pint and a quiet smoke. With half an hour to spare before the start of play I could enjoy my pint and pipe, soak up the atmosphere and chat with a few friends. How wrong can you be, up came Twiggy with that smile that says he's after something. So much for my plans, within five minutes I was put in charge of the P.A. system. No notebook, pencil, team sheets or anything to guide

## A Village at Lord's

me! Two lists of names eventually arrived. J.Angell was easy (as were all the Goatacre lads). If Jon walked to the wicket I simply had to introduce him as Pringle! But N.Smith — who was he? What did he look like? Kirsten Purnell, scoring for Tiddington, was just as much in the dark as I was about Adrian Manger's possible batting order. I'm no Alan Curtis, and I'm not blessed with his invaluable blotting paper memory. Still it was an experience, you do see life in village cricket.

And so to the match. The visitors won the toss and invited us to field. Dawson and Spencer contained the batting, and between them they had claimed three victims for nineteen by the end of the seventh. Rosie continued the good work, taking out three of the middle order, whilst Jon Angell held a smart caught and bowled to dismiss opener Anderson for a dogged 23 in 71 minutes. With seven wickets down for 99 in the twenty-fifth, things were looking good for the home team. But, The South African JT. had warned me about was at the wicket. He had played his first ball outside off stump, Wilkie had somehow managed to get a hand to it, but it just didn't stick. All changed after the hundred came up. Lock had played himself in by then, together with Paul Manning he put on an eighth wicket partnership of 56 in the next ten overs. Smith joined Lock after Manning had departed, and helped bring the score to 195 in the thirty-ninth, before he was out. The cool South African was their last wicket down, but not before he had helped himself to another six and four, to close the innings on 209.

Adrian Manger bowled Graham Iles without scoring. John Spencer looked in control with two confident fours, before Lock caught him off the bowling of Manger for 13. Paul Rose started in fine style with two successive fours, but became Manger's third victim. He had scored 12 of his 14 from boundaries when the third wicket went down. At 54 for 3 in the twelfth we were still ahead on run rate. Anchor man Hunt was still there and starting to open out, when he hit Goatacre's only six. Single handed he

## A Villager on the Boundary

took the total to 69 before John Haines was bowled without scoring. Kevin Iles started cautiously, then hit two successive boundaries. Meanwhile Bunter had been run out for a patient 38. At this point we were on 97 for 5 in the twenty-third (Tiddington at the same stage had been 99 for 7). With the captain still there anything could happen. It did. Lock had him caught before the score had moved on. Only the extras moved the score board, as the last four batsmen went without scoring. Lock mopped up the tail. His final figures were 4.1 – 1 – 7 – 3 as we finished on 104 all out in the thirty-first.

Many home supporters were "subdued" in the bar afterwards. In the space of half an hour they had seen possible, some say probable, victory turn to defeat. The local paper was not too kind in the match report that followed. It also left a vacuum for some supporters who knew little about cricket, but enjoyed the excitement and comradeship the competition had injected into our community. Cricket is a game of ups and downs. That day Charlie Lock, if not Tiddington, was definitely on an up. If Wilkie had held that early chance it could have all been different. But that's cricket.

No village side can sustain a good team without the essential nucleus of youth. I'm sure "Grampy" Iles, the founder of Goatacre CC. more than sixty years ago, would agree. They're never too young to start training. So it was great to see teenager Andrew Donegan receive the supporters' player of the year award in 1991. His mum, dad and older brother were very proud of him.

It was a welcome relief to many village clubs throughout Britain that the competition had attracted a new commercial sponsor for 1992. We were looking forward to visits from company personnel, which always add to the occasion. Rothmans had their own plans, as I explained earlier. We also had a new youngster in the side. During the latter stages of 1991, a tall blond teenager named Paul Clifford had demonstrated his ability as a natural fast bowler. His batting was also developing quite well under the

## A Village at Lord's

watchful eye of Goatacre's coaching stalwarts.

The first round match was a repeat of last year's county final, with a visit to Witchampton. By all accounts it was a more exciting affair, producing a 42 run victory. Eleven bowlers turned their arm in the match, and club secretary Eddie Jenkinson making a rare appearance, had the best figures of the day, with 3 for 28. Eddie is Goatacre's equivalent to Bill Thomas of Gowerton. I refer of course to his bowling action, he draws the line at wearing half mast creams and the editor's sunshade.

We played Beanacre at the attractive sports ground on the edge of Melksham, a typical Wiltshire market town. It was a pleasant early summer day, and for a change Pauline decided to come with me. Our total of 250 for 6 was always too much for the home team. They collapsed from 64 for 2 to 97 all out. Eddie "The Lobber" only bowled seven balls, but took two wickets. The first home tie saw a visit from Shrewton. An opening partnership of fifty helped set up a final total of 243. With the heavy atmosphere it proved too much for our Wiltshire neighbours. They were all out in the thirty-seventh, giving us victory by 74 runs. Eddie did it again, with 2 for 3 off only five balls. Top scorer in the match was Bunter with 65.

A slow wicket with low bounce at Winterslow, did not prevent Mark Hunt and Pete Leavey putting on a first wicket partnership of eighty. Once Pete had gone, having scored three sixes in his 38, John Spencer kept up the momentum. He departed with the score on 124 for 2, scoring 22 himself. Fry was delighted to capture the skipper's wicket, with only two singles to his name. Mark Hunt went soon after with the total on 136. Yet another typical Bunter innings where he scored a half century. Of the remaining batsmen only John Haines reached double figures as we ran out of overs on 194 for 8. Winterslow's reply was hampered by their losing three early wickets. A fourth wicket partnership was shaping up, but when it reached 45 Spencer snapped up Annetts for 24. On 68 for 4 it was not all over by

## A Villager on the Boundary

any means, particularly as Burton joined Dixon and they saw their team's total past the hundred. But 32 overs had gone, and in the thirty-third Burton was run out for 14. When Dixon went for a valuable 37 in the next over, and the total on 123, we were beginning to anticipate the county final. Willis and Sillence wagged the tail for 10 and 23 respectively, but the Winterslow innings closed on 168 for 8.

Let's forget the Lord's final for just a moment. Over the years, it is fair to say that entries have averaged about 700, but the 32 group finals have remained unchanged. These have always been a bit special, win it and you are over the threshold say many. Just to compete in it whets the appetite of a village to enter again. The winner, as I said has crossed the threshold. If it is in a year of commercial sponsorship, they have a trophy to hang on the clubhouse wall. Over the years it may begin to look a little forlorn, but it can rekindle the spirit several years later, when another group final is just two weeks away — weather permitting.

The group final against Fonthill was memorable in several ways. It was one of those days just made for village cricket. The boundary around Goatacre's compact ground was tightly ringed with spectators. Hardly a blade of grass was visible (except on the field of play), because of deckchairs, picnic hampers and sunbeds. Ken Butler could be seen putting the finishing touches to the wicket markings. The stumps were in place and a small band of knowledgeable spectators were pacing pensively around the square. It looked full of runs, was the consensus of opinion, as the five minute warning bell went. At which point Mel. Wilkins gave his a final polish ready for action. Fonthill's captain was marshalling his fielders into position in consultation with his opening bowler. A great cheer went up as Mark Hunt and Pete leavey stepped out into the bright sunlight, heralding battle was about to commence. And what a battle it was to be!

Fonthill seized the early advantage. Jenkins bowled his first two overs without conceding a run off the bat. He also bowled

Pete Leavey for five in his second. Eleven for one. John Turner joined Hunt, and after an early tactical struggle the bat began to dominate. When JT departed for 39 in the eighteenth, there were 85 runs on the board. The captain and Bunter stepped up a gear in the next nine overs. They shared a 74 run partnership of nearly eight an over. Then, much to the relief of Fonthill, their skipper Steer caught ours behind the stumps off the bowling of Slade, for 37. From 155 for 3 Andy Dawson helped Bunter take the score to 193, before the Steer-Slade combination struck again, dismissing our ever reliable opener. Forty-eight of his seventy-one had come in boundaries, including four huge sixes. At 193 for 4 in the thirty-third, Goatacre supporters were anticipating a hefty total. But John Spencer went first ball, and Andy Dawson ran out John Haines before he had a chance to face the bowling. When he was out for 30, at a run a ball in the thirty-sixth, Fonthill had succeeded in applying the brakes. Three overs previously the home team were coasting at 193 for 3, now the scoreboard read 205 for 5 in the thirty-sixth. However our two youngsters gave an impressive wag of the tail. Paul Clifford hit a boundary before being run out for nine, and Andrew Donegan hit a four and a six to be left not out twelve at the close. Forty overs had produced 234 runs for the loss of nine wickets, a healthy total indeed. What might it have been but for Fonthill's tenacity in the field?

    I needed a beer in the tea interval, firstly to quench my thirst, and secondly to calm my nerves. Mel was at the bar, "Cor blimey," he said "I've had to screw that bloomin' bell handle back on four times already!" A smiling Tony Donegan stood in the doorway with pint in hand, no doubt celebrating his son's mature performance with the bat.

    Fonthill's openers set about their reply purposefully, with nine off the first two overs. This included an ominous cover drive to the boundary from Scott-Gall. Dawson struck in the third, when Turner took a smart catch at slip to dismiss Jenkins for a single.

### A Villager on the Boundary

Delahaye joined Scott-Gall. They stayed together for the next thirteen overs, which saw an enthralling tactical battle between bat and ball. Kevin Iles entered the attack during this period and brought on young Clifford as well.

The drinks interval brought a welcome relief to proceedings at the end of the fifteenth over. I quickly compared run rates, Goatacre had been 64 for 1 at this stage, Fonthill were 54 for 1. Pauline wanted an ice cream and I needed a pint. "Right" I said to her "you look after the score sheet while I'm gone." "A Bacardi and coke. with lots of ice for me!" Julie called after me. My it was hot that day, in more ways than one. My girls had their sustenance courtesy of JT's younger son Robert. He acted as waiter whilst I discussed proceedings in the middle with Mel and Paul Clifford's dad. Len Clifford looked twitchy and a little preoccupied. This was because Paul was in the bowling attack. Mel found it all too much, and left me in charge of the bell while he went off in search of alcoholic relief. He obviously missed his cousin Wilkie who was not playing that day.

The sixteenth over brought the Wiltshire supporters to their feet, and I had my first experience of ringing that bell. Paul Clifford first had Delahaye caught behind by Bunter, who was substituting for Wilkie. Chris Weir edged a single to open his account, then Clifford disposed of opener Scott-Gall, when Dawson caught him at mid on for 35. Adam Iles joined Clifford in the attack and promptly bowled a maiden. Next over Clifford intensified the already electric atmosphere by removing the Rigiani brothers with consecutive balls. Dawson was beaming as he took up position in the deep. Clapping his hands together sharply, he typified the fielders' attitude, they were on their toes not wishing to let anything slip. The scoreboard looked healthy for us at the half way stage, reading 67 for 5.

Eddie Pool had joined Chris Weir, much rested on their shoulders and they knew it. Pool's tactics were to take the game to Goatacre. He dispatched Clifford to the boundary twice, then

## A Village at Lord's

Adam Iles for three fours in quick succession. It was time to bring Turner back into the attack, he succeeded in removing Weir, caught behind by Hunt for 29. The pair had put on 74 in twelve overs!

Another drinks interval at the end of the thirtieth saw new batsman Wilkins in earnest conversation with his partner Pool. They looked at the scoreboard, which read 134 for 6. By this time I had made it back to the comfort of my own chair. Amidst all the excitement my wife had maintained an accurate account of proceedings on our makeshift score sheet. Kevin Iles could be seen marshalling the fielders in preparation for the defence of our total. At this point the game was tilted in Goatacre's favour, with Fonthill needing to score at ten an over to wrench the Wiltshire title from us.

The next five overs saw the match slipping away from us. Both batsmen were in determined and belligerent mood. Pool hoisted Turner for six out of the ground, then pulled the next square for four. Wilkins took two sixes and a four off our skipper. At the end of the thirty-fourth, when ten came off the over, our front-line pace attack of Spencer and Dawson returned. The relentless batting barrage continued in the thirty-fifth. Wilkins hit the luckless Dawson for two successive sixes, as sixteen came off the over. There was tense silence as Spencer thundered in to bowl to Wilkins. He had occupied the crease for just twenty-five minutes, faced only twenty-five balls, and here he was needing two for his fifty. Would he continue to maul our bowling?, I thought to myself. He certainly tried, hoisting Spencer high into the deep field. It would have been a magnificent way to chalk up a half century by hitting his seventh six. But Donegan lived up to the occasion, he timed the catch beautifully, then fell back on the turf with relief. A delayed explosive roar came from the throats of Goatacre.

It took a while for things to settle down following Wilkins departure. He had shared with Pool a valuable 67 run partnership

## A Villager on the Boundary

in six overs. Pool however was not finished. He hit Spencer for two more fours as he continued to keep the scoreboard moving. Eight runs came in the thirty- seventh, and twelve in the thirty-eighth, to see the scoreboard standing on 218 for 7. Seventeen to win off two overs, and the thirty-ninth was full of incident. It produced one huge six from Pool, which was to be his last scoring stroke. Hunt's safe hands behind the wicket saw to that. A magnificent innings of 83 off 66 balls will long be remembered. He had almost seen his side home, and the crowd stood to applaud his exit. It is true Dawson had taken the wicket of Fonthill's hero of the hour, but it is an over Andy will readily admit as one he would prefer to forget. Of the thirteen runs accredited that over, four were no balls and one was a wide. Also during the course of that lengthy penultimate over, some quick thinking by Kevin Iles allowed Bunter to run out Paul Slade. So the start of the final over needed three runs for victory. Spencer was cool, the first three were pitched right up to the bat. Following the fourth ball of the over, that old scenario of "yes, no, get back", echoed round the ground. It was all to no avail, as wicket keeper Bunter flicked off the bails. Goatacre had won an absolutely enthralling match by the narrow margin of three runs.

The celebration in recognition of both teams sterling efforts went on far into the night. It was nine o'clock before Andy Dawson began to unwind, he felt he had let the team down with what he described as his diabolical bowling in the penultimate over. His description was more colourful than I can put into print! Bunter celebrated with his grandmother (affectionately known to us all as Gran). He had good reason, having followed his 71 with 5 victims from behind the stumps. The Rigiani brothers stayed late and added sparkle to the sing song.

We crossed the borders into Wales a fortnight later, to take on Llanarth from Gwent. Our coach arrived at 12.45 p.m., only to find that the bar didn't open until 2.30 p.m. Mel Baker and Dave Strange, fearing they may be entering a dry county, had brought their own supply. An inspection of the wicket revealed a distinct slope, but lack of bounce. Returning to the clubhouse we found our hosts had kindly opened the bar an hour early. We took full advantage of the situation of course, and a discussion over a pint led us to the conclusion that it was likely to be a low scoring match.

Llanarth had won the toss and invited us to bat. I settled in my chair, checking the makeshift score sheet was in order, and tightened the handle on Mels bell. He'd been on bar duty Friday night and asked me to take charge of it, as he had tug-of-war duties and wouldn't be able to make the match. As he put it, the lads wouldn't feel at home without it. I was to discover during the afternoon, it was going to cause a few problems.

Very early on it was evident batting conditions were not easy. Our openers batted sensibly but had to graft for their runs. When the first wicket went down on 80 Goatacre were in their twenty-third over. Pete Leavey had been at the wicket for 88 minutes, in facing 56 balls for his 15. With the score on 93 in the twenty-sixth, Bunter was bowled by Richards for 45. The skipper didn't fare very well when Watkins caught him off Teer for 16. In facing 22 balls he had uncharacteristically only scored one boundary. Of our other batsmen, only Andy Dawson seemed to have mastered the conditions. He was still there at the end on 33 off 32 balls, including the only six of Goatacre's innings. The bell had been very quiet for the last two and a half hours.

During the tea interval, I appeared to be in the minority. One hundred and sixty-six for eight, in some people's eyes, was not enough, I felt it was. One Llanarth supporter had tracked down the bell as he headed for the bar. "You gonna ring that in our innings too boyoh?" he asked in a soft Welsh lilt. "Sure I am," I replied. "Good, cos. we hope to get more boundaries than you did." My retort was instantaneous. "No sir, I intend to ring it precisely ten times, one for each of your wickets." He gave me a mocking glare as he disappeared into the clubhouse. I heard

## A Villager on the Boundary

his voice again some ten minutes later, whilst at the bar. He told the barman not to serve me, as I had the opposition's secret weapon and intended to use it. The barman took him seriously for a second, but just a second.

Teer and Powell started much in the same vein as our openers, although Teer did reach the boundary in the first over. Dawson had just bowled a maiden in the fourth, to restrict the home side to 12 without loss, when Bunter's dad passed my chair on his way to the loo. He tapped me on the shoulder whispering "I hope to hear that bell ringing before long." It did, three times in Dawson's next over. He had Teer caught behind by Wilkie, Teague lasted three balls before Bunter caught him without scoring. Llanarth captain Dewfield was run out first ball, when a smart throw from our skipper shattered his stumps.

This sequence of events caused great delight to the Goatacre supporters around the boundary. It also caused some commotion in the gents. loo. There were two windows overlooking the field of play, the one by Bunter's dad was sealed up awaiting repairs. The triple ringing of Mels bell had been too much for him to stand, and three Goatacre supporters left the building with trousers and shoes slightly wetter than when they went in.

Opener Powell continued to defend, but in the seventeenth was fifth wicket down, caught by Iles off Paul Clifford for 21. The total stood at 38 for 5. Jones played a dogged innings for his 29, before becoming JT's first victim. He had faced 75 balls, hit one four and the only six in Llanarth's innings. Turner was taking full advantage of the situation. His final figures of 4 for 24 in 9 overs demonstrated how difficult he was to score off. Baxter managed a four off him in his 19 not out. So did Watkins before Turner trapped him LBW. The ball had very definitely dominated proceedings, as our hosts finished on 113 for 9. It was almost 8 p.m. when the match finished. We still had time however to enjoy some Welsh hospitality before setting off home, to prepare for another battle against St.Fagans.

## A Village at Lord's

Our coaches left Wiltshire on an overcast Sunday morning. The clouds were still with us when we reached Cardiff. St.Fagans large ground had changed little since 1989. Many of our supporters remembered that last visit, and were out for revenge. Whatever the outcome was to be, it was set to be a battle. Some may say a clash of the Titans. It certainly looked that way, as Ricky Needham came out to open the Welsh innings with his partner Bell. I had watched Needham take the field in the 1991 final, he had certainly looked more relaxed then than he did on this occasion.

He and his partner saw their side past the half way mark, when Dawson bowled him in the twenty-first, he had scored 34 off 53 balls. It took until the twenty-ninth before the scoreboard showed treble figures at 100 for 4. What would the final surge produce? Clifford had Davies caught behind in the thirtieth for 22, with the score on 106. Powell shared a valuable 55 run partnership with Lewis before he went in the thirty-eighth over, with the score on 161. Spencer bowled the thirty-ninth, yielding just three runs. In the final over Rosser hit the only six of the game, and Lewis was justifiably rewarded for his 50 off only 39 balls, as St.Fagans innings closed on 182 for 6. Paul Clifford was pleased with his 4 for 39 in 9 overs.

Many of our supporters felt we were still capable of winning, being psychologically better equipped than in our last encounter. I'm sure St.Fagans also fancied their chances of containing us. The weather however had the last word, it rained during the tea interval and the match was abandoned at 6.45 p.m., without another ball being bowled. It was a miserable end to a day which had been further marred by the sudden death at the ground of past club chairman Fred Jennings' brother-in-law.

The rescheduled match saw Goatacre's ground packed to capacity, even though it was a Friday. The crowd basked in sunshine, and the wicket looked full of runs. It was a good toss to win, which St.Fagans did — Needham had no hesitation in electing to bat.

## A Villager on the Boundary

Ricky Needham I fancy gave himself a good talking to during the week, because he looked altogether more composed as he walked to the wicket. He hammered the first three balls from Andy Dawson to the boundary. By the tenth over the opening pair had put on 71. They did not slow down! At the end of the sixteenth the rate had been pushed to more than 7.5 an over. With the score on 128 in the next, it was captain against captain. Needham on 89 had his century in sight. But Kevin Iles won that particular round by bowling him. Needham had faced only 59 balls and hit one six and eighteen fours. Bell kept up the momentum, but his partner Davies struggled a little. When JT caught him off Jon Angell for 5, it was 148 for 2, and there were still eighteen overs to go. Lewis joined Bell to take their partnership to 48 at the start of the thirtieth. Clifford caught Bell off the bowling of Spencer for 76. He had mainly stayed in his captain's shadow in the early stages of the match, but had taken command following his departure. It had in my view been a very cultured innings.

So here we were with 200 on the board for the loss of three wickets, and still ten overs to go. Were we to see Goatacre chasing 300 plus to win? Graham Lewis obviously thought so, as he lofted John Spencer to the boundary. Our skipper then deceived him with one, and Wilkie made a fine stumping to dismiss him for 15, with the score on 208 in the thirty-first. One run later Kevin ran out Stevens for 6. Spencer immediately deceived Rosser, who was LBW without scoring. Goatacre were starting to apply the brakes. 210 for 7. Nine runs later the next wicket went down when Dawson's vociferous appeal saw the raised finger to Jones, who departed for 9. Powell was still keeping the scoreboard moving, as he saw Kevin Iles take a fine catch off Clifford's bowling, to dismiss Markinson for a single. In the penultimate over Dawson bowled Powell for 19. He had hit two sixes in his attempt to maintain the momentum. With the score on 239 for 9, the last pair added a further ten runs in the last

# A Village at Lord's

over before Madley was caught by substitute Graham Iles for six, off the penultimate ball of the innings. During the tea interval the general view was — honours even. The experience of St.Fagans opening pair had ensured they were off to a flying start. But Goatacre's guile and experience in the field over the last ten overs prevented a rout. Two hundred and fifty to win was within their capabilities, and both sides knew it.

Makinson and Rosser started with a maiden apiece before Bunter cut loose in the third with a boundary. Madley caught him off the bowling of Rosser in the sixth, with the score on 20. Tight bowling kept Turner and Spencer tied down until Spencer's frustration cost him his wicket, when he holed out to Bell off the bowling of Hardwick for twenty. He had however struck two sixes to increase the run rate. Next over our other opener Turner also went for twenty. 54 for 3. A maiden in the fourteenth was not good for our nerves.

The bowling and fielding remained tight, as at the half way stage we only had 84 on the board. Kevin Iles had opened his account with two sixes off Jones before he was fourth wicket down at 85. There were 19 overs to go, and Dawson took over to hit Jones for four then six, but with the score on "Nelsons" Lewis snapped a fine catch to dismiss him for 29. Jon Angell joined Wilkie. In nine overs they put on 61 before Angell was caught, his 28 had been one of some urgency, as it included four sixes. Now Wilkie was looking ominously dangerous. The next over produced ten runs, and the next, mostly from our wicket keeper's lethal bat. During this time John Haines had obviously been giving Wilkie the strike. He may have been out for four, but he had done his job. To quote Wilkie's cousin Mel, who said after the match "Our John played out of his skin." Ten further runs came in the thirty-eighth to 212 for 7. A further fourteen in the thirty-ninth, and sixteen in the final over. Goatacre had lost by seven runs.

The crowd rose to applaud John Wilkins off the field. He

walked towards the clubhouse raising his bat in both hands behind his head. In this way his elbows shielded the tears of disappointment that were welling up in his eyes. Everyone on the ground felt for him. He had finished with eighty to his name. His last six strokes had been six, two, two, six, six, and off the last ball when he knew all was lost, just a single. Wilkie had simply run out of balls, and Goatacre out of luck. It was a fine exhibition of cricket in which the Welshmen JUST had the edge. There was no doubt in my mind that the crowd that day had seen two of the strongest village teams in the country, give of their best. Sadly someone had to lose. Will Goatacre grace the hallowed turf again? Only time, which will one day be history, can tell. St.Fagans bowed out of the National Village Cricket Championships when they lost in the semi- final to eventual champions Hursley Park.

After the annual Goatacre dinner in November, our reliable opening bat Bunter was rumoured to have muttered something about wanting everyone to buy him silver polish for Christmas. Not an unreasonable request, as he almost swept the board during the trophy presentations for achievement in 1992. The New Year heralded good news. Somerset had signed Paul Clifford on a two year contract. I'm off now to finish the final two chapters and get the manuscript completed. Then I can watch Goatacre begin the long journey once more, in the hope of reaching St.John's Wood in 1993. Will they make it? I don't know, but if they don't it won't be for lack of commitment from players, officials and supporters which make up the Goatacre team!

*The Tavern at another place.*

*How to bridge the generation gap.*

### THE PREMATCH PHOTO CALL
*Himley CC in the Lord Harris Memorial Garden.
Front row centre, Captain Andy Shorter, 221 (see statistics).*

LEFT
A proud Scottish supporter.

BELO...
The Whitbread shi...
waiting to enter Lord...

ABOVE
The Scots announce their arrival at Lord's.

RIGHT: GOOGLIE THE GOAT
Goatacre's high smelling mascot.

COLLECTORS CORNER
*A collection of one sponsor's awards and memorabelia.*

*One of the other competitions.*

'HOWZAT'
*For supporters enthusiasm.*

A SCOTTISH WELCOME
*Pipe major Alistair Pirnie welcomes Freuchie in 1985.*

A GREAT MOMENT IN SCOTTISH SPORTING HISTORY
*Freuchie's triumphant captain after the 1985 final.*

**YESTERYEAR**
*Chiswell Street at it was before conversion to the Banqueting suite.*

**TODAY**
*Whitbread Banqueting suite at Chiswell Street.*

An Eve of final banquet in progress at Chiswell Street.

A CHARACTER ON THE BOUNDARY
'Mel The Bell' at Lord's.

## THE ORGANISERS
*A Rare opportunity to see the organising team before the camera. Note, Belinda Brocklehurst, second from the left, Ben fourth from the left and Malcolm Lukey, Norsk Hydro's anchorman for the sponsors, second from the right.*

## NOT LONG TO GO NOW
*Last minute preparations before a final.*

*A Happy group of supporters preparing to enjoy a very special match at Lord's.*

A PRESENTATION CEREMONY AT BECKENHAM
*Not every final finished at Lord's.*

## CHAPTER EIGHT

# Tales from the Hedgerows

The final each year comprises two village sides making one fixture. Working backwards to the second round, the number of fixtures doubles each time. This produces 629 fixtures. The first round however has to be an estimate. In the early years some 800 villages entered, which was later cut to 630. Some sides, and even groups, had byes to the second round. I would think therefore that an estimate of 170 first round fixtures is not over ambitious. This would produce some 17,000 fixtures in total since the competition began way back in 1972.

That means a tremendous number of people have been involved in some way or other, both on and off the field. It stands to reason therefore there must be some interesting tales to tell. Just a few are contained in this chapter.

### CAUGHT UNAWARES.

During a very hot Sunday afternoon, a quite unassuming ice cream sales man turned up at a village cricket match to ply his merchandise. The weather, he thought, was just right to make a few bob. Poor chap, he was unaware that it was a semi-final in the National Village Cricket Championships. He didn't stay long, following an initial onslaught on the unsuspecting salesman things quietened for a few moments. The final straw came when one of the assembled spectators, who was part of a large

## A Village at Lord's

*"I ONLY ASKED FOR 27 CORNETS"*

contingent of supporters took a head count. He promptly ordered twenty-seven large ice cream cornets. This was all too much for him. I suspect the next time he ventures to trade at a village cricket match, he will ensure his van is down on it's springs with stock stacked to the roof.

## A TALE FROM THE MEDITERRANEAN

I have already told the tale of Forge Valley's secretary, who ran up a £27. 'phone. bill to hear of his teams semi-final victory in 1986. In the words of comedian Jimmy Cricket — "And there's more".

The news that Valley were going to Lord's raised an impromptu celebration Cypriot style. The Almonds were spending time with two ex village players and their families, who were service men stationed on the island. Tony Kennedy and Steve Marshal decided to tempt the wrath of their respective spouses and spend special concessions time travelling thousands of miles to watch a village cricket match!

How did they placate those left behind? They promised a suitcase full of essential luxuries, like peppermint creams, Ariel (to remove the red earth from white school socks), my little pony

"WHO CARES IF WE FORGOT THE LITTLE PONY'S PEPPERMINTS ?!!"

stickers, and luxury of luxuries dried soup with croutons. Both lads arrived by different means, Tony opted to share a Hercules with an assortment of Army hardware, enduring an eight hour concessionary flight to the U.K. Steve travelled in comfort on a civilian flight, but had to go via Vienna.

They had a wonderful time, what they could remember of it. Their suitcase full of goodies on the return journey contained sufficient quantities of Panadol and Aspirin to cater for the reunion headaches. It also contained the Ariel, but nothing else. Still, one out of four wasn't bad! They had also brought back their memories to retell.

## THE ANONYMOUS LADY

Of necessity the participants in this particular tale must remain anonymous. The reasons will become clear as the story unfolds. 1976, as many will remember, produced one of the hottest and driest summers on record. On the particular Sunday this match was being played, the sun was continuing its unrelenting bombardment of parched outfields and bare pitches.

It was a match in the latter stages of the championships. The umpire was in regulation shirt sleeves buttoned to the wrist. Nothing untoward had happened in the first twelve overs. As he took up his position behind the stumps at the start of the

"HASN'T SHE GOT ANY ON THEN DEAR?—WELL, LET'S HOPE THE BOWLER'S SHORTSIGHTED!"

thirteenth, there was a great mechanical commotion from the car park. Most spectators (and there were a few thousand), and players alike, were distracted momentarily. An old Morris shooting break came to rest with relief, followed by a delayed emission of black smoke from the exhaust as the engine died. A large lady of mature years alighted, sporting a multi-coloured voluminous frock.

Play continued and the umpire followed the third ball of the over to the boundary. There he noticed the lady setting up her deckchair in line with the stumps. The over concluded, our umpire mopped his brow on the way to square leg. What he was about to see was to make him even more hot and bothered than he already was. He lined himself up with the popping crease and glanced in the direction of the stumps to make sure. By now the lady was well settled, intent on enjoying her day. The flowing dress fluttered in the slight breeze that had sprung up from nowhere then disappeared. But not before the umpire learnt she had nothing on under her frock.

The over concluded, he returned behind the stumps. There had been no change in the bowling since the start of the match. This continued as the opening bowler came from extra cover, which had been his fielding position from the start. He advised the umpire he was changing his delivery, as he returned to the stumps to check his run up the umpire commented to him on the lady in the deckchair. A nonchalant glance in the general direction, brought a mumbled reply but not a glimmer of change in his countenance. At the end of the over the umpire again spoke to him, and asked what he thought of the situation. At first he looked puzzled, but as the conversation continued a look of panic flashed across his face. "Here ump." he whispered urgently, "Don't let on about this please. You see I enjoy my cricket, and although no Ian Botham I do contribute something to our game, but the skipper hasn't discovered I'm a little short sighted."

With that he went off to indulge in earnest deliberations with his captain. The start of the fifteenth over saw a new fielder at extra cover. Our short sighted bowler had done a direct swap with his colleague from square leg. As the over progressed he went deeper and deeper. At the end of the over he had to be called urgently to prevent time wasting. This was no time to engage in polite conversation with a lady spectator on the boundary. Satisfied he had saved the lady any further undue embarrassment, he took a wicket in each of his last two overs.

## THE GHOST VILLAGE.

In a little village near Thirsk, where the residents number just 450, it is a little after noon on August Bank Holiday Monday. "The Spirit of Cricket" was there and observed a silence and

## A Village at Lord's

uncanny quiet that had prevailed all morning. There had been a young girl on the cricket pitch walking her dog. A few children peddled their tricycles and bicycles with total disregard for traffic hazard. There was no need to worry for there was neither car nor bus to be seen moving. Hold all, said the spirit to himself. I can hear an engine, of course it is the coach on it's market day run from Thirsk, this'll bring a bit of life back into the village. But no, the engine stopped and only the driver sat in his empty bus. No one got on or off as driver Joe read his paper, obviously expecting no trade. He had but three passengers all day.

The spirit shook his head, I will try the clubhouse, Bank Holiday Monday, beer, willow and leather, he thought, bound to be. Here he found the pitch deserted, the towels on the pump in the bar and nothing stirring. A telephone rang, he followed the sound and ghosted his way over the garden gate at Linden Lee Cottage. He heard a voice answering the call, saying everything was in order then pausing. A question was obviously being asked, to which it replied "Ahm not raht interested in crickett". Aribert Bean replaced the 'phone. in it's cradle. His daughter Sally had lunch ready, so they could clear up early ready to listen to the local radio station.

The spirit decided to visit the bowling green in the hope of finding some sign of life. On the way he saw Margaret Harper and sister-in-law Hilary, tidying their garden. Both looked tanned, they had just returned from holiday, which explained the garden's unkempt look. At the bowling green there was a message hanging on the notice board, perhaps that would explain what was happening. No, it only had a warning about Dutch Elm disease. A policeman knocked on Bertha Wedgewood's charming cottage, apparently to check that everything was OK. That is the only sign of life the spirit of cricket could find in that tiny Yorkshire village that day.

Not for the first time that day our spirit shook his head sadly. He decided to retire to a stack of hay and sleep. He would not be disturbed, for there was no sign of the farmer either. He felt cold and unwanted. What would Thomas Lord of Thirsk say if he could see a Yorkshire village devoid of life and cricket on such a summer day? For that matter he thought, what would the village forefathers have to say. The likes of George Freeman and the Clayton dynasty, many of whom were buried in the churchyard. The spirit slept a long long time.

It was chilling and dark in the small hours of the morning when the spirit was woken by the sound of lengines. Signs of life at last. Cars were arriving, so were coaches. All seemed cheerful, something was definitely happening. Ah yes, said he I recognise that lady, it's Mrs. Margaret Flintoff, she's a marvellous tea lady. What's that she's showing to Aribert's daughter? My, what a beautiful powder compact.

Despite the chill air as dawn broke, the spirit felt warmer than he had felt in the hot sun the previous afternoon. As the day wore on he felt more cheerful, bunting was erected and villagers

# A Village at Lord's

were happily milling around. The clubhouse saw the towels come off the pumps, but there were no stumps, umpires or players. It was obvious no cricket was being played that afternoon.

He noticed the villagers were becoming more excited. The sound of a bus, hooting of horns, and great cheers greeted the Sessay first eleven returning victorious from Lord's. Then the spirit woke up, it had all been a dream. The spirit of cricket in Sessay had been to Lord's for a holiday, but left a ghost behind, because cricket never really leaves Sessay.

## BEHIND THE BOWLERS ARMS

An infuriating habit which cricket has to endure, is the spectator who walks behind the bowler's arm. It is an irksome and unnecessary incident that can spoil a batsman's concentration.

*"I WONDER IF DRAKE HAD THE SAME PROBLEM WITH THE ARMADA?"*

The Lancashire village of Alvanley had an away match at a ground located by the side of a canal. The club chairman Percy

Ainsworth, was at the wicket, and there was no sight screen. As the bowler went back to his mark a ship came into view. The home team and their umpire clearly demonstrated this was one of those peculiar local conditions. Many villages have equally bizarre conditions which are normally of a static nature. Chairman Percy accepted the kind offer to wait until the ship had passed. It was not a ship, but a liner! After what seemed like an age, the game recommenced. Percy took his guard and was comprehensively bowled first ball.

## THE MISSING CRICKET BALL

Many cricket balls are lost in the fields and hedges, and are found by another generation. At Great Alne in Warwickshire a shuttle rail service ran past the ground. In one match a huge six was struck and the ball deposited in a passing train. No need to hunt for it, it had gone forever. No it wasn't, twenty minutes later the train passed the ground on its return journey. The ball was thrown back by the guard, who was a member of the club!

## WHISKY GALORE

Chinese whispers took hold as John Haig and company's generous sponsorship reached alarming proportions at Draycott C.C. They were not in the competition at the time. Their request for an entry form was prompted by the club secretary, after a conversation he had in the pub., with a local sage, following his side's latest defeat. I believe the conversation went something like this:-

## Tales from the Hedgerows

Sage- "Are you in the Haig?" Sec- "No" Sage — "Well you oughta be" The sage at this point agreed to supply the address to write to, in exchange for a pint. As he passes the information over he continues :- "You gotta be quick, cos they want the entries in by the end of October, if not sooner." Sec — "Yes, I'll be as quick as I can, if not quicker." Sage — "Oh, if you do get accepted, it'll do you the power of good. D'you know, every club entering gets 73 cases of whisky a week for the next ten years!" Sec — "Really? Well that is a good incentive. Do they supply the glasses?" The sage puzzles for a moment, then replies hesitantly "No, I don't think so. I 'spose they expect you to supply them yourselves out of yer increased bar takings."

A MUSICAL INTERLUDE

"...NEIGH!" "BAAAS!"
"EVERYBODY NEEDS GOOD...."
(AND NEIGHBOURS BECOME GOOD FRIENDS!"
— SO DO VILLAGE CRICKETERS!!)

We all know the Welsh have a passion for music, but in this competition it was not their exclusive right. Freuchie, after winning their semi-final, set about composing a tune especially for the final. Local villager Jack Crawford may well have made a fortune had it taken off. As it was, their amateur recording expert had to take over a local warehouse to keep up with demand. The English weren't to be outdone either. When Oxford Downs was founded in 1923 it was named after a local breed of black faced sheep. Some of their cricketers were red faced in a match against Shrivenham. Reeling at 3 for 3 several musical pundits retired to the bar. As the score board clicked up 5 for 5 some few minutes later, the following lament could be heard from the bar:- "We're poor little lambs who have lost our way; Baa, baa, baa. We're the Oxford Downs who have gone astray; Baa, baa, baa. Villager batsmen, out on a spree, With the score reading three for three; Lord have mercy on such as we, Baa, baa, baa."

## A FOUR-LEGGED TWELFTH MAN

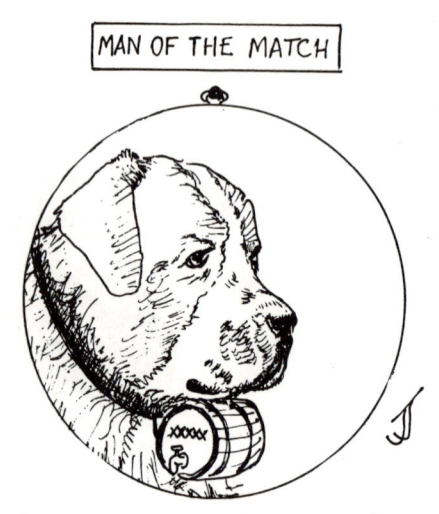

"So - your twelfth man can fetch a ball - you try the refreshments ours brings on!!"

In 1977 Newick C.C. beat Glynde in the Sussex final. This was a memorable occasion for them, in more ways than one. Newick had been in the competition since the beginning and had never been beaten, except by Glynde. And Glynde had never been beaten, except by Newick.

I am indebted to David Wickens of Newick for his tale of that match. Glynde batted first. When Ian Winchester and Graham Baker came together they put on a thrilling 125 run partnership. Baker finished in fine style, with a six over cover off the last ball of their innings. This left Newick requiring 166 to win.

In reply, Newick faced a fearsome pace attack. With two wickets down, and five an over needed, Caldwell came to the wicket. His innings was inspired, it included five consecutive sixes. The second six was a huge blow into a field adjacent to the ground. It appears the gathering gloom provided a sense of urgency, in order to beat the weather, so a lost ball could have been a problem. No one need have worried, Newick's twelfth man was an astute black labrador of obvious working stock. The ball was back in play in the twinkling of an eye. Newick went on to win the match. I wonder if eleven pints and a bowl of beer were on the bar at close of play, for the victorious team?

## SARTORIAL ELEGANCE

On one occasion at a final, a policeman spoke to me just as the cup was being awarded to the victorious team. He had been at several finals over the years, and commented to me on the smartness of most people. That is true, the Scottish side came to London in traditional Highland dress. Matching blazers and flannels for the teams has become the norm.

This is highlighted as being of particular importance by one situation that arose. Mike Almond was about to leave his hotel in Cyprus on the Thursday before the end of their holiday, when he was paged by the reception to take an urgent call from

# A Village at Lord's

*"UM — WHEN I PHONED — YOU SAID 69 LONG — ER — PERHAPS YOU MEANT CENTIMETRES!"*

England. Fearing tragedy or burglary, he rushed to the 'phone. It was Dave Long the team secretary, wanting his chest size and inside leg measurement.

It even goes one stage further, a family were on the train from Yorkshire to Lord's, when the mother spotted (horror of horrors), that her immaculately dressed son was wearing dirty plimsolls. It was no good, the train had to stop at Leeds to buy him new shoes. He was not going to be allowed to let down the image of his village.

## A WORD FROM THE SPONSORS

Whitbread's hospitality was of the highest standard, always. They were ever ready to ensure the rural visitors had nothing at all to worry about. This was ably demonstrated in 1983, when 90 guests found themselves marooned in the Metropolis (on their way to the eve of match banquet). Although only five miles from Chiswell Street, they may as well have been in another country! A fleet of taxis was sent to rescue them, thus ensuring the evenings festivities went without any further hitch.

Sam Whitbread said to me that it never ceases to amaze him

....."HOW LEVEL HEADED AND PRACTICAL VILLAGE CRICKETERS WERE."

how level headed and practical village cricketers were. This was particularly obvious after one banquet when Longparish's captain thanked him profusely for the meal. Sam acknowledged but looked puzzled, the man was obviously dressed for the night air. He certainly was, he was on his way home to Hampshire to tend his pheasants at dawn. He may have been captain of the village team, but he was also the local gamekeeper. His problem, and he dealt with it in his own way. Next morning he was in the Lord Harris Memorial garden for the team photograph.

Norsk Hydro's northern representative was their trading manager Tony Martin. He readily admitted to knowing precious little about the game (even though he hailed from a cricketing village). He was totally out of his depth at the start, but Forge Valley soon took him in hand. He has many fond memories of the games, particularly the spirit in which they were played. He recalled the occasion in one match, when a six entered the score box and knocked the poor scorer off his stall. There was some delay whilst the scorer was placed back on his perch and the lost ball sought. By the time he reached the final he had been well educated in the ways of village cricket. he virtually lived in Forge Valley for days after the final. He became an honorary member of the club, and was presented with his own bat.

GRATEFUL BENEFACTORS

When Sessay reached the final in 1976, the grandson of George Freeman (Yorkshire and England) presented the club with a framed picture of Lord's as it was a hundred years ago. This is at present on loan to the local museum in Thirsk. The village also erected a clock on the pavilion which was watched over by a wrought iron replica of Father Time.

"TWEEDLEDUM & TWEEDLEDEE"
(OR TWO FORGE VALLEY MEN AFTER
MRS. GLAVES SUPPER!!)

After Forge Valley won the title their club president Philip John Glaves, (sadly no longer alive), considered his team's victory his greatest moment of glory. His son Stephen had previously played at Lord's with Scarborough, but this was different. He wined and dined everybody before the match in fairytale fashion. After their win he presented every club member and associate with engraved momentoes of the glorious occasion. His wife cooked delectable breathtaking suppers for everyone at their home, until even the biggest appetite was satisfied.

## IT'S JUST NOT CRICKET

Many matches over the years have been played in unbelievable weather conditions. One of the most remarkable was a fixture between my own Wiltshire village and the champions of Oxford. This was played before I became involved with the team. Twiggy recalled it well. Apparently the scheduled fixture at Oxford Downs was rained off. The following Sunday the weather was just as atrocious in Wiltshire. Despite this a fair sized crowd watched a reduced match of thirty-two overs a side, which was to be played to a finish no matter what the conditions. It was more like water polo than cricket.

"NAH!! HE'S NOT IN DISTRESS — HE'S THE UMPIRE!"

# A Village at Lord's

The Oxford team batted first and clocked up an amazing 259 for 8. In reply Goatacre chased valiantly. When captain Kevin Iles came to the wicket he was armed with a pitchfork! This he pushed into the turf and asked the opposing captain did he still wish to continue. Following an answer in the affirmative, Kevin sent for his bat and promptly hit 133 runs to become the first player in the history of the competition to have five centuries to his name. The scores level Goatacre had lost six wickets with eight balls to go. All they had to do was play out the remaining few balls to win, or scrape a quick single. Ken Butler would have none of it, he thumped a six to record a memorable victory, then went off for a shower.

Obviously there was no cricket played in Wiltshire at all that day, except between these "sheep" and "goats." And the weather was so appalling an SOS went out to local villages for a loan of their whites, to enable players to frequently change into dry clothes. I also assume several spare bats were on hand, as our opening bat's sodden willow simply went dead.

## JAKE'S TALE

I promised to tell you the story Jake told me when we visited Grampound Road. I was standing on the pavilion steps minding my own business, quite early on in proceedings. An elderly gentleman from Devon was standing next to me, it appears he had nothing to do with the home team, but had heard a big village match was on, so came to watch.

"You'm be a Goatacre supporter be ye?" I acknowledged in the affirmative. "Tell me," he continued "Is yon kiddie opening the batting, an all rounder?" I replied that whilst he was deceivingly quick in the field, he was not renowned for his bowling. The old boy shook his head. It appears Bunter bore a striking resemblance to a player that had been involved in a match near Chumleigh in 1947. I felt a story coming on, and I was right.

Apparently Bunter's double was participating in a match where the opposition's bowling attack was almost as ferocious as Marshall and Garner are today. With his side reeling at 5 wickets for 4 runs, the intrepid all rounder came to the crease. He kept his head down for a few overs while taking stock of the situation. Then he began to take the game to the opposition. Before long he was in his usual belligerent mood, striking fours and sixes to all parts of the ground. At one particular point he struck the ball which went higher and higher, and further and further. It disappeared from view into the adjoining gardens. Before long there was a tinkling of glass — one greenhouse slightly the worse for wear. All applauded the shot, except square leg umpire, he scowled momentarily, then the incident passed.

"Come tea interval," the old boy continued, "Twenty-two players and one umpire went in to tea. Him from square leg went over the boundary, through the hedge and was gone. After tea twenty-two players and two umpires took the field. Where he came from I don't know, but he just appeared as if by magic."

Nothing further happened until Bunter's double was called upon to bowl. Whereupon the scowling umpire promptly no balled him four times in his first over. Being a gentleman he did not remonstrate or show the slightest sign of dissent.

The match over, everyone was in the bar enjoying a drink. When the intrepid all rounder spotted the umpire in the corner of the bar, filling his pipe, he decided to chance his arm and speak to him, as he was quite alone. His request as to why the umpire had no balled him produced a simple and succinct answer, which had nothing to do with the laws of cricket.

## A Village at Lord's

"You can break every window in my house, as many times as you like. You can even break the glass in my greenhouse. But, when you follow that up by pulverising my prize marrow entered for next week's agricultural show, I reserve the right to punish you in the best way suited to me!"

"STUFFED MARROW!!"

# CHAPTER NINE

# A Crystal Ball with no Snowflakes

Do you remember the old village scene set in a crystal ball, the one which when shaken produces an instant snowstorm? Of course you do. If you were to ask a gypsy fortune teller to gaze into her crystal ball today, what do you think she would see as the future for The National Village Cricket Championships? It need not be the vision of a perfect summer day, with white clad cricketers playing on the village green. There is no guarantee she won't see a game being played in a snowstorm. It has happened in the past, remember Rowledge's first match in 1981? If I were to be the one to ask, I would hope to hear her reply "I can see no end to it."

In my introduction I referred to the Village Championships as having become an established part of our National Cricketing Calendar. Imagine a season without Test Matches, the County Championships, or our three limited overs competitions. In recent years we have also had the introduction of One Day Internationals, which sees visiting Test Teams display their alternative skills in the limited overs game. They too I would suggest, have become part of the National Cricketing Calendar. They prove it by the attendance figures and gate receipts.

The first class fixtures to which I refer all have one thing in common — SPONSORSHIP. Without sponsors how many would have survived? In 1963, the first year of the "Gillette Cup", the company invested £6,500 in the competition. When they relinquished their involvement at the end of the 1969 season,

National Westminster Bank took over. The bank's financial commitment to the "Nat.West.Trophy" now exceeds £250,000 annually. Indeed had it not been for the introduction of limited overs cricket, I wonder where the game would be today. In 1950 county championship gates were approaching 2,000,000. By 1963 (when limited over cricket first became part of the scene), gates barely topped 700,000. In fact within the next three years they were to drop by a further 200,000 before an upward curve emerged. TIME is the measurement of change, and cricket has been around for a long time. The change today is that sponsorship is here to stay in all forms of sport. For without it I fear, sport will have great difficulty in surviving.

We talk affectionately of Hambledon being the cradle of cricket. This is due mainly to the chronicles and records which began under the expert quill of John Nyren, in the Bat and Ball Inn, where he recorded the events on Broad Halfpenny Down. The late John Arlott referred to his book "The Cricketers of My Time", as a classic to grace the book shelves with other immortal classics, worthy of recognition by a single word. In Arlott's opinion along with Gulliver, Oliver, Whittaker and Pickwick goes Nyren. Village cricket was played in the Weald of Kent and Sussex, long before the Hambledon chronicles, but are mainly forgotten events, as records are so scant.

Time is indeed the measurement of change, but measurement is not equally progressive. In the case of village life, it certainly has not been so. For centuries the rural way of life was virtually static, but saw change which has accelerated over the last 50 years. It has affected many aspects of rural tradition including village cricket and the image it portrays. Do not be fooled by that changed image however, in the majority of cases the game is still played for the fun it engenders, and the spirit is still sporting. It has been demonstrated many times since 1972, and commented on by the National Media.

We have all had to make adjustments to our everyday lives,

in order to cope with ever increasing and accelerated variations. Brought about by "progress", which means different things to different people. Cricket is no exception, from Test Match level to the grass roots, adjustments have been called for. Today we see many village clubs in local leagues. Where's the harm in that? It helps improve their game, which can lead to other things that can be of benefit to both individual and community. Many county coaches are increasingly looking to "club" cricket for young talent. First let us look at talent —

In the early days of the competition the Buckinghamshire village of Frieth had a young West Indian in their side. His name was Wilfred Slack. His name can be seen in the middle of competition records for batsmen, with 140 to his credit, which he achieved against Maids Morton in 1974. He also scored 111 against the strong Oxfordshire village of Horspath. Wilf went on to play for Middlesex and England. I watched him at Lord's on several occasions, and he always struck me as being a player who really enjoyed his cricket.

When he wrote the foreword to the 1984 annual he referred to his time at Frieth, saying that it had taught him a lot, and had laid the foundations for his future. Sadly his untimely death at the age of 35 prevented aspiring youngsters of future generations learning from him. I am sure his Buckinghamshire colleagues will long remember him.

Now let us look at the community — The village hall is more often than not the hub of village life. Many cater for the skittle team in Winter and the cricketers in Summer. In the situation where sport flourishes, so does the community, and along with that often their finances. In these days of national non-domestic rates (the business rate), it can be important. The Inland Revenue will view a cricket pavilion or village hall with the cold heartless valuer's eye. He then imposes on it a financial burden which has to be met. He gives not a jot whether the club has an unhealthy overdraft or a modest surplus. It is not for him to pay the bill, only decide what has to be paid.

Perhaps this is one of the reasons that has led to some village sides progressing to top class league cricket. I say top class deliberately, for league cricket takes many forms. One such club has aspired to dizzy heights. They are no longer in the village competition. It was from their local newspaper's office that the village trophy was stolen in 1989. There were rumours that someone may have been holding a grudge against the team, which was confirmed by an anonymous letter received at The Cricketer magazine. I am referring to the Cheshire village of Toft.

Today they are in the Cheshire County League, a natural progression, having won the Cheshire Cricket League. But, ask their chairman Peter Hornsby what the team's proudest achievement was, and he will tell you the two occasions they played in the championship final at Lord's. The club emblem is a Roebuck, and Peter says that perhaps you could detect a smile on the Roebuck's face the year they beat Hambledon to become National Champions.

At their Booth Park ground, Saturday morning is practice time for the youth. At times as many as a hundred young cricketers from the tender age of eight can be seen testing their skills under the watchful eye of club members. If you visit a Saturday game, you can enjoy a meal in the club bistro afterwards. I can assure you Toft still play their cricket for the enjoyment it gives.

This unique competition has brought passion, joy and pride to many village clubs, their supporters and counties (minor as well as first class). One club chairman recalls some memories of the day his village played at Lord's. He was a keen sportsman — as a younger man he had played football for Derby County and England. One of the team who was playing in the final had also played for "The Rams". He recalls their meeting Tom Graveny at the eve of match reception. It was, as he put it, three Gloucestershire lads reminiscing together, soon joined by another old (young) friend Cliff Morgan, to make it a perfect evening. He also found the morning of the final an emotional experience. I have in my records many of his thoughts and experiences as he walked round the hallowed ground that morning. The sight that brought a lump to his throat was his village flag fluttering in the breeze over his team's dressing room. He wanted everyone to see it, then his attention was distracted by clapping and cheering, as his team took the field. He remembered thinking that no team could have taken the field at Lord's looking smarter.

I recall a cryptic filler in a magazine which went something like this — In days before our advanced communications network, more than half the world did not know the other existed, let alone how they lived. Today we have that communication, not only do they know they exist but how they exist. Yet many do not have the inclination to care. The day may well come when communications are so advanced that everyone will have instant access to a central terminal, to pass information back and forth. This will prevent The Cricketer receiving a telephone call at eleven p.m. from Scotland. The match has just finished in daylight, yet in the heart of Kent it is pitch black.

Communication today is far enough advanced for a hamlet in the Highlands to know how other rural communities exist over the border. And they do care. There are as I have already said, villages many miles apart who have become firm friends, looking forward to friendly fixtures. To the outsider it could be viewed as a David and Goliath affair, in terms of cricketing skill, who cares! Village cricket is much more than cricketing prowess, it also includes mutual respect and comradeship.

I mentioned cricketing prowess deliberately. There has I believe been the rare occasion when a professional foul has caused the offending team to be brought to book. In the context of the sheer size of the competition, these have been few and far between. Maybe there are villages who feel they have been wronged, but if they have they must report the facts to the organiser and the opposing team. The rules are quite clear, the organiser's decision is final, but an anonymous letter of disgruntlement gives nothing on which to act.

Muddying the waters in this obscure area is the question of league cricket. This has become a fact of life which cannot be escaped. It is a vehicle which provides a fixed, defined annual schedule of fixtures in which the team can compete and hopefully improve their game. Yes, it can be fiercely competitive in some quarters. Many villages consider the relaxed spirit of the village championships a welcome relief. The ideal image of the parson, publican and farmer sharing pads, bats and the communal cricket bag, are becoming a rarity. True some villages still play for fun, and only fun, but they are becoming fewer.

As for those sides who have joined league cricket, it does not necessarily follow they have become gladiators of the game. League cricket is progressive. There is a vast difference between a local group of teams competing for top of the table honours, and a county league not far short of minor county status. There appears to be a core who recognise or consider (call it what you like) that they have outgrown the competition and bowed out. So for the future I sense a breeze of change.

These championships have also brought other opportunities, not dreamed of twenty years ago, for teams and individuals. 1980 champions Marchwiel went to Holland, where they contested a match against the Excelsior Club of Rotterdam, captained by Clive Lloyd. The following year, St. Fagans played a Whitbread eleven, captained by Jim Parks (England and Sussex wicket keeper). 1982 saw a Sam Whitbread invitation eleven selected from players who had competed in the championships take on an Old England eleven. The following year a repeat of this highly successful event was washed out by torrential rain, which fell the whole day. Nevertheless they enjoyed conviviality, an excellent lunch and recalled memories well into the afternoon.

So, to the architect Ben Brocklehurst and all his staff, I hope

## A Crystal Ball with no Snowflakes

you succeed in retaining sponsorship for the future. Keep up the good work. Plum Warner would have been proud of your efforts and achievements on behalf of the grass roots of the game. Let us not forget past sponsors, who brought their own individual styles, particularly to the finals. In the lean years it cannot have been easy. But Freuchie's imagination brought memories of Whitbread days, when they played at Lord's. To Rothmans, let us hope the Cavaliers' return will be a long one. Perhaps that gypsy woman will say "I can see no end to it", and there won't be.

## REFLECTIONS

I have attempted to include something from the competition to interest everyone. The dedicated spectator who can recall more youthful times, when he could run from first slip to long off without laboured breath and aching limbs. Also the young lad who received his first bat (one he could call his very own), at the start of the season. Some day he hopes to replace dad in the first eleven. For now he will have to be content as manager of the scoreboard, until called to play for the youth team. But he will continue practising while he dreams and hopes.

Those tea ladies and the other essential backroom folk, without whose untiring work village cricket would not be village cricket. Nearing the close of their innings the home team may be cheered from the boundary, to score a dozen or so more runs. Excitement is mounting, everyone is watching the game. They do not see the tea ladies slip away to prepare the brew which is to accompany the sandwiches and cakes. Nor the groundsman who steals away to his shed, looking over his shoulder at the game in progress. Someone has to roll the pitch and touch up the white markings during the interval.

There are also those supporters who appear unique to this competition, and possibly The Cockspur Cup (the national town equivalent of the N.V.C.C.). Their knowledge of the game is limited, yet they still manage to obtain immense enjoyment and excitement, just the same as their more knowledgeable fellow spectators. Freuchie C.C. kindly sent me a video, along with all their other stories. At the presentation ceremony a cameraman focused on a strapping twenty year old Scot, waving a tartan banner. It all became too much for him and he unashamedly broke down in tears, why should he care, his face was a mess anyway, having discharged himself from hospital the day before, following a nose operation. He was determined to be there and

## A Crystal Ball with no Snowflakes

cheer his team on, even though he readily admitted knowing nothing about cricket, but vowed it was a great day for Freuchie.

Last but not least, the statistical fanatic. He is the spectator who can normally be relied upon to give anyone a comparison run rate at any time during the second innings. How many more does the opening bat need for his fifty?, or how near are our lads to the hundred partnership? Official scorers are busy people. Not only do they need to keep tabs on what is going on in the middle, but need to know who is out there. To those stalwart scribes on the boundary, I apologise for any error they may spot. It is difficult to judge, with three different local match reports, and three combinations of the score in the thirty-fourth over. It is just not possible to nip up the motorway and check the official score book of a village in, say the Lake District, to check the facts.

I have strived to mention as many village sides as possible. By the very nature of the book, and the size of the competition, many have had to go unrecorded, but not unnoticed. Their names dance from the list of first round fixtures year by year. No doubt they gain a mention in their local weekly newspaper. Many names are so unique they conjure up some thoughts in my imagination. Our cricketing cousins in other lands use the affectionate term "the eccentric Brits.". Some, no doubt prompted by seeing a village match advertised as Warkworth v Backworth Percy, or Stobswood Welfare v Wylham.

I would love to know how some villages came by their names, Scone Palace, Burn Yates, Youlgrave, Hooten Pagnell, the list is endless. When I saw teams like Cumberworth United I thought perhaps they once played football, and gave it up for cricket, retaining the name for posterity. I could go on, but I won't. Instead I'll leave the last words to a village, any village, it could be yours, mine or any of those charming names, some of which are not pronounceable..........

## A VILLAGE'S EYE VIEW.

Just think of Lord's as an island,
Surrounded by an uncharted sea.
The ships that sail on those waters,
are villages like you and me.

Each Spring we start on a voyage,
The route of which is unclear.
Of our destination we're certain,
It's Lord's at the end of the year.

The cargo is leather and willow,
But that's not all that's on board.
The crew is our white clad heroes,
Plus their exuberant hoard.

We engage in many a battle,
And some of us go to the wall.
Of one thing we can be certain,
The crew will give of their all.

As we get closer to harbour,
Our route becomes more clear.
The crew it continues to battle,
Whilst the hoard increases it's cheer.

And so the penultimate battle,
With Grace Gates harbour in sight.
'Tis time for just one last effort,
Willow wielded with all of it's might.

## A Crystal Ball with no Snowflakes

At last we are safe in the harbour,
Two villages at journeys end.
This one is not such a battle,
More time to make a new friend.

To the village that started its journey,
But never quite made it to shore.
I say to you keep on sailing,
The voyage is never a bore. .

To those who have lifted the trophy,
To their hoard's tumultuous cheers.
Spare a thought for those valiant helpers,
Who've toiled all over the years.

This is the end of my story,
And one I trust you've found fun.
To those of you wishing to enter,
I hope you enjoy a good run.

                                      D.P.D. April '93

# Appendices

**APPENDIX I**   THE CHAMPIONSHIP RECORDS 1972-1992

| | |
|---|---|
| THE BATSMEN | 197 |
| THE BOWLERS | 199 |
| THE ALL-ROUNDERS | 201 |
| THE FIELDERS | 202 |
| THE SIDES | 203 |
| MATCH AGGREGATES | 204 |
| WINNING MARGINS | 205 |
| PARTNERSHIPS | 206 |

**APPENDIX II**   THE FINALS

| | |
|---|---|
| ROLL OF HONOUR | 207 |
| INDIVIDUAL PERFORMANCES | 208 |
| TEAM PERFORMANCES | 208 |

**APPENDIX III**   THE OTHER COMPETITIONS   210

**APPENDIX IV**   SOURCES OF REFERENCE   212

INDEX   214

QUOTE: "THERE ARE THREE KINDS OF LIES; LIES, DAMN LIES & STATISTICS."
Attributed to Benjamin Disraeli (1st. Earl of Beaconsfield 1804–1881) in Mark Twain's Autobiography of 1924.

AS FAR AS THE AUTHOR CAN SAY THE STATISTICS THAT FOLLOW ARE NEITHER LIES NOR DAMN LIES.

NOTES:- In the early years there were merit tables of successful village teams. These were omitted eventually because they were not considered to be reliable, as records could not be accepted as totally comprehensive. Troon were the top team for several years. If the tables were to be introduced again, it is thought St. Fagans would be favourites to go top, however neither team remain in the competition.

Page 000 is the authors view on merit order of all-rounders and not as shown in the annuals. Priority is given to the highest score from the bat in preference to bowling performance. The qualification of 50 runs and 5 wickets still stands. Where one player has an identical score and bowling analysis to another, they are placed in the table in date order, but share the same position.

# Appendix I

## CHAMPIONSHIP RECORDS

### THE BATSMEN

ALAN WADE 239 NOT OUT FOR GOLDSITHNEY AGAINST RUAN & PHILLEIGH MAY 3rd 1992.

| | | |
|---|---|---|
| A.SHORTER 221* | HIMLEY | 1988 |
| M.HOPKINS 214 | COOKLEY | 1978 |
| J.CUMMINGS 211* | CLEATOR | 1990 |
| T.BOTTING 206 | BALCOMBE | 1977 |
| T.CANNON 203* | COKENACH | 1977 |
| R.NEEDHAM 201* | ST.FAGANS | 1985 |

| | | | | | | |
|---|---|---|---|---|---|---|
| 189* | T. HARRISON | NASSINGTON | 1989 | 156 N. MEDD | IGHTHAM | 1986 |
| 188* | D. BARKER | HOUGHTON | 1982 | 156 R. SMITH | PLUMTREE | 1992 |
| 186 | A. TOMSON | SUTTON | 1973 | 155 W. MURDOCH | BUCKMINSTER | 1986 |
| 185* | R. MORRELL | WINSLEY | 1981 | 153* R. JAMES | DREFACH | 1990 |
| 179* | D. STITSON jnr. | HORNDON ON THE HILL | 1990 | 153 D. FAIRBAIRN | GREAT PRESTON | 1979 |
| 179 | D. LAWSON | BLUNHAM | 1974 | 153 S. POLLARD | COLEMANS HATCH | 1988 |
| 178* | J. BLAGDEN | TREETON WELFARE | 1989 | 151* S. WILLIAMS | BLEDLOW | 1979 |
| 173* | A. SELDON | DELABOLE | 1978 | 151* J. GRIEVESON | LULLINGTON PARK | 1992 |
| 172 | K. HILL | BLYTH | 1985 | 151* S. WILLIAMS | BLEDLOW | 1979 |
| 167* | D. HINDLE | READ | 1976 | 150* R. THOMAS | TONDU | 1989 |
| 166* | P. COLLIER | HAROME | 1991 | 150* D. PULLEN | GLYNDE & BEDDINGHAM | 1991 |
| 165* | N. YOUNG | BODICOTE | 1990 | 150 A. GUYVER | BUTLEIGH | 1991 |
| 164* | C. LONGBOTTOM | BARKISLAND | 1989 | 149 A. HUDSON | BRAMSHALL | 1987 |
| 162 | J. CAPON | ROSEMARKET | 1974 | 148* M. RICHARDSON | DELPH & DOBCROSS | 1981 |
| 161* | A. BOWES | BARDSEY | 1990 | 148* J. RAWSON | TONG PARK | 1991 |
| 161 | P. MAY | WERRINGTON | 1989 | 148 S. CARPENTER | WEDEN | 1988 |
| 158* | J. LIGHTFOOT | COPLE | 1984 | 147* P. FLYNN | LONG HANBOROUGH | 1984 |
| 158 | D. DIXON | SWARKESTONE | 1986 | 147* R. FLOREY | OXFORD DOWNS | 1982 |
| 158 | T. PITMAN | BARRINGTON | 1987 | 147* C. METCALFE | POYNINGS | 1991 |
| 157* | R. SHIRLEY | GREAT & LITTLE CHEW | 1982 | 147 W. SCOTT | MEIGLE | 1982 |
| 157* | S. HOYES | SPARSHOT | 1991 | 147 A. PHILLIPS | RUSHTON | 1989 |

| | | | | | | | |
|---|---|---|---|---|---|---|---|
| 146* K. SUTCLIFFE | LONGPARISH | 1990 | 142 A. PRIOR | ROWLEDGE | 1992 |
| 146 M. THURLOW | POTTERNE | 1992 | 141* P. TESKEY | FECKENHAM | 1987 |
| 145 M. FOOTE | LYDFORD | 1986 | 141* R. HANSON | BOCONNOC | 1982 |
| 145 S. WILLIAMS | BLEDLOW | 1991 | 141 T. BOTTING | BALCOMBE | 1975 |
| 144* K. HINKLEY | ALVANLEY | 1972 | 141 J. TURNER | GOATACRE | 1986 |
| 144* P. TUGWELL | BURRIDGE | 1990 | 140* A. PENGELLY | ST. BURYAN | 1992 |
| 144 R. FLOYD | BLEDLOW | 1985 | 140* K. SUTCLIFFE | LONGPARISH | 1992 |
| 143* R. MOULDING | TOFT | 1986 | 140 K. ILES | GOATACRE | 1983 |
| 143 C. MEGONE | ESCRICK PARK | 1990 | 140 W. SLACK | FRIETH | 1974 |

No less than 52 other batsmen have scored 130 or more in the first 21 years of the competition.

7 Centuries K. Iles (Goatacre)
5 Centuries R. Phillips (Fillongley)
4 Centuries B. Carter (Troon), D. Luff (Longparish), R. Mc.Queen (Aston Rowant), T. Croxton (Great Braxted), and C. Yates (Rowledge).
3 Centuries T. Botting (Balcombe), D. Gallagher (Fenns Bank) D. Stitson jnr. (Horndon on the Hill), S. Williams (Bledlow), and R. Needham (St. Fagans).

NOTE:- These records may have been superceeded since these statistics were compiled. Also some years records of century makers were not fully recorded. If any reader is aware of a player having scored three or more centuries in the competition, the publisher would like to hear from them.

The chairman of The Cricketer is anxious to know of any batsman over the age of sixty who has scored an innings at least equal to his age.

*Appendix 1*

# THE BOWLERS

## QUALIFICATION: 8 OR MORE WICKETS IN AN INNINGS.

STEVE JAMES 9 WICKETS FOR 7 RUNS FOR PLUMTREE AGAINST LEAKE & LEVERTON ON JUNE 24TH. 1990.

| | | | |
|---|---|---|---|
| J. DUNLOP | 9 FOR 14 | GOLDSITHNEY | 1979 |
| I. ENTERS | 9 FOR 14 | ALFRISTON | 1977 |
| J. BOBBINS | 9 FOR 15 | MULBARTON | 1972 |
| D. FENTON | 9 FOR 15 | SOUTH WEALD | 1992 |
| J. WESTGARTH | 9 FOR 17 | CLARA VALE | 1986 |
| G. HAMILTON | 9 FOR 34 | HORSPATH | 1984 |

| | | | | | | | |
|---|---|---|---|---|---|---|---|
| 8-1 | S. BROWN | RUSHTON | 1979 | 8-16 | M. ROBINSON | CUMBERWORTH | 1991 |
| 8-2 | N. HARDING | TEMPLE CLOUD | 1973 | 8-17 | A. GWYVER | BUTLEIGH | 1972 |
| 8-2 | I. YOUNG | BURES | 1972 | 8-17 | B. GRAY | TEMPLE CLOUD | 1972 |
| 8-4 | A. HUDSON | BITTESWELL | 1979 | 8-17 | D. WILLIAMS | OLD NETHERSEAL | 1984 |
| 8-5 | R. ARNOLD | TERRINGTON ST. CL.* | 1978 | 8-18 | A. WISHART | CLEATOR | 1974 |
| 8-5 | I. BAILEY | GRETTON | 1984 | 8-18 | R. GIBSON | CLOUGHTON | 1984 |
| 8-5 | A. WILTON | FENITON | 1986 | 8-19 | A. JONES | HATHERLEIGH | 1986 |
| 8-6 | C. MERRY | AUDLEY END | 1986 | 8-20 | K. BAKER | STAPLETON | 1980 |
| 8-6 | E. LANGFORD | CATTISTOCK | 1980 | 8-20 | A. PINNEY | BENHALL | 1972 |
| 8-7 | A. GARSTANG | WITHNELL FOLD | 1975 | 8-22 | R. FENWICK | BACKWORTH PERCY | 1976 |
| 8-7 | J. REYNOLDS | BRADFIELD | 1977 | 8-22 | D. GIBSON | YETHOLME | 1987 |
| 8-12 | A. NICHOLSON | MELPASH | 1975 | 8-23 | P. BEVAN | OVERTON | 1979 |
| 8-13 | A. BAKER | FOLKTON & FLICKTON | 1972 | 8-25 | B. FACER | KIMBOLTON | 1975 |
| 8-13 | R. JONES | BEAMINSTER | 1979 | 8-25 | R. THOMPSON | STAXTON | 1983 |
| 8-13 | M. WOODWARD | COOKLEY | 1982 | 8-30 | T. WOODHOUSE | HALLBOWER | 1980 |
| 8-15 | P. BROWN | FORDHAM | 1981 | 8-32 | A. GODMAN | ALVANLEY | 1983 |
| 8-16 | J. PATEL | TINTWHISTLE | 1985 | 8-33 | K. MOORE | WERRINGTON | 1991 |
| 8-16 | L. SMITH | CUCKNEY | 1986 | | | | |

NOTE:-* Refers to the village of TERRINGTON ST. CLEMENTS.

## FOUR WICKETS IN FOUR BALLS

| | | |
|---|---|---|
| P. BENHAM | HEMPSTEAD | 1976 |
| C. COCKERTON | TUDDENHAM | 1986 |
| H. DICKENS | ROBOROUGH | 1974 |
| G. HEARTON | LANGTON HERRING | 1987 |
| L. Mac.FARLANE | ABTHORPE | 1978 |
| D. TUSON | WOODHOUSE | 1975 |
| P. WEBB | EARLS COLNE | 1976 |

THERE HAVE BEEN MORE THAN 150 HAT TRICKS RECORDED IN THE HISTORY OF THE COMPETITION. ONLY ONE PLAYER HAS TWO TO HIS NAME. J. LAWTON OF WOORE ACHIEVED HIS FIRST IN 1981 AND SECOND IN 1982.

ANOTHER NOTABLE ACHIEVEMENT IS THE BOWLING OF D. GORDON OF EDENHILL IN 1989 WITH THE FIGURES OF 9 OVERS 8 MAIDENS 1 WICKET FOR 1 RUN.

N. BOWDEN OF FAILAND & PORTBURY HOLDS THE DISTINCTION OF HAVING TAKEN FOUR WCKETS IN FIVE BALLS.

NOTE:- If there are any records which a reader considers should be included in the above. The Cricketer would like to hear from them in order that the records can be amended accordingly.

# Appendix 1

## THE ALL-ROUNDERS

| | | | | |
|---|---|---|---|---|
| 1. T.BOTTING | 128* | & 7-15 | BALCOMBE | 1975 |
| 2. D.EDWARDS | 117 | & 5-15 | BENENDEN | 1972 |
| 3. S.NIGHT | 115* | & 5-6 | HORSEMONDEN | 1973 |
| 4. C.KNIGHTLY | 113* | & 5-50 | DUMBLETON | 1992 |
| 5. R.PITCHER | 106* | & 6-43 | NETTLEBED | 1976 |
| 6. R.BARBER | 105 | & 5-29 | HILTON | 1979 |
| 7. P.CONNOLY | 97 | & 6-22 | CHASLY/CORBT # | 1986 |
| 8. C.FOULDS | 97* | & 5-19 | STONYHURST | 1992 |
| 9. R.HARWOOD | 96* | & 5-24 | GREAT PRESTON | 1980 |
| 10. M.EMBURY | 93 | & 7-15 | CANON FROME | 1980 |
| 11. A.FREEMAN | 93 | & 6-35 | SOUTH NUFFIELD | 1987 |
| 12. C.BOULTER | 91* | & 5-37 | DUNSTALL | 1990 |
| 13. K.JONES | 90 | & 5-46 | NEWS'D COL'RY | 1982 |
| K.ILES | 90 | & 5-46 | GOATACRE | 1988 |
| 15. W.COPPLESTON | 88 | & 5-13 | ABINGER | 1978 |
| 16. I.BROOKBANK | 83* | & 5-12 | WOLVESTON | 1991 |
| 17. R.BULLOCH | 83* | & 5-38 | BARRINGTON | 1978 |
| 18. P.DAVIES | 82* | & 6-13 | HOCKLEY HEATH | 1980 |
| 19. M.ADAMS | 80* | & 5-23 | WOODVILLE | 1984 |
| 20. D.RUTT | 80 | & 5-23 | BLEDLOW | 1985 |
| 21. C.RADFORD | 79* | & 6-34 | FECKENHAM | 1991 |
| 22. S.LORD | 78 | & 5-38 | STEWARDS END | 1990 |
| 23. M.LEEVES | 77* | & 5-9 | FLETCHING | 1990 |
| 24. N.WHITEHEAD | 77 | & 5-16 | COTTERED | 1990 |
| 25. B.JACKSON | 77 | & 5-27 | SESSAY | 1977 |
| 26. G.GARNER | 73 | & 5-17 | WOODHOUSES | 1990 |
| 27. S.JAMES | 72 | & 9-7 | PLUMTREE | 1990 |
| 28. E.Mc.CRAY | 72 | & 5-6 | TOFT | 1988 |
| 29. R.RICHARDSON | 71* | & 6-27 | KINGTON | 1972 |
| 30. D.COWAN | 71* | & 5-31 | FREUCHIE | 1992 |
| 31. S.TALLENTIRE | 70* | & 5-1 | LANDS | 1983 |
| 32. C.SHREEVE | 69 | & 6-22 | BRADFIELD | 1975 |
| 33. E.LANGFORD | 67 | & 5-29 | CATTISTOCK | 1980 |
| 34. A.MOGDEN | 66 | & 5-25 | FILLISGH | 1984 |
| 35. J.SENWICK | 66 | & 5-34 | OUTWOOD | 1982 |
| 36. J.LODGE | 65* | & 6-22 | RICKLING | 1980 |
| 37. W.TAYLOR | 65 | & 6-24 | NASSINGTON | 1988 |
| 38. C.BAKER | 64* | & 5-23 | LEIGH | 1977 |
| 39. J.EVANS | 63 | & 6-31 | CANON FROME | 1978 |
| 40. M.FOWLER | 63 | & 6-61 | WILBY | 1978 |
| 41. G.FOGG | 63 | & 5-18 | RUFFORD | 1987 |
| 42. N.LAMOUR | 62 | & 5-33 | ESCRICK PARK | 1990 |
| 43. R.HIBBERD | 62 | & 5-42 | SHIPTON | 1972 |
| 44. D.CHAPMAN | 61 | & 6-30 | MARSHAM | 1979 |
| 45. D.GALLAGHER | 61 | & 5-15 | FENNS BANK | 1972 |
| 46. G.CARR | 61 | & 5-32 | CHECKLEY | 1986 |
| 47. K.KITCHEN | 60 | & 6-16 | TROON | 1983 |
| 48. G.PEARCE | 60 | & 5-15 | SHORTON | 1981 |
| 49. P.BROWN | 60 | & 5-21 | FORDHAM | 1984 |
| 50. P.ORCHARD | 60 | & 5-47 | WINSLEY | 1987 |
| 51. K.JONES | 59 | & 5-32 | WALTON | 1975 |

| | | | | | |
|---|---|---|---|---|---|
| 52. | S.BURNLEY | 58 | & 5-21 | ONNELEY | 1977 |
| | P.HULL | 58 | & 5-21 | COPLE | 1988 |
| 54. | N.HOWARD | 57 | & 5-20 | BUCKMINSTER | 1984 |
| 55. | T.DREYER | 57 | & 5-22 | BROMARSUND | 1980 |
| 56. | D.DANIELS | 57 | & 5-39 | HARTING | 1972 |
| 57. | J.HAYNES | 55 | & 5-15 | PLUMTREE | 1991 |
| 58. | J.OSMOND | 55 | & 5-21 | BARCOMBE | 1982 |
| 59. | J.WARNE | 55 | & 5-26 | GMPND. ROAD # | 1982 |
| 60. | J.CORCORAN | 54 | & 6-9 | GOLDSBORUOGH | 1990 |
| 61. | R.PICKFORD | 54* | & 6-22 | HORSPATH | 1984 |
| 62. | W.TAYLOR | 54 | & 5-29 | NASSINGTON | 1988 |
| 63. | E.Mc.CRAY | 53 | & 6-8 | TOFT | 1988 |
| 64. | P.LULOW | 53 | & 5-10 | DINTON | 1991 |
| 65. | S.MURRAY | 53 | & 5-18 | ELVASTON | 1991 |
| 66. | C.RASLEIGH | 52 | & 5-22 | TROON | 1980 |
| 67. | D.HUGHES | 52 | & 5-25 | RODE PARK | 1983 |
| 68. | S.SKINGLEY | 52 | & 5-36 | AUDLEY END | 1986 |
| 69. | T.TALBOD | 51 | & 7-3 | CHASLY/CORBT # | 1973 |
| 70. | R.RIDGEWAY | 51 | & 5-2 | HURLEY | 1989 |
| 71. | R.LOWE | 51 | & 5-13 | OXFORD DOWNS | 1985 |
| 72. | J.NEWPORT | 51 | & 5-34 | BOOKER | 1977 |
| 73. | W.KNIGHT | 50 | & 6-19 | LINDAL MOOR | 1986 |
| | D.WILLIAMS | 50 | & 6-19 | MOORHOLM | 1986 |
| 75. | M.BURFORD | 50 | & 5-21 | WITCOMB | 1990 |
| | J.HOWELL | 50 | & 5-21 | FOCHABERS | 1990 |
| 77. | T.CLACEY | 50 | & 5-23 | FARLEY HILL | 1992 |

NOTES:- # Positions 7 & 69 refers to the village of CHADDESLEY CORBETT, position 13 refers to the village of NEWSTEAD COLLIERY and position 59 refers to thevillage of GRAMPOUND ROAD.

## THE FIELDERS
## THE WICKET-KEEPERS

| | | | |
|---|---|---|---|
| T.GOUGH | PINKNEY GREEN | 3CT. & 4ST. | 1974 |
| R.CHATTERTON | NASSINGTON | 7CT.   – | 1990 |
| M.ROBERTS | ARMITAGE BRIDGE | 6CT. & 1ST. | 1992 |
| P.ARNOLD | FORDHAM | 2CT. & 4ST. | 1979 |
| J.CARTER | SYREHAM | 6CT.   – | 1975 |
| A.DEW | GOWERTON | 6CT.   – | 1973 |
| A.FAIRBROTHER | OLD NETHERSEAL | 1CT. & 5ST. | 1976 |
| G.HARTLEY | TOLLESBURY | 1CT. & 5ST. | 1974 |
| H.HAYES | CHARLESWORTH | 6CT.   – | 1978 |
| J.NEWPORT | BOOKER | 5CT. & 1ST. | 1976 |
| T.TIDEY | REED | 4CT. & 2ST. | 1988 |
| S.VOSS | EAST LULWORTH | 6CT.   – | 1987 |

NOTES:- There have been many recordings of a wicket-keeper achieving five dismissals in an innings.
Also worthy of note is J.Carters six dismissals for Syreham in 1975-a special achievement as he had never kept wicket before.

N. SOMERTON OF HATHERSAGE IS THE ONLY FIELDER TO HAVE HELD SIX CATCHES IN AN INNINGS, WHICH HE ACHIEVED IN 1989. THREE WERE CAUGHT & BOWLED, HE FINISHED WITH FIGURES OF 4 FOR 14. S.KNAIRA OF BOXTED TOOK FIVE CATCHES AND SCORED 73 IN A MATCH. WHILE M.BELLING OF GORRAN AND J.HAIG OF BROMARSUND EACH TOOK FOUR CATCHES IN AN INNINGS.

*Appendix 1*

## THE SIDES HIGHEST SCORES
### QUALIFICATION 300 OR MORE.

| | | | | | | |
|---|---|---|---|---|---|---|
| 440-5 BARKISLAND | v OLD SHARLSTON | 1989 | 314-7 PONTBLYDDYN | v HAWK GREEN | 1992 |
| 419-6 CANON FROME | v MUCH MARKLE | 1980 | 314-8 SOUTH MILFORD | v HUBY | 1984 |
| 415-5 PLUMTREE | v LEAKE & LEVERTON | 1991 | 312-3 TONG PARK | v CROSS ROADS | 1991 |
| 407-4 ESCRICK PARK | v WIGHALL PARK | 1990 | 311-7 PLUMTREE | v LEAKE & LEVERTON | 1990 |
| 404-1 GOLDSITHNEY | v RUAN & PHILLEIGH | 1992 | 310-1 LULLINGTON PARK | v CLIFTON | 1992 |
| 376-7 LYDFORD | v ASH | 1990 | 310-4 KINGTON | v BADSEY | 1992 |
| 346-4 POTTERNE | v EAST LULWORTH | 1992 | 310-4 TREETON WELFARE | v WADWORTH | 1989 |
| 343-0 HIMLEY | v OVERTON ON DEE | 1988 | 310-6 LUCTONIANS | v PRESTEIGNE | 1982 |
| 339-4 KILDALE | v CARLTON & FACEBY | 1980 | 310-6 GOATACRE | v REDLYNCH | 1990 |
| 339-7 BUTLEIGH | v WEARE | 1989 | 309-5 SONNING | v DONNINGTON | 1987 |
| 335-4 BARDSEY | v CROSSROADS | 1990 | 309-5 HAVERING/BOWER* | v RICKLING | 1976 |
| 332-7 CHEW MAGNA | v FITZHEAD | 1991 | 307-4 ST.FAGANS | v WENVOE | 1985 |
| 332-9 LYDFORD | v FITZHEAD | 1986 | 306-5 BARKISLAND | v CUMBERWORTH | 1988 |
| 331-6 CANON FROME | v FLYFORD FLAVELL | 1978 | 305-2 BELFORD | v BELTON | 1976 |
| 330-1 CLEATOR | v THRELKELD | 1990 | 304-3 POYNINGS | v HANDCROSS | 1991 |
| 328-4 FECKENHAM | v WARREN | 1986 | 304-4 ASTON ROWANT | v DORCHESTER | .1972 |
| 326-1 WERRINGTON | v BOCONNOC | 1989 | 304-4 LANGLEY | v AUDLEY END | 1985 |
| 325-3 CROSTON | v NEWBURGH | 1990 | 304-8 COOKLEY | v HEWELL | 1979 |
| 321-5 FROCESTER | v TIDDENHAM | 1982 | 303-5 TEMPLE CLOUD | v DULVERTON | 1972 |
| 319-5 BLEDLOW | v BRADENHAM | 1991 | 302-2 ST.BURYAN | v BUTLEIGH | 1992 |
| 319-7 ADDINGHAM | v WOOLLEY | 1988 | 301-2 THORPE ARNOLD | v BELTON | 1981 |
| 318-5 SUTTON-on-the-HILL | v HILTON | 1973 | 300-3 BUTLEIGH | v TINTINHALL | 1991 |
| 318-6 COOKLEY | v WOOLHOPE | 1978 | 300-4 BEDALE | v MIDDLETON TYAS | 1992 |
| 317-4 ROWLEDGE | v DONNINGTON | 1992 | 300-5 FAILAND & P'TBURY† | v WEARE | 1990 |
| 314-2 PLUMTREE | v STRAGGLERS | 1992 | 300-8 TUDDENHAM | v GREAT LEIGH | 1991 |

NOTE:- Forty-six further teams have scored 280 or more in the competition.
    * is the village of Havering-atte-Bower.   † is Failand & Portbury

## THE SIDES LOWEST SCORES
### QUALIFICATION 15 RUNS OR LESS

| | | | | | | |
|---|---|---|---|---|---|---|
| 6 MARSTON ST LAW[1] | v ABTHORPE | 1978 | 12 TIDDENHAM | v WOODCHESTER | 1981 |
| 7 LITTLE EATON | v QUARNDON | 1976 | 13 FLECKNOW | v NEWBOLD | 1983 |
| 8 FARTHINGHOE | v RUSHTON | 1978 | 13 EST HOATHLY | v BOLNEY | 1976 |
| 8 DONNINGTON | v TETNEY | 1991 | 13 WARSLOW | v RODE PARK | 1986 |
| 9 BELFORD | v BOTTESFORD | 1980 | 13 WARREN | v ALVELY | 1985 |
| 10 FARTHINGHOE | v BUGBROOKE | 1972 | 14 ALBOURNE CMN[3] | v POYNINGS | 1975 |
| 10 CAUNTON | v NORTH WHEATLEY | 1974 | 14 WESTMILL | v LANGLEBURY | 1981 |
| 10 BILLESDEN | v CROPSTON | 1979 | 14 EAST LULWORTH | v CATTISTOCK | 1990 |
| 10 WHITWELL | v ESSENDEN | 1983 | 15 FLEUR DE LYS | v CHIPPING W.[4] | 1975 |
| 10 HALWILL | v FENITON | 1986 | 15 HIGHAM | v BITTESWELL | 1978 |
| 10 BURTON | v HALE | 1990 | 15 WEELEY | v STOCK | 1976 |
| 11 HADDENHAM | v TERRINGTON st. cl[2] | 1972 | 15 BOLTON PERCY | v STILLINGTON | 1986 |
| 11 WEELEY | v ROXWELL | 1990 | 15 CHIPPING | v GT.ECCLESTONE | 1988 |
| 12 STANSFIELD | v TUDDENHAM | 1986 | 15 LEAKE & LEVERTON | v PLUMTREE | 1990 |
| 12 WICK & DISTRICT | v ROSEMARKET | 1972 | | | |

* NOTE ABBREVIATIONS:- 1. MARSTON ST.LAWRENCE (6) 1978  2. TERRINGTON ST.CLEMENTS (11) 1972.
    3. ALBOURNE & SAYERS COMMON (14) 1975. 4. CHIPPING WALDEN (15) 1975.

203

# A Village at Lord's

## MATCH AGGREGATES.
### QUALIFICATIONS 470 OR MORE.

| | | | | |
|---|---|---|---|---|
| 570 | BARKISLAND 440-5 | OLD SHARLESTON 130 | | '89 |
| 564 | FECKENHAM 285-7 | BRAMSHALL 279-5 | | '87 |
| 550 | ASTON ROWANT 277-4 | OXFORD DOWNS 273-3 | | '83 |
| 544 | ESCRICK PARK 407-5 | WIGHALL PARK 137-9 | | '90 |
| 542 | DELPH & DOBCROSS 271-2 | GREENMOUNT 271-8 | | '81 |
| 526 | CHEW MAGNA 332-7 | FITZHEAD 194 | | '91 |
| 525 | HESLERTON 266-5 | GOLDSBOROUGH 259-3 | | '88 |
| 524 | GOATACRE 265-6 | OXFORD DOWNS 259-8 | | '88* |
| 521 | BARKISLAND 271-9 | THORNTON 250 | | '91 |
| 520 | WOODHOUSES 260-7 | READ 260 | | '75 |
| 517 | KIRKBY 259-7 | PENDLEFOREST 258-3 | | '91 |
| 513 | WERRINGTON 326-1 | BOCONNOC 187-7 | | '89 |
| 513 | PLUMTREE 415-5 | LEAKE & LEVERTON 98 | | '91 |
| 512 | HIMLEY 343-0 | OVERTON ON DEE 169-9 | | '88 |
| 512 | DUNSTALL 258-4 | TREETON WELFARE 254 | | '90 |
| 507 | BARKISLAND 289-6 | BLACKLEY 218-5 | | '92 |
| 507 | ST.BURYAN 303-2 | BUTLEIGH 205 | | '92 |
| 498 | SONNING 309-5 | DONNINGTON 189-6 | | '87 |
| 498 | BUTLEIGH 339-7 | WEARE 159 | | '89 |
| 498 | OMBERSLEY 273-4 | BADSEY 25-7 | | '92 |
| 496 | METHLEY 268-6 | THORNTON 228 | | '88 |
| 495 | KILDALE 339-4 | CARLTON & FACEBY 156 | | '80 |
| 495 | TREETON WELFARE 310-4 | WADWORTH 185-9 | | '89 |
| 494 | CLEATOR 285-3 | BURNSIDE 209-9 | | '80 |
| 490 | GOATACRE 262 | FROCESTER 228 | | '90 |
| 489 | COALPIT HEATH 246-8 | BARRINGTON 243-7 | | '87 |
| 488 | WEST ISLEY 246-7 | MORETON 242-9 | | '89 |
| 485 | ROXWELL 244-8 | GREAT BURSTEAD 241 | | '85 |
| 484 | BUCKMINSTER 262-4 | KINETON 222 | | '88 |
| 484 | BEDALE 300-4 | MIDDLETON TYAS 184-9 | | '82 |
| 484 | THORPE ARNOLD 269-7 | TAMWORTH IN ARDEN 215-5 | | '92 |
| 484 | WINTERSLOW 251-3 | SPYE PARK 233-6 | | '92 |
| 483 | HOMDON ON THE HILL 281-8 | GREAT WALTHAM 227-8 | | '89 |
| 479 | WORFIELD 278-7 | FENNS BANK 201-8 | | '79 |
| 479 | HOMDON ON THE HILL 281-8 | ROXWELL 198-7 | | '89 |
| 479 | HOMDON ON THE HILL 279-5 | ROXWELL 200 | | '90 |
| 478 | SUTTON ON THE HILL 318-5 | HILTON 160 | | '73 |
| 477 | BUCKMINSTER 243-6 | FULBECK 234 | | '74 |
| 476 | CANON FROME 419-6 | MUCH MARKLE 57 | | '80 |
| 475 | HOLMEWOOD & HEATH 249-5 | CROMWOOD MEADOWS 226-7 | | '86 |
| 472 | CHADDESLEY CORBETT 239-8 | BURGHILL & TIDDINGTON 233-9 | | '87 |
| 472 | HAROME 294-0 | FOLLIFOOT 178-3 | | '92 |
| 471 | HORSPATH 246-5 | BLETCHINGTON 225-8 | | '90 |
| 471 | NORTH PERROTT 237-7 | KILVE 234-4 | | '91 |
| 470 | ROCHE 287-1 | STOKE CLIMSLAND 183-8 | | '84 |

\* The match aggregate of 524 between Goatacre & Oxford Downs was scored off a reduced match of 33 overs a side.

## Appendix 1

## WINNING MARGINS
### QUALIFICATION 220 RUNS OR MORE

| | | |
|---|---|---|
| 362 CANNON FROME 419-6 | bt. MUCH MARKLE 57 | '80 |
| 352 GOLDSITHNEY 404-1 | bt. RUAN & PHILLEIGH 52 | '92 |
| 335 LYDFORD 376-7 | bt. ASH 41 | '90 |
| 317 PLUMTREE 415-5 | bt. LEAKE & LEVERTON 98 | '91 |
| 310 BARKISLAND 440-5 | bt. OLD SHARLSTON 130 | '89 |
| 305 CANON FROME 331-6 | bt. FLYFORD FLAVELL 26 | '78 |
| 295 PLUMTREE 311-7 | bt. LEAKE & LEVERTON 15 | '90 |
| 289 CLEATOR 330-1 | bt. THRELKELD 41 | '90 |
| 283 ADDINGHAM 319-7 | bt. WOOLEY 36 | '88 |
| 283 POTTERNE 346-4 | bt. EAST LULWORTH 63 | '92 |
| 281 FROCESTER 263-3 | bt. TIDDENHAM 30 | '82 |
| 278 ROXWELL 289-2 | bt. WEELEY 11 | '80 |
| 277 THORPE ARNOLD 301-2 | bt. BELTON 24 | '81 |
| 276 BOTTOSFORD 285-4 | bt. BELTON 9 | '80 |
| 274 BELFORD 305-2 | bt. BELTON 31 | '76 |
| 274 SARISBURY ATHLETIC 294-4 | bt. HARTING 20 | '73 |
| 270 ESCRICK PARK 407-4 | bt. WIGHALL PARK 137-9 | '90 |
| 267 SOUTH MILFORD 314-8 | bt. HUBY 47 | '84 |
| 261 COOKLEY 318-6 | bt. WOOLHOPE 57 | '78 |
| 260 FECKENHAM 328-4 | bt. WARREN 68 | '86 |
| 260 COOKLEY 304-8 | bt. HEWELL 44 | '79 |
| 249 BRILL 299-6 | bt. BRADENHAM 50 | '89 |
| 244 BOMARSUND 266-3 | bt. MITFORD 22 | '80 |
| 242 OXENHOPE 281-5 | bt. HORBURY BRIDGE 39 | '81 |
| 242 PONTYBLYDDYN 300-6 | bt. HAWK GREEN 72 | '92 |
| 239 FAILAND & PORTBURY 300-6 | bt. WEARE 61 | '90 |
| 238 ARDINGLY 271-5 | bt. ASHURST 33 | '90 |
| 230 NASSINGTON 272-2 | bt. PYTCHLEY 42 | '85 |
| 227 REED 256-6 | bt. ELSENHAM 29 | '92 |
| 226 ASTON ROWANT 304-4 | bt. DORCHESTER 78 | '72 |
| 225 HAROME 293-2 | bt. MIDDLEHAM 68 | '91 |
| 224 CROSTON 325-3 | bt. NEWBURGH 101 | '90 |
| 223 COWPEN BEWLAY 291-8 | bt. BURNT YATES 65 | '73 |
| 220 OUTWOOD 288-6 | bt. SHAMLEY GREEN 68 | '84 |

## PARTNERSHIPS

### QUALIFICATIONS 200 RUNS OR OVER

| | | | | |
|---|---|---|---|---|
| 373* | FOR 1ST. | I.KITCHEN 118 | A.WADE 239* | GOLDSITHEY | 1992 |
| 343* | FOR 1ST. | A.SHORTER 221* | S.WALKER 109* | HIMLEY | 1988 |
| 310 | FOR 1ST. | P.MAY 161 | A.SHOPLAND 128* | WERRINGTON | 1989 |
| 304* | FOR 2ND. | P.GOUGH 135* | J.GRIEVSON 151* | LULLINGTON PK. | 1992 |
| 294* | FOR 1ST. | G.STRICKLAND 136* | D.GREENLAY 135* | HAROME | 1992 |
| 288 | FOR 2ND. | J.CUMMINGS 211* | M.GREEN 96 | CLEATOR | 1990 |
| 274 | FOR 2ND. | C.LIBBY 132* | D.HOLLYOAK 130 | ROCHE | 1984 |
| 270* | FOR 1ST. | D.PULLEN 150* | M.SUTTON 112* | GLYNDE | 1991 |
| 268 | FOR 3RD. | A.KIDD 125 | P.DIBB 124* | WARKWORTH | 1988 |
| 255 | FOR 1ST. | I.SIM 135 | S.TIFFIN 133* | BELFORD | 1976 |
| 253 | FOR 1ST. | K.SUTCLIFFE 146* | J.HEAGREN 82 | LONGPARISH | 1990 |
| 243 | FOR 1ST. | C.DAVIS 132 | D.PRICE 114 | LUCTONIANS | 1982 |
| 240 | FOR 2ND. | P.STIBLEY 96 | C.MEGONE 143 | ESCRICK PARK | 1990 |
| 240 | FOR 3RD. | T.JONES 120 | R.PITCHER 106* | NETTLEBED | 1976 |
| 233* | FOR 3RD. | R.PHILLIPS 119* | A.WOOD 118* | FILLONGLEY | 1979 |
| 231 | FOR 2ND. | C.BUXTON 130 | G.SPAWTON 126 | THORPE ARNOLD | 1981 |
| 227 | FOR 2ND. | B.WILLIAMS 118 | A.PENGELLY 140* | ST. BURYAN | 1992 |
| 225 | FOR 1ST. | N.TAYLOR 123 | R.SHIRLEY 91 | GREAT & LITTLE TEW | 1985 |
| 225 | FOR 1ST. | K.POLLARD 128* | S.ENLY 101 | FULBECK | 1990 |
| 220 | FOR 1ST. | G.HANCOCK 122 | B.KINGSLEY 116 | LANGLEY | 1982 |
| 219 | FOR 1ST. | N.PARRISH 116* | R.CLARKE 82 | ROXWELL | 1980 |
| 217 | FOR 2ND. | S.LOCKE 137 | S.EMM 80* | STEEPLE LANGFORD | 1989 |
| 216 | FOR 1ST. | M.RAYNE 139* | M.LANFIELD 69 | MIDDLETON TYAS | 1983 |
| 216* | FOR 1ST. | T.RICHINGS 131* | W.GUNYON 80* | SPARSHOT | 1990 |
| 215 | FOR 2ND. | R.FLYNN 147* | R.BUSBY 93 | LONG HARBOROUGH | 1984 |
| 214 | FOR 1ST. | D.GREEN 136 | C.LONGBOTTOM 164* | BARKISLAND | 1989 |
| 214 | FOR 1ST. | A.BAIRD 119 | R.BROWN 81* | GLENDELVINE | 1991 |
| 213 | FOR 2ND. | M.RICHARDSON 143* | R.ANCHOR 104 | DELPH & DOBCROSS | 1981 |
| 209 | FOR 1ST. | J.IRVINE 105* | S.POULTER 101 | MAINSFORTH | 1985 |
| 209 | FOR 1ST. | A.HUDSON 149 | A.HALL 67 | BRAMHALL | 1987 |
| 208* | FOR 2ND. | T.HARRISON 189* | W.TAYLOR 65* | NASSINGTON | 1988 |
| 205 | FOR 1ST. | B.JACKSON 120* | D.LAWSON 72 | ALNE | 1992 |
| 204 | FOR 1ST. | R.SMITH 156 | R.BRYANT 65 | PLUMTREE | 1992 |
| 204 | FOR 2ND. | M.THURLOW 146 | R.DUNFORD 89 | POTTERNE | 1992 |
| 203 | FOR 1ST. | P.SHAW 139 | A.TISO 66 | LULLINGTON PK. | 1989 |
| 203 | FOR 2ND. | A.THOMAS 186 | C.BUCKSTON 70 | SUTTON On the Hill | 1973 |
| 203 | FOR 4TH. | D.TAYLOR 112 | P.MAY 103 | WERRINGTON | 1991 |
| 201 | FOR 1ST. | S.BARNES 120 | W.FOOTE 112 | KYDFORD | 1980 |

*DENOTES NOT OUT BATSMAN AND/OR UNBROKEN PARTNERSHIP

NOTE:- There are 31 further village teams in the championships who have recorded a partnership of 180 runs or more.

# Appendix II

## LORD'S MCC GROUND

## The National Village Cricket Championships

### ORGANISED BY THE CRICKETER
### THE FINALS

| | | | | |
|---|---|---|---|---|
| 1972 | TROON | v | ASTWOOD ROWANT | HAIG |
| 1973 | TROON | v | GOWERTON | HAIG |
| 1974* | BOMARSUND | v | COLLINGHAM | HAIG |
| 1975 | GOWERTON | v | ISLEHAM | HAIG |
| 1976 | TROON | v | SESSAY | HAIG |
| 1977 | COOKLEY | v | LINDAL MOOR | HAIG |
| 1978 | LINTON PARK | v | TOFT | CRICKETER |
| 1979 | EAST BRIERLY | v | YNYSYGERWN | WHITBREAD |
| 1980 | MARCHWEIL | v | LONGPARISH | WHITBREAD |
| 1981 | ST. FAGANS | v | BROAD OAK | WHITBREAD |
| 1982 | ST. FAGANS | v | COLLINGHAM | WHITBREAD |
| 1983 | QUARNDON | v | TROON | WHITBREAD |
| 1984 | MARCHWEIL | v | HURSLEY PARK | WHITBREAD |
| 1985 | FREUCHIE | v | ROWLEDGE | CRICKETER |
| 1986 | FORGE VALLEY | v | YNYSYGERWN | NORSK-HYDRO |
| 1987 | LONGPARISH | v | TREETON WELFARE | NORSK-HYDRO |
| 1988† | GOATACRE | v | HIMLEY | NORSK-HYDRO |
| 1989‡ | TOFT | v | HAMBLEDON | NORSK-HYDRO |
| 1990 | GOATACRE | v | DUNSTALL | CRICKETER |
| 1991 | ST. FAGANS | v | HAROME | CRICKETER |
| 1992 | HURSLEY PARK | v | METHLEY | ROTHMANS |

\* The 1974 final was played at Edgebaston a week late after being rained off at Lord's.
†The 1988 fial was played at the Midland Bank Ground, Beckenham after being abandoned due to rain. It is the longest final lasting over 9 hours and 121 overs.
‡The 1989 final again at Beckenham, 1st innings interuppted by rain at Lord's.

# THE FINALS 1972-1992

## HIGHEST INDIVIDUAL SCORES

| | | | |
|---|---|---|---|
| 123 K.M.ILES | FOR GOATACRE | AGAINST DUNSTALL | 1990 |
| 91* K.M.ILES | FOR GOATACRE | AGAINST HIMLEY | 1988 |
| 79* T.CARTER | FOR TROON | AGAINST ASTWOOD BANK | 1972 |
| 76* C.SURRY | FOR HURSLEY PARK | AGAINST METHLEY | 1992 |
| 75 S.A.WALKER | FOR HIMLEY | AGAINST GOATACRE | 1988 |
| 70* T.CARTER | FOR TROON | AGAINST GOWERTON | 1973 |

## BEST BOWLING PERFORMANCES

| | | | |
|---|---|---|---|
| 6-24 R.COULSON | FOR LINDAL MOOR | AGAINST COOKLEY | 1977 |
| 4-17 J.P.G.SYLVESTER | FOR ST.FAGANS | AGAINST HAROME | 1991 |
| 4-18 J.ANGELL | FOR GOATACRE | AGAINST DUNSTALL | 1990 |
| 4-23 B.MOYLE | FOR TROON | AGAINST SESSAY | 1976 |
| 4-24 I.TREWARTHA | FOR FREUCHIE | AGAINST ROWLEDGE | 1985 |
| 4-32 A.MORRIS | FOR MARCHWIEL | AGAINST HURSLEY PARK | 1984 |
| 4-38 I.CURTIS | FOR YNYSYGERWN | AGAINST FORGE VALLEY | 1986 |
| 4-40 C.WESTBROOK | FOR HURSLEY PARK | AGAINST METHLEY | 1992 |
| 4-46 K.M.ILES | FOR GOATACRE | AGAINST HIMLEY | 1988 |

## BEST ALL ROUND PERFORMANCE

### 91* & 4-46 K.M.ILES FOR GOATACRE AGAINST HIMLEY IN 1988

### TEAM PERFORMANCES    HIGHEST SCORES

| | | | |
|---|---|---|---|
| 267-5 GOATACRE | AGAINST | DUNSTALL | 1990 |
| 217-8 DUNSTALL | AGAINST | GOATACRE | 1990 |
| 216-4 EAST BRIERLEY | AGAINST | YNYSYGERWN | 1979 |
| 193-6 GOATACRE | AGAINST | HIMLEY | 1988 |
| 192 HIMLEY | AGAINST | GOATACRE | 1988 |

NOTE:- HIMLEY SCORED 207-6 IN THEIR ABANDONED FINAL AGAINST GOATACRE AT LORD'S IN 1988.

### TEAM PERFORMANCES    LOWEST TOTALS

| | | | |
|---|---|---|---|
| 82-9 LONGPARISH | AGAINST | MARCHWIEL | 1980 |
| 90 TREETON WELFARE | AGAINST | LONGPARISH | 1987 |
| 95 SESSAY | AGAINST | TROON | 1976 |
| 104 HAMBLEDON | AGAINST | TOFT | 1989 |
| 109 COLLINGHAM | AGAINST | BOMARSUND | 1974 |
| 110 LINDAL MOOR | AGAINST | COOKLEY | 1977 |

## Appendix II

### HIGHEST AGGREGATES

| 484 | GOATACRE | 267-5 | BEAT DUNSTALL | 217-8 | 1990 |
| 385 | GOATACRE | 193-6 | BEAT HIMLEY | 192 | 1988 |
| 340 | TROON | 176-3 | BEAT GOWERTON | 164-5 | 1973 |
| 340 | EAST BRIERLEY | 216-4 | BEAT YNYSYGERWN | 124 | 1979 |

### BIGGEST VICTORIES

| 92 RUNS | EAST BRIERLEY | 216-4 | BEAT YNYSYGERWN | 124 | 1979 |
| 79 RUNS | MARCHWIEL | 161-8 | BEAT LONGPARISH | 82-9 | 1980 |
| 76 RUNS | LONGPARISH | 199 | BEAT TREETON WELFARE | 90 | 1987 |

NOTE:- THE CLOSEST FINAL WAS THE 1985 FINAL, WHEN ROWLEDGE SCORED 134 ALL OUT. IN REPLY FREUCHIE SCORED 134 FOR THE LOSS OF EIGHT WICKETS AT THE CLOSE OF THEIR REPLY. SO THEY WON BY HAVING LOST FEWER WICKETS.

# Appendix III

IN THE EARLY YEARS OF THE COMPETITION HAIG WHISKY'S SPONSORSHIP INCLUDED A CONTEST IN WHICH SELECTED VILLAGERS WERE INVITED TO THROW THE CRICKET BALL. I HAVE BEEN ABLE TO LOCATE THE FOLLOWING RECORDS.

1972:- THE COMPETITION WAS WON WITH A THROW OF 106 YDS. 2FT. 1 INCH. THE NAME OF THE WINNER HAS NOT BEEN LOCATED.

1973:- THE COMPETITION WAS WON BY BARRY HAYWARD OF SHRIVENHAM WITH A THROW OF 103 YDS. 11 INCHES.

1974:- THE COMPETITION WAS WON BY TERRY TREWARTHA OF FREUCHIE WITH A THROW OF 105 YDS. 2 FT. 1 INCH.

NOTE:- Roger White of Tetsworth was third in 1973 with a throw of 93 yds. 1 ft. 5 inches, he actually threw further but was adjudged a foul as the ball was thrown to the wrong end.

ALSO DURING HAIG WHISKY'S SPONSORSHIP (1975) THERE WAS A COMPETITION FOR THE TEA LADIES. TEAMS WERE INVITED TO SUBMIT ENTRIES. THESE WERE JUDGED BY A PANEL, COMPRISING WENDY BURROUGHS (HAIG WHISKY), BELINDA BROCKLEHURST (THE CRICKETER), MICHAEL HENDERSON (HAIG WHISKY), BRIAN JOHNSTON (THE CRICKETER) AND COLIN INGELBY Mc.KENZIE (FORMER CAPTAIN OF HAMPSHIRE AND INTERNATIONAL CAVALIER).

The nominations from the villages were quite interesting by all accounts. Here are just a few of the ladies who presented the judges with the difficult task of choosing the winners: Mrs.May of Spye Park, then sixty, she did the teas for the first and second eleven, which she had been doing since 1939. Mrs.Eleanor Allen of High Etherley aged seventy-one bakes delicious cakes. Mrs.Osgood of Brayswood regularly did a barbecue for 250 with two daughters to help, as well as doing the teas. Mrs.Heather of Burford provided teas with the aid of her eighty-five year old mother. One lady tended the pitch with her 'special' compost. Janice Beard of Grampound Road was the youngest entrant at sixteen, she had regularly score for the second eleven for six years. A white haired grandmother was also nominated, she was the club umpire!

## Appendix III

The winner was Mrs.Cynthia Gypps of Samfords C.C. in Essex. Apart from the teas, Mrs.Gypps sold the raffle tickets, washed umpires' coats and was the team barber. She was also an organiser of the annual dinner and dance. If that wasn't enough she was also the vice-captain of the ladies' team. The judges never did find out who did the scoring on those occasions.

Second prize went to Mrs.Angela Farey of Breedon C.C. in Gloucestershire. Tea lady and seamstress she may have been, but I suspect she was more famous for her home made bread, and if a match finished early the players were invited home to sample her husband's home made beer.

Third prize went to Mrs.Patsy Lewis of Falconhurst C.C. in Kent, her delicious home made chocolate cakes were renowned (Johnners on the panel I suspect had some influence here). She was also the first aid expert, provided a great barbecue and was general cheerer-upper.

The ladies were invited to Lord's for an interview. First prize of a luxury weekend for two in London was declined by Mrs.Gypps as she was unable to get away, so she accepted a luxury hamper similar to the two other winners. Twenty runners up received a powder compact.

IN 1987 NORSK HYDRO RAN A PHOTOGRAPHIC COMPETITION IN CONJUNCTION WITH "AMATEUR PHOTOGRAPHER' AND "THE CRICKETER". THIS RESULTED IN A SUPERB CALENDAR IN 1988, WITH THIRTY-SIX PHOTOGRAPHS DEPICTING THE MANY FACETS OF VILLAGE CRICKET. THERE WERE SIX FIRST PRIZES OF 200 EACH, AND SIXTEEN RUNNERS UP WHO EACH RECEIVED 25. ALL NAMES WERE ACKNOWLEDGED ON THE FRONT OF NORSK HYDRO'S 1988 CALENDAR.

### FIRST PRIZE WINNERS

K.R.EBSWORTH, HAROLD WOOD, ESSEX.
R.J.BENZIES, COUPAR ANGUS, PERTHSHIRE.
MRS.J.DUNN, TELFORD, SHROPSHIRE.

MRS.M.MARLOW, PORTSMOUTH, HAMPSHIRE.
M.KIPLING, GUISBOROUGH, CLEVELAND.
P.A. BRECKON, MIDDLESBROUGH, CLEVELAND.

# Appendix IV

Sources of reference:-

"Double Century" by Tony Lewis.
"The Essential John Arlott" edited by David Rayvern Allen.
"The Haig Book of Village Cricket" by J.P.Fogg.
"Barclay's Book of International Cricket" edited by E.W.Swanton.
"The Cricketer Annuals" 1973-1993.

I am indebted to the following for their assistance, encouragement and material supplied to complete the book:-

The staff of The Cricketer.
Whitbread
Norsk Hydro
Rothmans
The Wiltshire Gazette and Herald.
Brian Johnston.
The Independent on Sunday.
The Daily Record - Glasgow.
The Evening Echo - Darlington.
Tony Huskinson.
Dunstall C.C.
Freuchie C.C.
Ynysygerwn C.C.
St.Fagans C.C.
Forge Valley C.C.
Sessay C.C.
Troon C.C.
Toft C.C.
Newick C.C.
Goatacre C.C.
Linton Park C.C.
Rowledge C.C.
Radio Wales.
Radio 2 - Charlie Chester.
Eric Marsh - Photographer.
Robert Hallam - Photographer.
Nick Redman - Archivist, Whitbread PLC.
And last but not least Jeremy Joslin - cartoonist.

**RECOMMENDED BOOKS ON VILLAGE CRICKET:-**

"**Village Cricket.**" by Dr.Howat — David & Charles 1980

"**The Haig Book of Village Cricket.**" by J.P.Fogg — Pelham 1972

"**Village Cricket.**" by A.J.Forrest — Hale 1972

"**The Cornerstone of Village Cricket.**" by Gerald French — Hutchinson 1948

**USEFUL ADDRESSES:-**

Lord's Cricket Ground, London, NW8 8QN

The Cricketer Magazine, Beechanger, Ashurst, Tunbridge Wells, TN3 9ST

The National Cricket Association:-
Lord's Cricket Ground, London, NW8 8QN

The Association of Cricket Umpires and Scorers:-
Leslie J. Cheeseman B.E.M., "Red Gables", 16 Ruden Way, Epsom
  Downs, Surrey, KT17 3LN

**USEFUL TELEPHONE NUMBERS:-**

Lord's Cricket Ground:-
  Pavilion Switchboard: 071-289-1611—5
  Club Office: 071-289-8979
  M.C.C. Shop: 071-289-1757
  Prospects of Play: 071-289-8011

The National Cricket Association:- 071-289-6098
  Competitions Office: 071-286-4766

# Index

Abberton 123
Aberdeen Football Club 105
Abinger 95
Abthorpe 95
Acton Andy 62
Addingham C.C. 61, 80
Ainsworth Percy 171
Alfriston C.C. 35
Ali Abid 110, 112
Allom Maurice 17
Allsopp 84
Almond Betty 74, 75
Almond Mike 74, 76, 175
Almond Pat xiii, 74
Alne C.C. 74
Alvanley C.C. 49, 96, 170
Ampfield 48
Anderson John 122, 148
Angell Jon ('Pringle') 112, 136, 143, 144, 146, 148, 159, 160
Angove J.P xiii, 33
Annetts 150
Arlott John vii, 26, 184
Armitage Bridge 121
Arnold Peter 42
Ashley 94
Aston Rowant 77, 97
Astwood Bank C.C. 22, 23, 24, 25
Audley End 123
Avon 114
Avoncroft C.C. 26
Aymes Adrian 68

Backworth Percy 191
Bailey 67, 99, 146
Baker Mel 155
Balcombe C.C. 35
Ball E 91
Ball J 91
Bannockburn 102
Barkisland C.C. 54, 82, 91, 121
Barnett K 73
Barrett Peter 50, 51, 54, 61, 68
Barrett Steve 50, 94
Barton 113
Bat and Ball Inn The 94, 184
Baylis David 73
Beacon C.C. 63
Bean Aribert 168
Beanacre 150
Beckenham 88, 90, 93
Bedale 74, 80, 82, 85
Bedfordhsire 67, 123
Bell John 50, 51, 68
Bell Kristian 115, 116, 158, 159
Bell Mary 50
Bennett 147
Benson & Hedges Cup 119
Berkshire 20, 123
Bevan 30

Billesdon 101, 102
Black 98, 99
Blackley 121
Blake 145
Bledlow C.C. 21, 99, 113, 123
Bletchley 100
Blundon 75
Blythe 99
Bolton Percy C.C. 73
Bomarsund 29, 52, 54, 92, 96
Bond 76
Booth Park 186
Boothroyd Allan 122, 126, 127
Boothroyd Graham 125, 126
Borthwick 34
Botham Ian 167
Botting Tim 95
Botting Trevor 35
Boulton Colin 107, 108, 111, 112
Bourne 122, 125
Bournemouth 127
Bowes Andy 86, 114, 116
Bowles 98
Bradenham 113
Bradford 137, 139
Brattle 98, 99
Brearley 99
Bredon 135
Brindley J 94
Bristol Channel 136
British Rail 23
Britton Reg 36
Broad Halfpenny Down 93, 94, 184
Broad Oak 52, 54, 55, 56
Brocklehurst Belinda ix, xii, 16,
Brocklehurst Ben ix, xi, xii, 9, 10, 11, 15, 19, 20, 29, 93, 94, 188
Brooke 56
Buckinghamshire 123, 185
Bunney 68
Burn Yates 191
Burnett 33
Burnmoor C.C. 32, 41
Burtenshaw 94
Burton Mail 91
Burton on Trent 107, 108
Butcher 64
Butleigh 121
Butler Ken ('Kenny') 89, 98, 134, 138, 140, 151, 180

Caldwell 175
Camborne 21
Cambridgeshire 29, 30, 32, 33, 108
Cannon Tim 35
Canon Frome 47, 66, 84, 91, 95, 121
Cardiff 52, 158
Carew 63, 115
Carlton 73, 75
Caro 94

Carson 51
Carter Brian 25, 27, 33, 34, 64, 65
Carter Brothers 48, 63, 66
Carter Terry 24, 25, 27, 33, 65
Castleford 124
Castleton 61
Cattistock C.C. 86, 138
Cavaliers The 120
Cawley 30
Cayton C.C. 74
Chaddesley Corbett C.C. 62, 75, 76, 78
Cherhill 110
Cheshire 41, 82, 92, 94, 96, 122, 186
Chester Charlie xiii,
Chew Magna 114
Chiddingstone C.C. 35
Chippings C.C. 85
Chiswell Street xii, 40, 45, 50, 68
Cholmondley 96
Christie Brian 104
Christie Dave xiii, 101, 102, 103, 104, 105
Chumleigh C.C. 67, 140, 181
Clark C 114
Clark David 66
Clayton dynasty 169
Claytons The 32, 74
Cleator C.C. 82
Clegg Dave 124
Cleveland 113
Clewley Frank 114
Clifford Paul 149, 152, 153, 157, 158, 159, 161
Clinton George 122, 124
Close 99
Cloughton 32, 67, 74, 77
Clwyd 41, 47, 49, 50, 51, 66, 122
Cockenach C.C. 35
Cockerton C 73
Cockspur Cup The 190
Coldstream Guards The 45
Cole 30
Collen L 33
Collen M 33
Collier Darren 86
Collier David 86, 114, 116, 122
Collier Peter 86, 113, 114
Collingham C.C. 23, 26, 29, 52, 57, 58, 60, 61
Colton 109, 110
Colwall C.C. 57, 108, 114
Constable Albert 35
Constantine Harry 9, 10,
Cookley C.C. 35, 36, 95
Cooper G 73
Cooper Rob 104, 109, 112
Copley 67, 106
Copplestone M 95
Corns John 142
Cornwall 10, 21, 25, 26, 28, 34, 63, 65, 137, 138

214

# Index

Corton House Kennels 129
Coulson 36
Coutts 99
Country Life 134
Cowan D 103, 104
Cowdrey Sir Colin 40, 78
Crackehall 80
Crawford Jack 174
Crawley Aiden 9, 18, 20,
Cressely C.C. 58
Crichton Andy 103, 104
Crichton George 104
Cricketer The ix, xiii, 9, 11, 15, 17, 18, 19, 20, 27, 36, 39, 41, 69, 71, 72, 78, 83, 90, 93, 95, 99, 106, 112, 115, 186, 187
Crompton Joe 22
Crookham Hill 107, 123
Crossland Charlie 110, 111
Crowther Leslie 87
Crumpton 24, 25,
Cuckney 73
Cumberworth 113
Cumberworth United 191
Cummings 83
Curtis Alan 6, 31, 110, 125, 148
Curtis Jeff 43, 44, 77, 78, 79
Cyprus 74, 76, 175

Dafen 52
Daily Express 25
Daily Mirror 29, 51
Daily Record The 103
Daily Telegraph 87, 93
Daniel Adrian 27, 30
Danston M.S. 21
Davey Brian 53
Davies 24, 44, 46, 115, 116, 158, 159
Davies Roy 50
Davis Tony 68, 96
Dawlish 23
Dawson Andy 111, 137, 139, 141, 145, 146, 148, 152, 154, 155, 156, 157, 158, 159, 160
Day John 85
De Manio Jack 19
Debrett's Peerage 15
Decent John 43, 46
Defoe Clive 45, 46, 47
Delahaye 153
Derbyshire 41, 49, 61, 62, 63, 64, 65, 66, 67, 106
Despres C xiii,
Devon 67, 140, 180
Dewfield 157
Dixon David 73, 151
Doggart Hubert 60, 84
Dolman Pete 132, 136, 142
Donaldson Mike 92
Donegan Andrew 143, 144, 145, 146, 149, 152, 154
Donegan Tony 143, 144, 152
Dorset vii, 21, 26, 127, 138, 144
Douglas Sir Robert 143
Doust Dudley 130
Dowson B 113, 114, 116, 122
Draycott C.C. 172

Driscoll Gavin 58, 59
Duffield M. 32
Duke Hotel The 129
Dumbleton 121
Dunbar Jim 11
Dunbar Neil 103, 104
Duncan Alan 104
Dunstall C.C 91, 92, 107, 108, 109, 110, 111, 112, 142, 143
Dunstan 34
Durham 3, 32, 54, 113
Dursley Gazette 91
Dyfed 43, 115

East Anglia 42
East Brierley C.C. 36, 40, 41, 42, 46, 47, 52, 112
Edgbaston 29
Edwards Chris 24, 25, 51, 54
Elliott Neil 122
Embry Maurice 47
England 4, 21, 31, 57, 111, 125, 176, 185, 186, 188
England Richard 57, 59
English Tourist Board 100
Enters Ian 35
Enville C.C. 49, 107, 108
Essex 48, 58, 97, 106, 115, 123
Etherley 32
Evans David xiv, 77
Evans R.D. 30
Evercreech C.C. 21
Excelsior Club of Rotterdam 188

Faithful 94
Farley Hill 106
Farmer 61, 65
Father Time 5, 59, 178
Feckenham & Bramshill C.C 91
Feniton 73
Fenton D 121
Field Pat 91, 104
Fife 101, 105, 122
Fillongley C.C. 67, 96, 97
Finch Kelvan 82
Fisons 72
Fitzhead C.C. 73
Flintoff Brian xiii, 32, 34, 62
Flintoff Margaret 169
Flintoffs The 31, 32
Floyd R.F 99
Flyford Flavell 95
Flynn P 67
Fogg John 17, 93
Fonthill 144, 151, 152, 153, 154, 155
Foote Max 73
Fordham C.C. 26, 42
Forest of Boland C.C.
Forge Valley C.C. xiii, 73, 74, 75, 76, 78, 79, 80, 164, 177, 178
Forrester Graeme xiii,
Fowler M 95
Fox 125
Freeman George 31, 169
Freeman Tony 49, 51
Freuchie xiii, 3, 75, 82, 101, 102, 103, 104, 106, 122, 123, 174,

189, 190, 191
Frieth 185
Frocester 43, 77, 91, 139
Froud 147
Fry 150

Gauna Tony 97, 98
Geohaghan A 43, 44, 46
Gibson Pat 93, 141
Gibson R 67
Gillette Cup 119, 183
Glamorgan 30, 40, 43, 57, 77, 87, 92, 106, 115, 117
Glaves Philip John 75, 178
Glaves Stephen 75, 79, 178
Glaves T.S 79
Glavin John 179
Glen Rothes 101
Gloucester 77, 139, 186
Gloucestershire 21, 43, 58, 135
Glynde & Beddingham C.C. 175
Goatacre C.C. xiii, 63, 84, 85, 86, 87, 88, 89, 90, 110, 111, 112, 127, 129, 130, 131, 133, 134, 135, 137, 140, 141, 142, 143, 144, 145, 148, 149, 150, 151, 152, 153, 154, 155, 156, 157, 160, 161, 180, 181
Goldsithney 121
Gordon P.C. Ian 102
Gowerton C.C. 26, 27, 29, 30, 150
Grace Gates 5, 40, 103
Grace W.G 31
Grampound Road 41, 95, 96, 138, 139, 140, 180
Grandstand The 5, 66
Graveney Tom 78, 186
Grayson Andy 79
Great Alne 172
Great Burstead 100
Great Durnford 134
Great Ecclestone C.C. 85
Greaves Alan 54, 55, 56
Green Stephen xii,
Greenlay 117
Gretton C.C. 67, 82
Gulliver 184.
Gwent 77, 155

Haig Whisky ix, xiii, 19, 20, 21, 27, 28, 29, 30, 36, 39, 40, 71, 172
Hailey 29
Haines John 146, 149, 150, 152, 160
Hall 99
Halwill 73
Hambledon C.C 1, 92, 93, 94, 137, 184, 186
Hamilton G 67
Hampshire vii, 1, 3, 26, 47, 50, 66, 68, 80, 81, 83, 84, 87, 92, 97, 106, 133, 137
Hanborough C.C. 67
Hancock 68
Hardwick 115, 116, 160
Harome C.C. 85, 86, 113, 114, 115, 116, 122
Harper Hilary 168
Harper Margaret 168

215

Harris (Quickie) 83
Harris Wayne 77, 78, 79, 97
Harrison D. 32, 34
Harrow 53
Hartley 76
Hatcher 141
Hathersage 121
Havering 97
Heagren John 48, 49, 51, 83
Heath 42
Helmsley 113
Henderson Michael 19, 20, 25, 37
Her Majesty The Queen 16
Hereford Times The 91
Hertfordshire 1, 41, 53, 63, 64, 77, 78, 123
Hesleden 82
Hey 56
Hibberd John 65, 81, 83
Hick 79
Higgott Tony 108, 110
Hill K 99
Hilmarton 129
Hilton 95
Himley C.C. 84, 85, 86, 87, 88, 89, 113, 121, 134, 142
Hockley Heath 22
Hogan Terry 44
Holland 98, 188
Hollis Steve 63
Hollyoak D 67
Holmes 56
Holmesfield 32
Hook Tony 103
Hopkins M 84, 95
Hopkinstown 114
Horbury 22
Hornden on the Hill 106, 121
Horner Dick 54, 55
Hornsby Peter 186
Horspath 42, 67, 185
Horton House 22
Houghton B.C. 30, 33
Houghton Barry 33, 42
Hovingham 122
Hoyle Simon 55
Hunt Mark (Bunter) 89, 110, 111, 132, 138, 140, 141, 143, 148, 149, 150, 151, 152, 154, 155, 156, 157, 160, 161, 181
Hursley Park 3, 8, 48, 66, 67, 68, 87, 97, 106, 123, 125, 126, 127, 131, 132, 133, 161
Huskinson Tony xiii, 27, 37, 78, 90
Hutton Richard 78
Hutton Sir Leonard 40, 78, 87, 138

Ightham 73
Iles Adam 145, 153, 154
Iles Court 130
Iles Graham 132, 133, 148, 160
Iles Grampie 149
Iles Keith 87
Iles Kevin 84, 88, 89, 111, 112, 132, 138, 139, 141, 146, 149, 153, 154, 155, 157, 159, 160, 180
India 4

Ingleby Greenhow C.C. 74
Inland Revenue The 185
Irvine J 100, 104
Isleham C.C. 30, 32, 33, 108

Jackman 97
Jackson 33, 34
Jacobs Nigel 84
James J 56, 77
James Steve 94, 121
Jarvis Andrew 122, 125, 126
Jarvis Paul 126
Jenkins 151, 152
Jenkins Cyril 80
Jenkins David 49
Jenkinson Eddie 124, 150
Jennings Fred 158
John Player League 119
Johns Peter 24, 34, 64, 65
Johnston Brian ix, xi, 78
Jones 50, 51, 55, 56, 122, 126, 157, 160
Jones Andy 48, 83
Jones David 49, 67, 125
Jones Gareth 53, 59, 81, 93
Jones Peter 64
Jones Wayne 30, 49

Kellaway 68, 125, 126
Kennedy Tony 164
Kent vii, 17, 20, 22, 26, 41, 96, 97, 99, 106, 140, 141, 187
Khan Imran 110
Kimble 123
Kimbolton C.C. 23
King 132, 133
Kington Bagpuize 138
Kington C.C. 85
Kirkburton C.C. 49
Kirkham J. 57, 58
Kirkley C.C. 57, 75
Kitchen 64, 65, 121
Knightley C 121

Ladcock 95, 96
Lake District The 191
Lambourne 98
Lancashire 41, 54, 170
Langley C.C. 58, 82
Langleybury C.C. 41, 44, 45, 52, 53, 54, 63, 64, 77, 78, 92, 97, 106, 123
Lawlor 114, 116
Leamington Spa 22
Leavey Pete 110, 141, 142, 150, 151, 152, 156
Leicestershire 101
Leigh 96
Lethard 41
Leverton 57, 113
Lewis Graham 59, 158, 159, 160
Lewis Simon 158
Lewis Tony 40
Libby C. 67
Lightfoot J 67
Lillie Dennis 22
Lindall Moor C.C. 35, 36,
Linsey 41

Linton Park C.C. xiii, 22, 41, 44, 96, 97, 98, 106, 140, 141
Little Durnford C.C. 43, 44
Little Harrowden C.C. 80
LLanarth 155, 156, 157
Llangwm 43
Lloyd Clive 47, 188
Loates D 57
Lock Charlie 147, 148, 149
Locke 94
Londesborough C.C. 32
London 3, 19, 88, 90, 102, 112, 113
Long Dave 176
Long Room The 15, 16,
Longbottom Craig 91
Longparish 47, 48, 50, 51, 52, 80, 81, 82, 83, 106, 177
Lord Harris Memorial Gardens 5, 177
Lord's Banqueting Suite 4
Lord's Day Observance Act 119
Loveridge Bryan 67
Lowe J 100
Luff Denis 48, 51
Lukey Malcolm xii, 94
Lydford C.C. 58, 73
Lyneham RAF 129

M.C.C. 1, 5, 15, 16, 17, 23, 39, 47, 60, 66, 84, 99, 111, 127
Mac Farlane L 95
Mac Haggis Hamish 102
Mackie A 114
Mackinson 116, 160
Madley 59, 160
Maids Morton 185
Mainsforth 100, 113
Malvern Hills 108
Manger Adrian 148
Manning Paul 148
Marchington 107
Marchwiel C.C. 3, 47, 49, 50, 51, 52, 54, 61, 66, 67, 68, 80, 85, 122, 188
Marden 26, 97
Markinson 159
Marshal Steve 164
Marshall 181
Martin 44
Martin Jenkins Christopher 15, 19, 78
Martin Tony 177
Marwood Charles 115, 116, 117
Marwood Chris 86, 114
Marwood Johnathan 86, 114
Marwood Tom 113
Mason 59
Matthews Pauline 130, 141
McCreadie 55, 56
McDonald 93
McKay Chris 44, 46
McNaughton Niven 103
McQueen 97
Mead Paul 132, 133
Meadows 83
Meagen 89
Meed Nick 73
Meigle 101
Melford Michael 25
Melksham 150

216

# Index

Melluish Michael 127
Methley xiii, 122, 124, 125, 126, 127
Middleham 113
Middlesex 119, 185
Middleton Tyas C.C. 61
Milford Hall C.C. 26, 66
Mills 126
Mims 42
Mitchell 116
Moreton 123
Moreton Hampstead 73
Morgan Cliff 187
Morgan John 25
Morrall Frank 22, 25
Morris A 68
Morris J 61, 62, 65
Morrit T.L 83
Moyle Brian 34
Much Markle C.C. 47, 66, 121
Muir 55
Mulholland 98, 99
Mundy Simon 81
Murray John 119

N.C.A. 9, 11, 20,
Nassington 100
Nat.West Trophy 119, 184
Needham Ricky 53, 54, 55, 56, 57, 58, 81, 99, 114, 115, 116, 136, 158, 159
New Mound Stand 5, 25, 87, 103, 110, 124
New Zealand 120
Newcastle Tyne & Wear 41
Newcombe 51
Newick C.C. xiii, 175
Neyrn John 94
Normanby 96
Norris Chris 86
Norsk Hydro ix, xii, 71, 72, 78, 84, 87, 90, 94, 106, 177
North Yorkshire (North) 31, 82, 122
Northamptonshire 21, 22, 58
Northrup Hill C.C. 41, 80, 106
Northumberland 3, 28, 32, 54, 57, 92
Nottinghamshire 23, 26, 29, 57
Norway 71
Nurse 42, 45
Nursery end 5, 7

Oakmere 121
Oakmoore 107
Oakwood C.C. 48
Old Netherseal C.C. 61, 73, 82
Old Sharlston 91
Oliver Mike 125, 126
Outwood C.C. 66, 100
Oval The 4
Oxford 136, 179
Oxford Downs 85, 86, 87, 100, 131, 138, 174, 179
Oxfordshire 43, 67, 77, 138, 147, 185

Paine Simon 83
Painter David 53, 54, 56, 59, 60
Palmer C.H. 47
Palmer Sean 53, 63, 78
Palmer Simon 77

Parfitt Peter 119
Parks Jim 188
Partridge Frank 7
Patel J 160
Paulton 127
Pay Colin 92, 94, 98
Peachy David 33
Pearson John 97
Pedlar 63, 65
Peebles Ian 26
Penberthy A.L. 21
Perran-A-Worthal 52
Pettit Nigel 76, 79
Phillips 97
Pickering 46
Pickles Canon viii,
Pickwick 184
Piper 99
Pirnie Pipe Major Alistair 102, 103
Pitt D 100
Plews Nigel 4
Plumtree 113
Pool Eddie 153, 154, 155
Pope 33
Poulter S 100
Powell Martin 114, 116, 157, 158, 159
Poynings C.C. 81
Prior Alan xiii, 103, 104
Prout Chris 79
Purnell Kirsten 148
Pytchley C.C. 80

Quarndon C.C., 41, 52, 61, 62, 64, 65, 66, 67, 106

Rain M 61
Rampley 42, 43
Rea The Hon.Findlay 11, 45, 69
Reddick Gordon 53, 64, 77
Redditch 22
Redlynch C.C. 135, 138, 144, 145
Redshaw P 73
Reed 123
Refuge Assurance 119
Reid Graham 77
Rentch (Spanner) 75
Rice 106
Rich Keith 122, 125, 127
Richards 84, 156
Ridsdale 79
Riffold 104
Rigiani brothers 153, 155
Roberts 50, 56, 67, 68
Roberts D 21, 56
Robertson 56, 59
Robinson 24, 25
Robinson Colin 22
Robinson M 24
Roche 67, 84
Rogers L 123
Rogers Steve 85
Rose Paul ('Rosie') 111, 132, 133, 134, 135, 143, 145, 148
Ross Gordon 69
Rosser 116, 158, 159, 160
Rothmans ix, xii, 115, 120, 127, 149, 189

Rotterdam 47
Rowledge xiii, 3, 81, 100, 101, 102, 103, 104, 106, 123, 126, 183
Roxwell 100
Royal Green Jackets 24
Ruan & Philleigh 121
Rushton 26

Sampfords 123
Sanderson 42, 43, 45, 46
Sarton 135
Scarborough 80, 178
Schofield M 75
Scone Palace 191
Scotland xiii, 3, 10, 101, 106, 122, 187
Scott-Gall 144, 152, 153
Scottish Rugby Union 105
Scrimshaw Stuart 109, 112
Sessay C.C. 31, 32, 33, 34, 52, 61, 62, 76, 170, 178
Shackleton 109
Shamley Green C.C. 66
Shepherdson Martin 75, 79
Shere 100
Sheriff Hutton Bridge C.C. 32, 113, 114
Shillingstone C.C. 21
Shilton Geoff 111, 112
Shipton David 110, 111, 142
Shorter Andy 84, 86, 88, 89, 90, 121
Shorter Darren 88, 89
Shrewton 150
Shrivenham C.C. 174
Sillence 151
Silver 104
Simpson 81, 103
Skyes T 91
Slack Wilfred 185
Slade Paul 152, 155
Slater Tina & Ken 88
Small Adrian 123, 126
Smallwood 97
Smart M 122
Smith 51
Smith Barry 81, 84
Smith Ian 81
Smith Les 73
Smith N 148
Soley 86, 87
Somerset 21, 26, 58, 114, 161
Somerton N 121
Souter Ian 145
South Africa 120
South Milford C.C. 61
South Weald 73, 121
South Yorkshire 61, 80, 113
Southwick 143
Sowden John 75, 76
Spain 96
Sparsholt 80
Spencer John 110, 135, 136, 139, 141, 143, 148, 150, 152, 154, 155, 158, 159, 160
Spinks Colin 123
Spittle 24
Spry J 48, 64, 65, 66

217

Spye Park 143
Sri Lanka 60
St.Boswell 106
St.Buryan 121
St.Fagans xiii, 52, 53, 54, 55, 56, 57, 58, 59, 60, 77, 81, 82, 92, 93, 99, 106, 114, 115, 116, 117, 123, 126, 136, 157, 158, 160, 161, 188
St.John's Wood 3, 45, 69, 102, 103, 111, 161
Staffordshire 22, 49, 84, 86
Stainborough C.C. 41
Stansfield 73
Stapleton 52
Star The 113
Staxton 61
Steep C.C. 26
Steeple Langford 134, 137
Steer 152
Stephenson Lt. Col. xii,
Stevens Roger 53, 56, 59, 81, 159
Stewart Nick 112
Stiles 94
Stillington 73
Stimpson 94, 96, 97, 98
Stitson D jnr 106
Stobswood Welfare 191
Stock C.C. 48, 115, 123
Stoke Climsland C.C. 67
Stollmeyer Jeffery 23
Stones C.C. 73, 91, 121
Stourbridge 107
Stragglers C.C. 57
Strange Dave 133, 137, 141, 155
Strickland Graham 116, 117, 122
Sturt 82, 83, 84
Sudbrook 58
Suffolk 123
Sunday Correspondent 130
Surrey vii, 66, 81, 102, 104, 119, 123
Surry Clive 126, 127, 132
Sussex vii, 35, 48, 175, 184, 188
Sutcliffe Keith 50, 51, 81, 82, 84
Sutton on the Hill 95, 114
Swansea 26
Swanton Jim 9, 20
Swarkeston C.C. 73, 106
Swindon 130
Swynnerton Park C.C. 22
Sylvester Jamie 115, 116

Tanworth in Arden 67
Tavern The 5, 24, 27, 36, 45, 87, 110, 124, 127
Taylor K 75
Taylor Phil 41
Taylor W 100
Teague 157
Teer 156, 157
Teskey Adam 73
Teskey Paul 73
Thirkell John xiii, 98, 99
Thirkell Nigel 99, 141
Thirkle Tim 99
Thirsk 31, 167, 178
Thirsk Lord Thomas of 31, 169
Thomas Bill 27, 30, 150

Thomas Cyril 137
Thomas Dave 46, 79
Thompson David 61
Thompson Ron 61
Thornham 54
Thorpe 83
Thow Frank 125, 126, 127, 132
Thrumpton 57
Tiddington C.C. 81, 136, 147, 148, 149
Tidhoe C.C. 54
Till Ian 32, 33
Tills The 31, 32
Titmus Fred 119
Toft C.C. xiii, 41, 75, 82, 92.93, 94, 96, 97, 98, 99, 106, 186
Tondu C.C. 58
Topp P 46
Toshack 55
Towler D 108
Treeton Welfare C.C. 57, 80, 82, 83, 84, 85, 106, 108, 109
Trewartha Terry 104
Troon C.C. xiii, 21, 23, 24, 25, 26, 27, 28, 31, 33, 34, 35, 41, 43, 48, 61, 63, 64, 65, 66, 67, 77
Truswell 76
Tubbs 146
Tuddenham C.C. 73
Tudhoe 96
Tunaley 64
Turner John 'JT' 87, 88, 89, 110, 111, 132, 134, 135, 139, 140, 141, 144, 146, 147, 148, 152, 153, 154, 157, 159, 160
Turner Robert 92
Turner Topsy 93, 94
Twigg Tony ('Twiggy') 131, 134, 135, 138, 144, 179

Underwood 61, 64, 65
Upwey vii,

Vency 72
Vienna 25, 165
Vincent Jim 25, 34

Wade Alan 121
Waite 122, 126
Wales 10, 30, 40, 44, 50, 57, 60, 63, 68, 117, 155
Walford S 106
Walker Steve 85, 88, 121
Walker York xiii
Wall Martin 76, 78
Wallbank Phil 108, 109, 111, 112
Wallis Darryl 67, 68
Walters Alan 87, 89, 132, 134, 135
Walwyn Murphy 42
Ward Tim 109, 142
Warkworth C.C. 113, 191
Warner Plum 189
Warren CC 73
Warren Jonathan 63, 65, 73, 100
Warwickshire 29, 58, 67, 172
Warwickshire C.C. 58
Wash The 10
Watkins 45, 156, 157

Wayman 146
Weald C.C. 73
Wedgewood Bertha 169
Weeks Nigel 57, 58
Weir Chris 153, 154
Welford Park C.C. 20
Wenvoe C.C. 99
Werrington C.C. 26, 63, 86, 115
West Indies 23, 33, 36, 120
West Yorkshire 49, 54, 66
Westbrook 125
Westmorland Hotel 103
Whatton & Aslockton C.C. 57
Whitaker 184
Whitbread ix, 39, 41, 45, 55, 62, 63, 64, 66, 68, 69, 71, 102, 138, 176, 188
Whitbread Samuel xii, 40
Whiteman John 53
Whitley Hall 106, 121
Whyte 141
Wickens David xiii, 175
Wilby 95
Wilford T 114
Wilkie Alan 102
Wilkie Mark 104
Wilkins John ('Wilkie') 111, 131, 132, 134, 138, 140, 144, 145, 148, 153, 157, 159, 160
Wilkins Mel 133, 135, 146, 151, 156, 157, 160
Williams Christopher 60, 65
Williams Geoff 29, 45, 46, 53, 56, 59
Williams P 59
Williams Revd.David 52
Williams Royston 77, 78, 79
Williams S 113
Wilson George 42, 104
Wiltshire 43, 44, 58, 63, 85, 87, 90, 123, 129, 130, 131, 134, 138, 139, 140, 141, 144, 150, 158, 179
Winchmore Hill C.C. 81
Winterbourne 72
Winterslow C.C. 58, 150, 151
Witchampton C.C. 26, 146, 147, 150
Witton A 73
Wolfesdon Ron 124
Wood Keith 53, 55, 56, 64
Woodhouse C.C. 41, 75
Woore C.C. 85, 107
Worcestershire 20, 22, 35, 57, 62, 75
Worcestershire C.C.C. 107
Wright 59, 68
Wylham 191

Yalding C.C. 41
Yates Chris 81, 104
Ynystawe 52, 77, 86
Ynysygerwn C.C. 28, 40, 43, 44, 45, 46, 52, 73, 77, 78, 79, 106
Yorkshire 31, 32, 33, 36, 40, 41, 46, 52, 54, 55, 56, 61, 62, 73, 75, 76, 79, 82, 83, 84, 85, 109, 113, 114, 115, 116, 122, 124, 125, 169, 176
Youlgrave 191
Yoxall John 22, 24, 25